# READY-TO-USE
# ESL
# ACTIVITIES
# FOR EVERY MONTH
## of the
# SCHOOL YEAR

## CAROL A. JOSEL

Illustrated by Carol and Gavrielle Josel

**THE CENTER FOR APPLIED**
**RESEARCH IN EDUCATION**
West Nyack, New York 10995

**Library of Congress Cataloging-in-Publication Data**

Josel, Carol A.
    Ready-to-use ESL activities for every month of the
school year / by Carol A. Josel ; illustrated by Carol and Gavrielle
Josel.
        p.   cm.
    ISBN 0-87628-848-4
    1. English language—Study and teaching (Elementary)—Foreign
speakers—Aids and devices.    2. Activity programs in education.
I. Josel, Gavrielle.    II. Title.    III. Title: Ready-to-use ESL
activities for every month of the school year.
PE1128.A2J65    1994                                        93-45738
428′.0078—dc20                                              CIP

Printed in the United States of America

10   9   8   7   6   5   4   3


C8484-2

ISBN 0-87628-848-4

**THE CENTER FOR APPLIED RESEARCH
IN EDUCATION**
West Nyack, NY 10994

On the World Wide Web at http://www.phdirect.com

## Dedication

*To Gavrielle and Alan, without whom there would be so little.*

# ACKNOWLEDGEMENTS

This book would never have been written were it not for the persistent encouragement of my initial editor, Sandra Hutchison. Indeed, she planted the seed for this project and never stopped believing in it—or me. Thanks also go to my present editor, Connie Kallback, for all her patient guidance.

I am grateful, too, to my friends and colleagues for their ideas and insights; their enthusiasm and helpful support were unflagging. In particular, I want to thank Sue Checcio whose artistic talents I occasionally relied on.

And very special thanks go to my students for teaching me so much and making these pages possible.

And finally, I must thank my husband and daughter. Although not a teacher by profession, Alan has taught me a great deal about living and people. He also ate countless cereal dinners, so that I could keep on writing. And I don't know what I would have done if I couldn't have kept on going to Gavrielle and asking, "Can you draw this for me?" She is everywhere in this book—and in my heart.

# About the Author

A graduate of the University of Maine (B.A.—English/French), Carol Josel also holds a Master of Education degree in Reading, as well as supervisory and principal certification from Beaver College. A teacher since 1966, she is currently a learning specialist with the Methacton School District (Pennsylvania), working with intermediate-aged children and their parents. Her writings have appeared in such professional journals as *Teaching K–8* and *The Journal of Reading,* as well as books and teacher guides for Merrill Publishing Company and Bantam Books, Inc.

# About This Resource

Children learn language through play and purposeful activity, naturally and in an environment that invites risk taking, poses no anxiety, and applauds all effort. And such learning is best served by teachers who always facilitate, guide, and model this process, while being expansive in their gestures, facial expressions, and tone of voice. With the focus always on what a child is trying to do, practice activities should be related to his/her actual language needs. This book, then, based on a whole-language, integrated approach to language development, is a starting place, filled not only with reading and writing activities, but with art, cooking, music, gardening, and drama, as well. You will find that most of these activities make collaboration unavoidable, helping your students acquire English naturally, even when cleaning up. Here, they will focus on how to do things, not just on how to describe them. Such nonthreatening opportunities to practice language will also serve to promote self-esteem and keep the wonder and fun in learning.

All current research in ESL teaching and learning supports such a model, including Tracy Terrell's *Natural Approach to Language Learning* and Stephen Krashan's *Acquisition Theory,* both of which are based on how children acquire their first language. The chief aim is genuine communication in a classroom devoted primarily to activities that foster acquisition. We need, therefore, to allow our students to respond either in English, in their native language, or in a mixture of the two. However, if your student(s) come to you knowing no English at all, I suggest that you first follow James Asher's Total Physical Response method (TPR). This instructional strategy is based on asking children to be silent and listen carefully to a command in English, and then act immediately. At least ten hours of such instruction should be provided before launching any program. In this way, your students will *see* the meaning of much of what they hear, and English will be learned a whole act at a time. By allowing your students to internalize their listening comprehension of English, they can more gracefully make the transition to production, reading, and writing.

By following these methods, your students will be ready to successfully participate in the activities offered in this book—and you will find a full array of them. By providing real experiences, they will add to the children's existing background knowledge, helping them more readily digest and comprehend the new learning. *Ready-to-Use Monthly ESL Activities for Every Month of the School Year* builds on that prior knowledge, reviews and expands on it, and offers connections and reinforcement. You will find that listening, speaking, reading, and writing are taught here as an integrated whole, encouraging children to respond to literature and their world in a variety of ways, asking them to explore and investigate, pose questions, and seek solutions. The focus, then, is always on meaning, making sense of things and connecting ideas, placing language in a social and personal setting.

Mother Goose rhymes and fairy tales dot each month's line-up, all appealing to the imagination with their interesting characters and action-packed vocabulary, while also providing a sequential buildup of plot, frequent repetitions, and fairly predictable consequences. And you will find the inclusion of story frames particularly helpful for your ESL learners, serving as a visual aid to comprehension, since the internal structure of stories may vary from one culture to the next.

Included, too, are suggested Learning Experience Approach activities (LEA), which allow students to build their language and literary skills based on what they know, enabling them to begin writing even before they are proficient readers, writers, or spellers. Drama activities and choral readings encourage your children to convey their messages symbolically and to experiment with moods, gestures, and postures, as well as words. Additional notes and activities for teachers are also provided each month.

The same can be said for all the other activities you will find, as well. Through music, cooking, gardening, and drawing, your students will explore, imagine, interpret, seek solutions, and find expression through their own creativity. And all the while, they will talk, enhancing their language learning and deepening their understanding. Remember, of course, that you need to reinforce and expand these experiences since only you know the true needs of your students. And all your efforts will be greatly enhanced by field trips, journal writing, classroom visitors, involved parents, and pairing your ESL learners with native English-speaking students. Thus, by actively engaging your students in their own learning and applauding their every attempt to communicate, you will be helping them to acquire their adopted language naturally and enjoyably.

*Carol A. Josel*

# Table of Contents

**Other Monthly Activities:**

**School Related Activities:**

**Story & Related Activities:**

# OCTOBER:

## Teacher Notes and Additional Activities . . . . . . . . . . . . . . .   **40**

**Monthly Activities:**

**Colors:**

**Shapes:**

# FEBRUARY:

## Teacher Notes and Additional Activities . . . . . . . . . . . . . . . . **160**

## MARCH:

## Teacher Notes and Additional Activities . . . . . . . . . . . . . . . . 190

## APRIL:

### Teacher Notes and Additional Activities . . . . . . . . . . . . . . . **220**

#### Monthly Activities:

#### World Languages:

#### Getting to Know You:

#### Story & Related Activities:

## MAY:

### Teacher Notes and Additional Activities . . . . . . . . . . . . . . . **246**

#### Monthly Activities:

## JUNE:

# SEPTEMBER

Teacher Notes and Additional Activities
Calendar
Numbers
Telling Time
Days of the Week
Months of the Year
Other Monthly Activities
School-Related Activities
Story and Related Activities

# SEPTEMBER
# Teacher Notes and Additional Activities

### September, September Calendar

Encourage children to decorate their calendars, noting important dates and birthdays. Make a large, classroom calendar, as well, and celebrate September birthdays.

Put the cloze passage on an overhead or copy onto chalk board and do as a group activity.

### Count On It, What We Did, More Numbers, Still Counting, Adding It All Up

Make up a command game (similar to Simon Says) using terms such as first, second, now, then.

Play **Odd or Even**: Pair the children, and give 10 or 15 pennies or beans to each child. One player closes his hand over some of his pennies and asks his opponent, "Odd or Even?" The opponent guesses. If the guess is wrong, the mistaken guesser hands over one penny. If right, the guesser is given a penny. This continues until one of the players runs out of pennies.

As a group activity, have children collect all the coins, pieces of chalk, pencils, crayons, etc., they can find. Then, have them count these items and record their findings on a chart in numbers and words.

**Ball Toss**: Call out a number and toss the ball to a student who must catch it before the second bounce. She comes up with another number and bounces the ball to someone else, and so on.

### "Hickory, Dickory, Dock"

Be sure to model this activity several times, encouraging the children to join in as soon as they feel comfortable. Then, let them do it on their own.

### Quarter Time

Give each child four popsicle sticks or tongue depressors, placed on the floor in front of them. When you call out your commands, such as "one-fourth," they should take three sticks away, etc.

Photocopy a large circle for each child. First, have the children make and number 60 small lines (as on a clock) around the outer edge. Then, tell them to fold the circle first in half and then in quarters. Next, call out "30," "one-quarter," etc., and have them hold their circles up accordingly. Finally, have your students color in each quarter of their circles and label, one-quarter, one-half, three quarters, whole.

Bring in a pie or cake (one that's easily cut is best) and cut it in quarters. Then cut each quarter in half and let the kids feast.

## What Time Is It?, All Day Long, In the Evening

Demonstrate the concept of time on a clock. Then have children stand in a circle, each holding a large card with a number on it, one through twelve. As you call out a time, the children with the appropriate cards should hold them up. Repeat by having students lie in a circle with feet toward the center. Again, call out different times and have the appropriate children sit up.

Outside on the parking lot, draw a large clock; under each number, 1 through 12, write the corresponding minutes (5 minutes under the 1, etc.). Call out different times, letting the children take turns going to the right place on the clock.

Make direction cards, such as "Go to bed." The child acts out your instructions, while the rest of the class guesses the activity and writes down what time it must be.

Have students sit with you in a circle and answer questions, such as "What time do you get up?" and "Do you eat breakfast *before* or *after* you get dressed?"

## Water Clocks

Ancient Egyptians used water clocks as timekeepers. Now your children can "watch" time slipping (flowing) away. After the children have made their water clocks, you can have them compare their timepieces with a kitchen timer to find out how long it takes for their clocks to empty. You can also have them make other water clocks, punching the hole a little higher each time. The higher the hole, the less time it will take for the water to stop flowing. Compare with an hour glass and sundial.

## Sundae on Any Day

Explain to students the difference between Sunday and sundae. *Ball Toss:* To reinforce learning, have children stand in a circle. You begin by saying **"Monday"** and tossing the ball to a student. She/he must catch the ball before the second bounce and correctly say the next day of the week, **"Tuesday,"** and so on.

## All Year Long

Bring in lots of hats, jackets, coats, sweaters, boots, rubbers, raincoats, shorts, etc. (Always keep them on hand.) Divide class into equal groups. Hand one child in each group a card with a month and a season on it. He must run up and dress appropriately, while the other children guess first the season, then the month. Continue till all have participated at least once.

## All in a Day's Work

Have your students do some role playing by handing each one a card with a different occupation on it and asking each to role play the part while everyone else tries to guess what she/he is supposed to be.

Once well acquainted with some jobs, pair up your students for some reciprocal role playing. Put these roles on cards, such as:

> dentist-patient
> doctor-patient
> teacher-student
> cashier-paying customer
> waiter-customer

As they are enacted, let the other children guess at the relationships being portrayed.

Ask children to make a list of all the things they might like to be when they grow up.

## Labor Day Crossword Puzzle

The puzzle can be done as a small-group activity, followed by completing the puzzle on an overhead with the whole group.

Photocopy various pages from the Yellow Pages and hand out to each student. Then ask such questions as, "I have a toothache. Whom should I call?" Students should look through their Yellow Pages and give the name, occupation, and phone number of the person they would call.

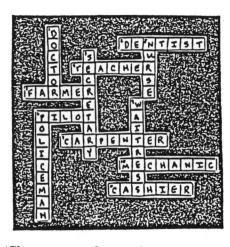

Give out a classroom job to each child, such as:

| | |
|---|---|
| paper distributor | timekeeper |
| clean up committee | board eraser |

(Change every few weeks)

## Card and Envelope Making

Put the names of all your students in a hat and let each child pick one and make a card for that person. You could also have the children do some interviewing, asking the person whose name they have drawn questions such as, "What is your favorite time of day?" "What is your favorite season?" "What is your favorite ice cream flavor?" "What is your favorite color?" etc. Answers can be pictured in their cards.

## School Days, My Classroom . . .

Label everything you can in the classroom, from floor to ceiling. Children can help you with this.

Using commands, have students enact together such "school" words as:

| | | | |
|---|---|---|---|
| stand up | read | sit down | answer |
| line up | walk | point to | write |
| start | stop | find | turn around |
| look up | draw | color | hurry |
| listen | show me | look at | slow down |

Have students gather the following items for you and put them on a large tray:

| | | |
|---|---|---|
| scissors | large paper clip | pencil |
| ruler | pen | notebook |
| stapler | rubber eraser | rubber band |
| small map | chalk eraser | crayon |
| book | piece of chalk | small pencil sharpener |

Give the children plenty of time to study all the assembled items. Then have them close their eyes while you remove one item. They then try to figure out what's missing.

Do a Language Experience Approach (LEA) activity with the students on "My First Day of School." Turn into a big book and illustrate.

Have students draw their classroom on butcher-block paper, labeling and coloring everything in it.

Tape the song "School Days," changing the lyrics to: "School days, school days, dear old teacher's rules days. Reading, and writing, and arithmetic, we have to learn it all so quick. You were the kid in the first row; I was your friend all along you know . . ." You can, of course, add to these words or come up with something better. Then put the words on the board and point to them as students follow along. Once ready, let them start singing along. Add some instruments. Can also be acted out.

## Cartooning

Bring in lots of comics from the Sunday paper to familiarize the children with "bubbles" and how the sequence of events are arranged.

Use comic strips as scripts and let the students act them out.

Photocopy a comic strip that needs an ending and let the students draw the last frame.

Have students complete their Flamingo Cartoons in the book, color them in and share them with the class.

## "The Little Red Hen"

Before getting the children involved in the action of the story, read it to them several times, modifying the story accordingly. Then model the various motions and change your voice to reflect the different characters.

Once very familiar with the story line, you're ready for some action. Assign parts to volunteers as noted in the version in the book, with all students participating in the "everybody" parts. Doubling up parts can ease anxiety. Repeat lots of times.

Take your students on a field trip to a farm.

Making bread is quite involved and time-consuming, so, instead, you might try bringing in some seeds (any kind), stalks of grain (or a picture), and flour, so that the children can "see" the process. Then, together bake several loaves of already prepared dough, eating the bread all up just like the Red Hen.

# SEPTEMBER

**What to do:** Use the calendar on the next page to complete this activity. Follow these steps:

1. Number the days of September.

2. Cut out and paste  on the first day of school.

3. Cut and paste  on Labor Day.

4. Cut and paste  on Grandparents' Day.

5. Cut and paste  on the first day of fall (autumn).

6. Cut and paste  on special September birthdays.

7. Color your calendar.   (Calendar is on next page)

Name _____

Date _____

## SEPTEMBER

| SUNDAY | MONDAY | TUESDAY | WEDNESDAY | THURSDAY | FRIDAY | SATURDAY |
|--------|--------|---------|-----------|----------|--------|----------|
|        |        |         |           |          |        |          |
|        |        |         |           |          |        |          |
|        |        |         |           |          |        |          |
|        |        |         |           |          |        |          |
|        |        |         |           |          |        |          |

# COUNT ON IT!
## (A Class Activity)

**Everybody:** (Follow the directions.)

Sitting in a circle,
everyone ties shoes

**One, two . . . TIE MY SHOE!**

One person shuts door;
rest clap hands once

**Three, four . . . SHUT THE DOOR!**

Picking-up motion        **Five, six . . . PICK UP STICKS!**

Everyone runs across room     **Seven, eight . . . DON'T BE LATE!**

Everyone returns to circle     **Nine, ten . . . DO IT ALL AGAIN!**

# WHAT WE DID, AND WHEN WE DID IT!

Fill in the blanks to show the order of activities in "Count on It," the class activity.

1. I tied my shoes.

2. _____

3. _____

4. _____

5. I did it again.

1. First, I _____

2. Second, I _____

3. Third, I _____

4. Fourth, I _____

5. Fifth, I _____

First, I _____. Next, I _____.

The third thing I did was _____. Then, I _____

_____. Finally, I _____.

© 1994 by The Center for Applied Research in Education

Name _____    Date _____

# NUMBERS AFTER TEN

◎◎◎◎◎◎◎◎◎◎ + ◎ =                    eleven (11)

◎◎◎◎◎◎◎◎◎◎ + ◎◎ =                   twelve (12)

◎◎◎◎◎◎◎◎◎◎ + ◎◎◎ =                  thirteen (13)

◎◎◎◎◎◎◎◎◎◎ + ◎◎◎◎ =                 fourteen (14)

◎◎◎◎◎◎◎◎◎◎ + ◎◎◎◎◎ =                fifteen (15)

◎◎◎◎◎◎◎◎◎◎ + ◎◎◎◎◎◎ =               sixteen (16)

◎◎◎◎◎◎◎◎◎◎ + ◎◎◎◎◎◎◎ =              seventeen (17)

◎◎◎◎◎◎◎◎◎◎ + ◎◎◎◎◎◎◎◎ =             eighteen (18)

◎◎◎◎◎◎◎◎◎◎ + ◎◎◎◎◎◎◎◎◎ =            nineteen (19)

## NOW YOU TRY IT:

ten + one   = _____        ten + two   = _____

ten + three = _____        ten + four  = _____

ten + five  = _____        ten + six   = _____

ten + seven = _____        ten + eight = _____

ten + nine  = _____        ten + ten   = _____

**Answers: 11; 13; 15; 17; 19; 12; 14; 16; 18; 20**

Name _____    Date _____

# STILL COUNTING

You can make new numbers by adding tens together. What other objects can you think of to show these numbers? Draw your own picture in the box beside the drawings here.

10 + 10 = 20 (twenty)

20 + 10 = 30 (thirty)

30 + 10 = 40 (forty)

40 + 10 = 50 (fifty)

50 + 10 = 60 (sixty)

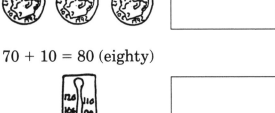

60 + 10 = 70 (seventy)

70 + 10 = 80 (eighty)

80 + 10 = 90 (ninety)

90 + 10 = 100 (one-hundred)

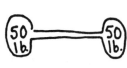

**Name** _____     **Date** _____

# ADDING IT ALL UP

**NOW YOU TRY IT:**

1.  ten + ten          = _____

2.  twenty + ten       = _____

3.  thirty + ten       = _____

4.  forty + ten        = _____

5.  fifty + ten        = _____

6.  sixty + ten        = _____

7.  seventy + ten      = _____

8.  eighty + ten       = _____

9.  ninety + ten       = _____

10.  twenty + twenty   = _____

11.  thirty + thirty   = _____

12.  forty + forty     = _____

13.  fifty + fifty     = _____

**Answers: 1. twenty (20); 2. thirty (30); 3. forty (40); 4. fifty (50); 5. sixty (60); 6. seventy (70); 7. eighty (80); 8. ninety (90); 9. one-hundred (100); 10. forty (40); 11. sixty (60); 12. eighty (80); 13. one-hundred (100)**

# HICKORY, DICKORY
## (A Class Activity)

**Everybody:**
(follow the directions.)

| | |
|---|---|
| Move heads from side to side | **Hickory, dickory, dock,** |
| Fingers climb up | **The mouse ran up the clock;** |
| Clap hands once and say, "Bonggggg" | **The clock struck one,** |
| Fingers move downward | **And down he run,** |
| Move heads from side to side | **Hickory, dickory, dock.** |

Name _____ Date _____

# QUARTER TIME

We tell time in hours and parts of hours. Look at the words by the first clock that show different ways to say one o'clock and then fill in the missing blanks.

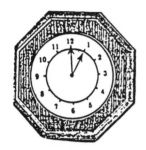

1 hour          1:00          one o'clock

¼ hour          _____          one-fifteen (quarter after one)

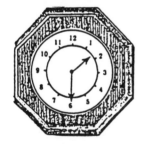

½ hour          1:30          _____ (half past one)

¾ hour          _____          one forty-five (quarter to one)

1 hour          2:00          _____

# WHAT TIME IS IT?

Write the time shown on each clock on the line.

1. _____

2. _____

3. _____

4. _____

5. _____

© 1994 by The Center for Applied Research in Education

© 1994 by The Center for Applied Research in Education

Name _____    Date _____

# ALL DAY LONG

Fill in the blank with the time shown on the clock.

1. I get up at _____

2. I eat breakfast at _____

3. My school bus comes at _____

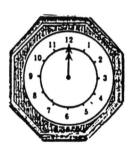

4. I eat lunch at _____

5. I come home at _____

# IN THE EVENING AND AT NIGHT

Fill in the blank with the time shown on the clock.

1. I start my homework at _____

2. I eat dinner at _____

3. I watch TV or read at _____

4. I go to bed at _____

5. By _____, I am sound asleep.

# WATER CLOCKS

Water clocks were used in ancient Egypt. Now you can make one and watch time pass by.

## WHAT YOU WILL NEED:

empty can or plastic bowl     plastic basin or sink
water     a hammer and a nail (or awl)
scrap paper     watch or clock

## WHAT TO DO:

1. Punch a small hole near the bottom of the can or bowl.

2. Place a paper plug in the hole.

3. Fill the can (bowl) with water and place in plastic basin or sink.

4. Take out the paper plug and watch your clock at work.

5. Refill your water clock. How many times can you clap before the water runs out?

    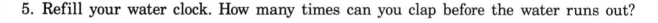

6. Refill your water clock again. This time see how many times you can jump up and down before the water runs out.

    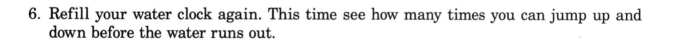

7. Refill your water clock again. Using your watch, count the number of minutes and seconds it takes before the can is emptied. Repeat to be sure.

    minutes: _____     seconds: _____

**Name** _____  **Date** _____

# A SUNDAE ON ANY DAY

**Days of the Week**

**Sunday**

**Monday**

**Tuesday**

**Wednesday**

**Thursday**

**Friday**

**Saturday**

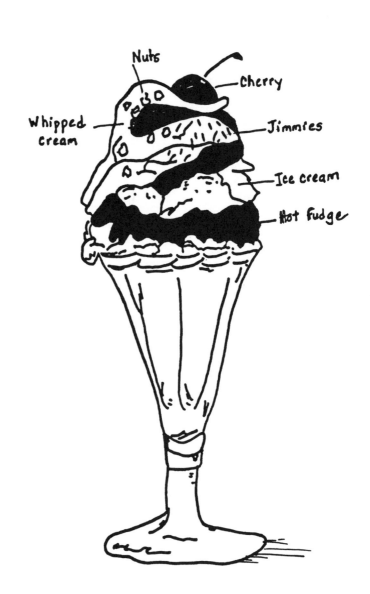

Nuts

Cherry

Whipped cream

Jimmies

Ice cream

Hot Fudge

**DIRECTIONS:**  Make your own sundae with:

1. your favorite ice cream

2. a topping of your choice, such as chocolate sauce
   pineapple
   butterscotch
   marshmallow
   strawberry

3. Add whipped cream, nuts, jimmies/sprinkles, and a cherry

4. Enjoy!

**Name** _____  **Date** _____

# DRAW AND COLOR YOUR OWN SUNDAE HERE:

## CIRCLE THE ONES YOU LIKE TO EAT:

Kind(s) of ice cream:     chocolate

vanilla

strawberry

_____

_____

Kinds of toppings:        chocolate/hot fudge          nuts

butterscotch                 jimmies/sprinkles

strawberry                   cherry

pineapple                    whipped cream

marshmallow

Name _____  Date _____

# ALL YEAR LONG

| Months of the Year | | The Four Seasons |
|---|---|---|
| January | (first—1st) | winter |
| February | (second—2nd) | |
| March | (third—3rd) | |
| April | (fourth—4th) | spring |
| May | (fifth—5th) | |
| June | (sixth—6th) | |
| July | (seventh—7th) | summer |
| August | (eighth—8th) | |
| September | (ninth—9th) | |
| October | (tenth—10th) | fall (autumn) |
| November | (eleventh—11th) | |
| December | (twelfth—12th) | |

Write the correct answer on the line.

1. September is the _____ (#) month of the year.

2. Last month was _____. (Name of the month)

3. Next month is _____. (Name of the month)

4. The first month of the year is _____. (Name of the month)

5. The last month of the year is _____. (Name of the month)

**Answers: 1. 9th month; 2. August; 3. October; 4. January; 5. December**

**Name** _____ **Date** _____

# ALL IN A DAY'S WORK

Here are people working in different kinds of jobs.

carpenter

nurse

police officer

cashier

teacher

pilot

mechanic

doctor

secretary

farmer

dentist

waiter

What other occupations can you think of?

Name _____    Date _____

# LABOR DAY CROSSWORD PUZZLE

**WORD BANK:**

carpenter
nurse
policeman
cashier
teacher
pilot
mechanic
doctor
secretary
farmer
dentist
waitress

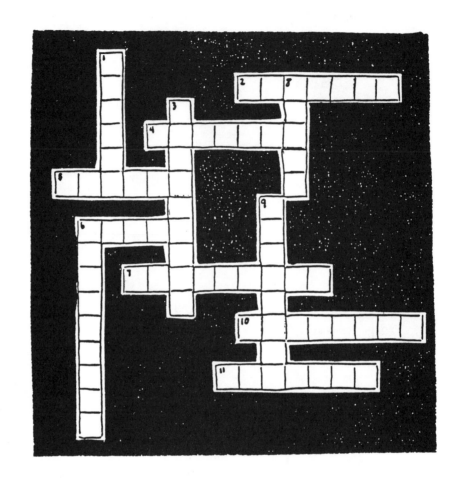

**DOWN CLUES**

1. cares for the sick
3. does a lot of typing
5. grows our food
6. keeps order and arrests people
8. works with doctors to make us well
9. (She) serves food in a restaurant

**ACROSS CLUES**

2. cares for our teeth and gums
4. helps students learn
6. flies airplanes
7. makes things out of wood
10. repairs cars and other machines
11. takes our money and gives us change

# CARDMAKING

**DIRECTIONS:**

1. Cut along dark, solid lines  ____
2. Fold along dotted lines    - - - - - - -
3. Write a message inside
4. Decorate the cover

# MAKING AN ENVELOPE

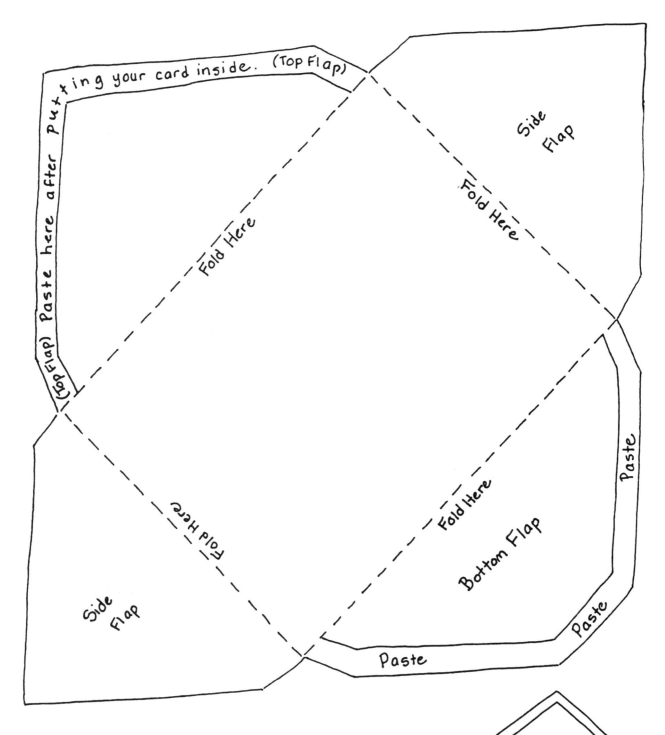

**How to make the envelope:**

A. Cut out along solid line ✂ _____

B. Fold side flaps along dotted line _____

C. Fold bottom flap along dotted line _____

D. Put card inside the envelope

E. Fold top flap down along dotted line ------ and paste

**Name** _____  **Date** _____

# SCHOOL DAYS

Check the words that are shown in this classroom.

_____ book

_____ bookcase

_____ calendar

_____ chair

_____ chalk board

_____ clock

_____ desk (teacher's)

_____ desk (students')

_____ door

_____ flag

_____ map

_____ newspaper

_____ pen

_____ pencil sharpener

_____ poster

_____ ruler

_____ scissors

_____ students

_____ table

_____ teacher

_____ wall

_____ wastebasket

_____ window

Name _____ Date _____

# MY SCHOOL, MY CLASSROOM

Fill in the blanks.

1. Where is your school? _____ (town/city)

   _____ (state)

2. What grade are you in? _____

3. What is your teacher's name? _____

Now, choose a partner to work with.

What is your partner's name?

_____

**WITH YOUR PARTNER, COUNT AND TELL ME . . .**

1. How many desks are in your classroom? _____

2. How many students are in your classroom? _____

3. How many chairs are in your classroom? _____

4. How many windows are in your classroom? _____

**NOW, COUNT THESE THINGS IN YOUR CLASSROOM:**

_____ flags                _____ plants

_____ pencils              _____ pencil sharpeners

_____ posters              _____ scissors

_____ chalkboards          _____ bookcases

_____ bulletin boards      _____ maps

_____ wastebaskets         _____ newspapers

_____ books                _____ pieces of chalk

# CARTOONING

**DIRECTIONS:** Make us talk! (Please color us, too.)

# THE LITTLE RED HEN
## (A Class Activity)

| | | |
|---|---|---|
| Narrator: | One morning the little Red Hen found some grains of wheat. | (Everybody: "Look what I found! Look what I found! Look what I found!") |
| Little Red Hen: | I think I'll plant them! | |
| Narrator: | But first she went to her friends for help. | |
| Little Red Hen: | Dear duck, will you help me plant these grains of wheat? | (Everybody: "Please, oh, please!" with begging motion) |
| Duck: | No, no! I have no time. Quack! Quack! | (Everybody: "Sorry! Sorry!" and shake their heads) |
| Little Red Hen: | Dear goose, will you help me plant these grains of wheat? | (Everybody: "Please, oh, please!") |
| Goose: | No, No! I have no time. Honk! Honk! | (Everybody: "Sorry! Sorry!" and shake their heads) |
| Little Red Hen: | Dear cat, will you help me plant these grains of wheat? | (Everybody: "Please, oh, please!") |
| Cat: | No! No! I have no time. Meow! Meow! | (Everybody: "Sorry! Sorry!" and shake their heads) |
| Little Red Hen: | Dear pig, will you help me plant these grains of wheat? | (Everybody: "Please, oh, please!") |
| Pig: | No! No! I have no time. Oink! Oink! | (Everybody: "Sorry! Sorry!" and shake their heads) |
| Little Red Hen: | Then I will plant them myself! | (Everybody: "Yes, I will!" with shoveling/planting motion) |
| Everyone shouts: | And she did! | |

| | | |
|---|---|---|
| Narrator: | Soon the wheat grew tall | (Everybody: Stands on their toes) |
| Little Red Hen: | Will you help me cut the wheat? | (Everybody: "Please, oh, please!" with begging motion) |
| Duck: | No! No! I have no time. Quack! Quack! | (Everybody: "Sorry! Sorry!" and shake their heads) |
| Goose: | No! No! I have no time. Honk! Honk! | (Everybody: "Sorry! Sorry!" and shake their heads) |
| Cat: | No! No! I have no time. Meow! Meow! | (Everybody: "Sorry! Sorry!" and shake their heads) |
| Pig: | No! No! I have no time. Oink! Oink! | (Everybody: "Sorry! Sorry!" and shake their heads) |
| Little Red Hen: | Then I will cut the wheat myself! | (Everybody: "Sorry! Sorry!" and shake their heads) |
| Everyone shouts: | And she did! | |

## THE LITTLE RED HEN, continued

Narrator: Now the wheat had to go to the mill to be made into flour.
Little Red Hen: Will you help me carry the wheat to the mill?
Duck: No! No! I have no time. Quack! Quack!
Goose: No! No! I have no time. Honk! Honk!
Cat: No! No! I have no time. Meow! Meow!
Pig: No! No! I have no time. Oink! Oink!
Little Red Hen: Then I will carry the wheat to the mill myself!
Everyone shouts: And she did!

(Everybody: "Please, oh, please!" with begging motion)
(Everybody: "Sorry! Sorry!" and shake their heads)
(Everybody: "Sorry! Sorry!" and shake their heads)
(Everybody: "Sorry! Sorry!" and shake their heads)
(Everybody: "Sorry! Sorry!" and shake their heads)

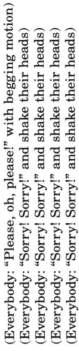

Narrator: Now the little Red Hen was ready to mix the flour into dough.
Little Red Hen: Will you help me make my dough?
Duck: No! No! I have no time. Quack! Quack!
Goose: No! No! I have no time. Honk! Honk!
Cat: No! No! I have no time. Meow! Meow!
Pig: No! No! I have no time. Oink! Oink!
Little Red Hen: Then I will make the dough myself!
Everyone shouts: And she did!

(Everybody: "Please, oh, please!" with begging motion)
(Everybody: "Sorry! Sorry!" and shake their heads)
(Everybody: "Sorry! Sorry!" and shake their heads)
(Everybody: "Sorry! Sorry!" and shake their heads)
(Everybody: "Sorry! Sorry!" and shake their heads)

## THE LITTLE RED HEN, continued

Narrator: After the little Red Hen had shaped the dough into a loaf
of bread, she was ready to bake it in her oven.

Little Red Hen: Will you help me bake my bread?
Duck: No! No! I have no time. Quack! Quack!
Goose: No! No! I have no time. Honk! Honk!
Cat: No! No! I have no time. Meow! Meow!
Pig: No! No! I have no time. Oink! Oink!
Little Red Hen: Then I will bake the bread myself!
Everyone shouts: And she did!

(Everybody: "Please, oh, please!" with begging motion)
(Everybody: "Sorry! Sorry!" and shake their heads)
(Everybody: "Sorry! Sorry!" and shake their heads)
(Everybody: "Sorry! Sorry!" and shake their heads)
(Everybody: "Sorry! Sorry!" and shake their heads)

Narrator: Finally, the bread was baked to a golden brown.
Little Red Hen: Who will help me eat my bread?
Duck: I will! I will! Quack! Quack!
Goose: I will! I will! Honk! Honk!
Cat: I will! I will! Meow! Meow!
Pig: I will! I will! Oink! Oink!
Little Red Hen: No, I will eat it myself!
Everyone shouts: And she did!

(Everybody: "Um! Um! It smells so good!" and rub stomachs)
(Everybody: "Yes! Yes!" and nod their heads up and down)
(Everybody: "Yes! Yes!" and nod their heads up and down)
(Everybody: "Yes! Yes!" and nod their heads up and down)
(Everybody: "Yes! Yes!" and nod their heads up and down)

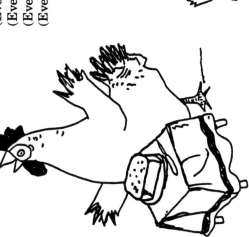
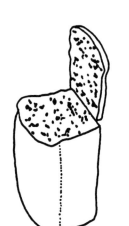

# THE LITTLE RED HEN BOOK

**PART ONE—**
**WHAT TO DO:**
**A. Carefully cut out the next page along the dotted line.**
**B. Then follow these directions to make your little book:**

1. Fold the paper you cut out in half lengthwise.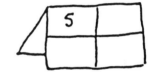

2. Fold it in half again, as for a book.

3. Fold it in half again.

4. Unfold the paper.

5. Fold in half widthwise.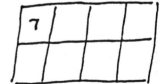

6. Cut the center crease from the folded edge to the X.

7. Open the paper again.

8. Return to the original lengthwise fold (as in Step #1).

9. Push the end sections together and it will fold itself into a little book. The cover should be on top.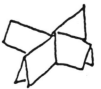

# THE LITTLE RED HEN BOOK

**PART TWO—**
**WHAT TO DO:**

1. Color the pictures below.
2. Carefully cut them out along the dotted lines. ✂ - - - - - -
3. Now paste them on the correct pages of your little book on the next page after you read the words carefully.
4. Finally, color the cover.

Next, she took the grain to the mill to be made into flour.

Then, she cut the stalks of grain.

After that, she made the flour into bread dough.

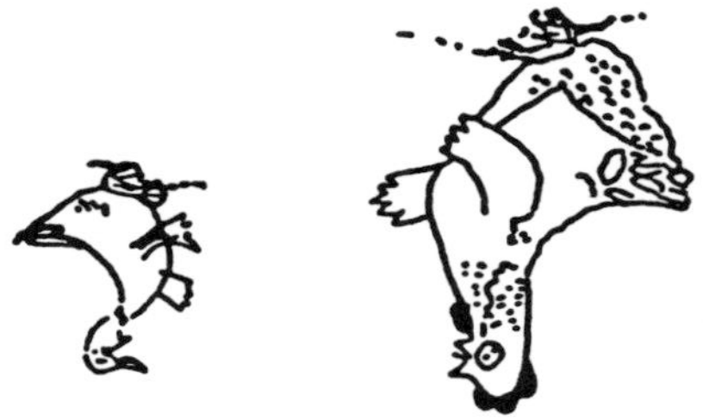

First, the little Red Hen found some seeds of grain and planted them.

Then, she put the bread in the oven to bake.

**THE LITTLE RED HEN**

Finally, she put the bread on the table and ate it all by herself.

↖ **CUT ON SOLID LINE** ↗

↖ **FOLD ON DOTTED LINES**

Name _____

Date _____

# SEQUENCE CHAIN FOR THE LITTLE RED HEN

**DIRECTIONS:** Step by step, tell what happened in the story using the boxes below.

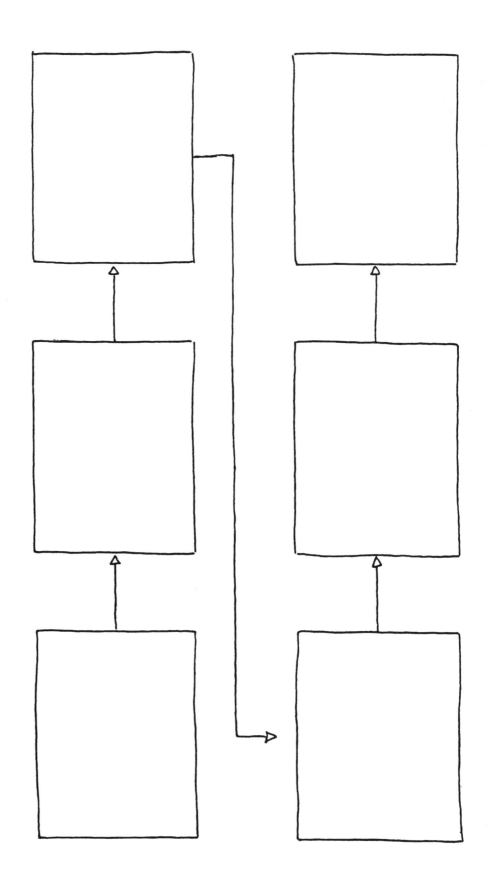

**Name** _____   **Date** _____

# BAKER'S CLAY

**WHAT YOU NEED:**  large mixing bowl     knife and fork
large spoon          cookie cutters
2 cups of flour      cookie sheets
1 cup of salt        aluminum foil
1 cup of water       rolling pin

**WHAT TO DO:**
1. Put salt and flour in large bowl. Mix well.
2. Add water, a little at a time. Mix as you pour.
3. Form into a ball.
4. Knead for 7 to 10 minutes until dough is smooth but firm.
5. Roll out the dough to about ¼ inch thickness.
6. Now using cookie cutters or a knife, cut out the little Red Hen and her friends.
7. Let your clay cutouts dry for 48 hours or bake them in the oven at 325 degrees for about 30 minutes or until golden brown.

**To knead dough:**

Place dough on lightly floured table. Fold it toward you.

With your palm, push it away. Give the dough a quarter turn.

Continue until dough is smooth and not sticky.

# OCTOBER

Teacher Notes and Additional Activities
Monthly Activities
Colors
Shapes
Foods and Related Activities
Story and Related Activities

# OCTOBER
# Teacher Notes and Additional Activities

### Another Day . . . , October Calendar

Do the circled year on an overhead, drawing an arrow to October and talking about the new season. Do the cloze passage together.

Talk about change, drawing a Venn Diagram on the board. Ask students to share "summer" and "autumn" words and list these. In the middle, put all words that pertain to both seasons, such as rain. It might be helpful if you bring in props such as an umbrella, shorts, bathing suit, sweater, etc.

Teach the song, "'Tis Autumn," by Henry Nemo (Ivan Mogull Music Corp.), putting the words on the board and pointing to the words as you go along. You might want to shorten the song and drop a few of the more difficult lines. Then have the children dramatize such words as Father Time by having the children nod their heads while saying "tick tock," and chirping birds, etc. Add some instruments.

Take the children to the library for some tree/leaf books. Then go outside and see how many types they can find. Press these on construction paper to make a leaf book.

To make scatter paint silhouettes, have the students place a few leaves on paper. Then, after dipping an old toothbrush in water color, have them scrape a piece of cardboard across it so the paint spatters around the leaves.

Turn the leaf walk into a Language Experience Approach activity.

Encourage children to decorate their calendars, noting important dates and birthdays. Make a large classroom calendar, too, and celebrate October birthdays.

### Christopher Columbus

Develop the concept of old and new by bringing in samples of each, such as a new and old book. Then give some background about the search for the New World and why we honor Columbus.

Once the children are familiar with the rhyme, add some motions to go with the words, such as waving their hands like the ocean's waves and putting up 3 fingers for the 3 ships, pointing to "you and me" at the end.

Trace Columbus' route on a large map.

Do some math, subtracting 1492 from the current year, etc. Use overhead for exercise.

Talk about heroes and have them share their's.

### Halloween Activities and "Peter, Peter"

Buy several pumpkins when you make jack-o'-lanterns together.

Save enough seeds for the Seed Art activity, as well as for roasting. Just coat them with a little cooking oil and roast on a cookie sheet in a 350 degree oven. Then sprinkle with salt and enjoy.

Celebrate with a party and encourage the children to dress up using such everyday items as pillowcases, sheets, and empty boxes. Make ghostly lollipop favors by tying a tissue around a lollipop and drawing a ghost face on it.

Cut out a large pumpkin on butcher-block paper and one stem for each child to play "Pin the Stem" on the pumpkin.

Make jack-o'-lantern pizzas by spreading English muffin halves with pizza sauce and cutting the stem and face out of cheese. Bake (450 degree oven) for about 10 minutes and enjoy.

Any of these activities will make excellent Language Experience Approach (LEA) activities.

Be sure to model the "Peter, Peter" activity several times, letting the children join in as soon as they feel comfortable. Then, let them do it on their own.

## Color Activities

You can also split white light into all the colors of the spectrum by filling a clear glass with water and holding it up to the sunlight. Rainbow patterns will appear on the floor and ceiling.

Make colorful creeping crystals by placing one tablespoon of salt and one table-spoon of water in a saucepan. Cook and stir over medium heat until the salt dissolves. Remove from heat and add ¼ teaspoon of food coloring (any color except yellow). Then pour the mixture into a jar lid, almost to the top. As the liquid evaporates, crystals will grow over the sides, lasting for months. Or, instead, use as paints. As the paint dries, wonderful crystals will form on the paper. Make several batches for lots of colors.

Take the children for a walk around the school to collect fallen leaves. Once back in the classroom, have them sort the leaves by color.

Write the names of the colors on oak tag and, under each one, have the children list things that are that color. This can be an ongoing activity.

Make edible finger paint in various colors: Mix 2 tablespoons instant clear gelatin; ¼ cup sugar; 1 pack unsweetened cold drink mix; and ¾ cup water.

## Shape Activities

Make shape mobiles.

Using different colored silk scarves, have the children move their scarves in the air to form the various shapes you ask for.

Working together, have the children form their bodies into the various shapes.

Once the children can differentiate between the shapes, let them begin the activities in the book. Use an overhead with most of these to insure understanding.

Find other examples of optical illusions; talk about what we think we see versus what is really there.

Make shape cards using large index cards and hand these out. Then let the children move around the room and then outside to find items that approximate the various shapes. Let them paste these to their cards, label, and display. These also make great mobiles.

## Money Activities, Food Activities

Do the money exercises with real currency and add to them. Great math practice fun!

Paste currency on construction paper to help children visualize the denominations and their relationships to each other. (These could also be drawn.)

Go around the classroom and tape prices on the various objects in the room. Then stage a mock garage sale, allowing the children to make their purchases with play money.

Make a group list of "eating" words, such as munching, swallowing, sipping, and licking. Have the children act each word. Milk and cookies make a great addition to this activity.

Have the children make food chains by vertically writing the names of different foods on strips of different colored construction paper, such as red for meats and white for dairy products. These can then be pasted into links and strung about the room.

Clip grocery coupons and ads from the newspaper and have the children go "shopping" and then let them tally their totals. These purchases can then be sorted into the major food groups, plus snack foods, of course. This makes a fine lead-in for a discussion about nutritious foods and healthy eating. Recommended daily servings are provided, together with pictures of many foods, on pages 63–67.

Have the children plan and make a luncheon. Take your students on a field trip to a grocery store to make their purchases. Keep it simple, of course.

Ask your students to keep track of everything they eat for 24 hours. Then share and categorize according to the major food groups.

Role play ordering food in a restaurant.

Have your students create TV ads for their favorite foods and videotape them.

The children can also create posters showing the major food groups and recommended daily servings.

## Measuring and Baking Gingerbread Man Cookies

Before involving the children with baking, they need to know a little about our system of measuring. Demonstrate these with water and, whenever possible, clear containers.

If your students are not ready for this activity, or you think making the gingerbread dough might be too involved or confusing, make the dough at home and bring it in, just having the children cut out their gingerbread men and baking them.

## "The Gingerbread Man" and Related Activities

A nice touch at the end of "The Gingerbread Man" is to let your children all be foxes and gobble up their cookies at story's end.

Before engaging your students in the motions that accompany my version of this story, it would be helpful to first read it out loud to them several times, modifying it accordingly, and letting them watch you do the actions first. Once they are very familiar with the story line, engage them in the actions themselves, with all students participating in the "everybody" parts. Doubling up parts can ease anxiety. Repeat lots of times.

Do "Another Look" on an overhead.

Using a Language Experience Approach (LEA) format, have the children retell the story, making sure to include the who, what, where, when, why, and how of the plot. Then help your students create wanted posters for the fox, complete with an illustration:

### WANTED:

**NAME OF CHARACTER:** _____

**REASON WANTED:** _____

_____

_____

**DESCRIPTION:**

      **HEIGHT:** _____    **WEIGHT:** _____

      **EYES:** _____    **HAIR:** _____

      **AGE:** _____

**DESCRIPTION OF CRIME:** _____

_____

_____

**WHERE LAST SEEN:** _____

_____

**REWARD:** _____

**CONTACT: (student's name)** _____

Model making the story cubes several times for the children before having them construct their own. When they are all done, these can be displayed on tables or used in mobiles.

Name _____  Date _____

# ANOTHER DAY, ANOTHER MONTH

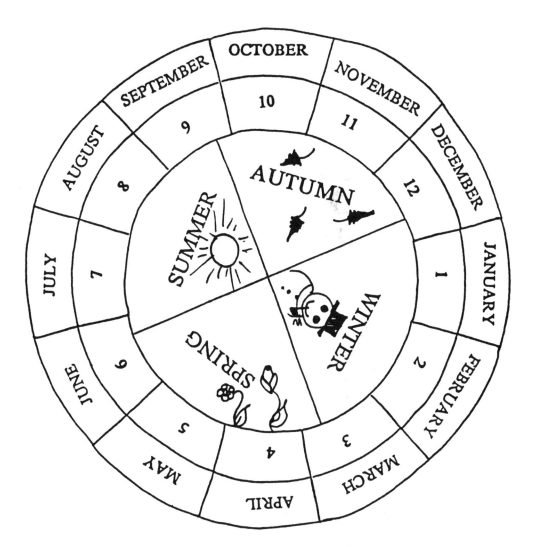

Fill in the blanks.

1. October is the _____ (#) month of the year.

2. Last month was _____. (Name of the month)

3. Next month is _____. (Name of the month)

4. This is the season of _____. (Name of season)

5. The second month of the year is _____. (Name of the month)

6. The eleventh month of the year is _____. (Name of the month)

© 1994 by The Center for Applied Research in Education

# OCTOBER

**WHAT TO DO:** Use the calendar on the next page to complete this activity. Follow these steps:

1. Number the days of October.

2. Cut and paste  on Columbus Day.

3. Cut and paste  on Halloween.

4. Cut and paste   on special birthdays.

5. Color your calendar.

(Calendar is on next page)

Name _____

Date _____

## OCTOBER

| SUNDAY | MONDAY | TUESDAY | WEDNESDAY | THURSDAY | FRIDAY | SATURDAY |
|--------|--------|---------|-----------|----------|--------|----------|
|        |        |         |           |          |        |          |
|        |        |         |           |          |        |          |
|        |        |         |           |          |        |          |
|        |        |         |           |          |        |          |
|        |        |         |           |          |        |          |

**Name** _____  **Date** _____

# CHRISTOPHER COLUMBUS

Santa Maria

**1492**

Columbus crossed the ocean blue
In fourteen-hundred and ninety-two. (1492)
Three ships came sailing with him, too,
To find the New World for me and you.

Pinta

Nina

Read each question and write your answer on the line.

**WHO** is the rhyme talking about? _____

**WHAT** did he do? _____

**HOW** did he cross the ocean? _____

**WHEN** did he do this? _____

**Answers: 1. Christopher Columbus; 2. found the New World; 3. in 3 ships; 4. 1492**

**Name** _____    **Date** _____

# JACK-O'-LANTERN

**What you need to make a Jack-o'-Lantern:**

a sharp knife

a large spoon

a black crayon

a large pumpkin

a collander

a flashlight

**NOW:**

1. With your crayon, make a circle around the stem.

2. Carefully cut along that circle and lift off the top.

3. Take out all the pulp and seeds and put in the colander. Set aside for the next activity.

4. With the crayon, make a face on your pumpkin.

5. Carefully cut out the face.

6. Turn on the flashlight. Put it inside the pumpkin.

© 1994 by The Center for Applied Research in Education

**Name** _____  **Date** _____

# SEED ART

**WHAT TO DO:**  1. Remove seeds from pulp.
2. Wash the seeds.
3. Place on paper towels to air dry (about 48 hours).
4. Paste seeds on colored paper.

# PETER, PETER
## (A Whole Class Activity)

**EVERYBODY SAY:**

Peter, Peter, pumpkin eater,

Had a wife and couldn't keep her.

He put her in a pumpkin shell,

And there he kept her very well.

| | | **EVERYBODY DO:** |
|---|---|---|
| (Low voice) | "Chomp, Chomp" | Eating action |
| (Low voice) | "What will I do? I love her!" | Fingers on temple and shake head |
| (Low voice) | "In you go!" | Pushing motion |
| (High voice) | "No, no! Please don't put me in that awful pumpkin shell!" | Outstretched hands |
| (High voice) | "This is terrible! Please don't leave me here." | Put head in hands and cry |
| (Low voice) | "This is wonderful! Now I always know where you are." | Laugh loudly |

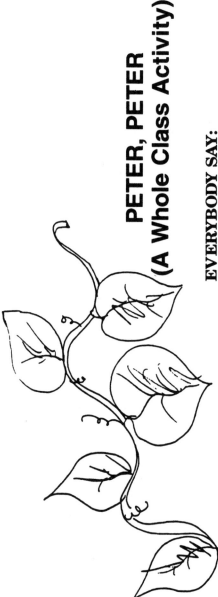

# COLOR IT!

Color the pictures using these colors.

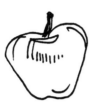

red     = apple

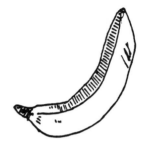

yellow  = banana

green   = leaf

white   = cloud

blue    = balloon

brown   = trunk

purple  = grapes

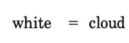

orange  = pumpkin

black   = witch

# MIXING IT UP

USING WATER COLORS, POSTER PAINTS, CRAYONS, OR COLORED PENCILS, FIND OUT WHAT THESE COLORS ADD UP TO.

RED + YELLOW =

BLUE + YELLOW =

BLUE + RED =

RED + BLUE + YELLOW =

BLUE + BLUE + BLUE + RED + RED + YELLOW =

# LIGHTEN UP

Adding white to a color makes a new color.

RED     + WHITE = PINK

BLUE    + WHITE = LIGHT BLUE

YELLOW + WHITE = LIGHT (PALE) YELLOW

GREEN   + WHITE = LIGHT GREEN

PURPLE  + WHITE = VIOLET

BROWN   + WHITE = TAN

BLACK   + WHITE = GRAY

Try it using water colors, poster paints,
crayons, or colored pencils.

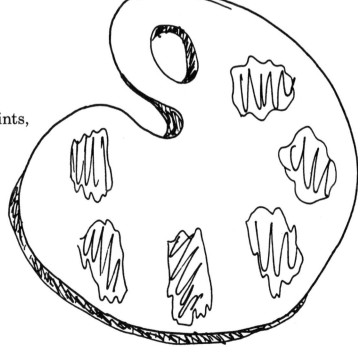

**Name** _____  **Date** _____

# SOAP CRAYONS

**To make a soap crayon for each color, you'll need:**

pure soap flakes
hot water
food coloring (red,
   blue, and yellow)

bowl
large spoon
measuring cup
measuring spoons
ice trays

**NOW:**
1. Pour 2 tablespoons of hot water into a bowl.
2. Add one cup of soap flakes.
3. Add about one teaspoon of food coloring.
4. Stir until you have made a thick paste. (This takes time.)
5. Press spoonfuls of the mixture into an ice-cube tray.
6. Place tray in a dry place for a day or two so the crayons can harden.
7. Bang the tray to loosen your crayons.

Reminder:   red + yellow  = orange
                 blue + red    = purple
                 yellow + blue = green

**Name** _____ **Date** _____

# MAKE YOUR OWN RAINBOW

**YOU'LL NEED:**

clear glass bowl
small mirror
water
sunny day

**NOW DO THIS:**

1. Fill the bowl with water.
2. Place the bowl in a sunny place.
3. Put a small mirror in the water, facing the sun.
4. Tilt the mirror at an angle.
5. When you get the angle right, you will see a rainbow of colors on the ceiling.

## RAINBOW COLORING

**WHAT TO DO:** Color this rainbow poem.

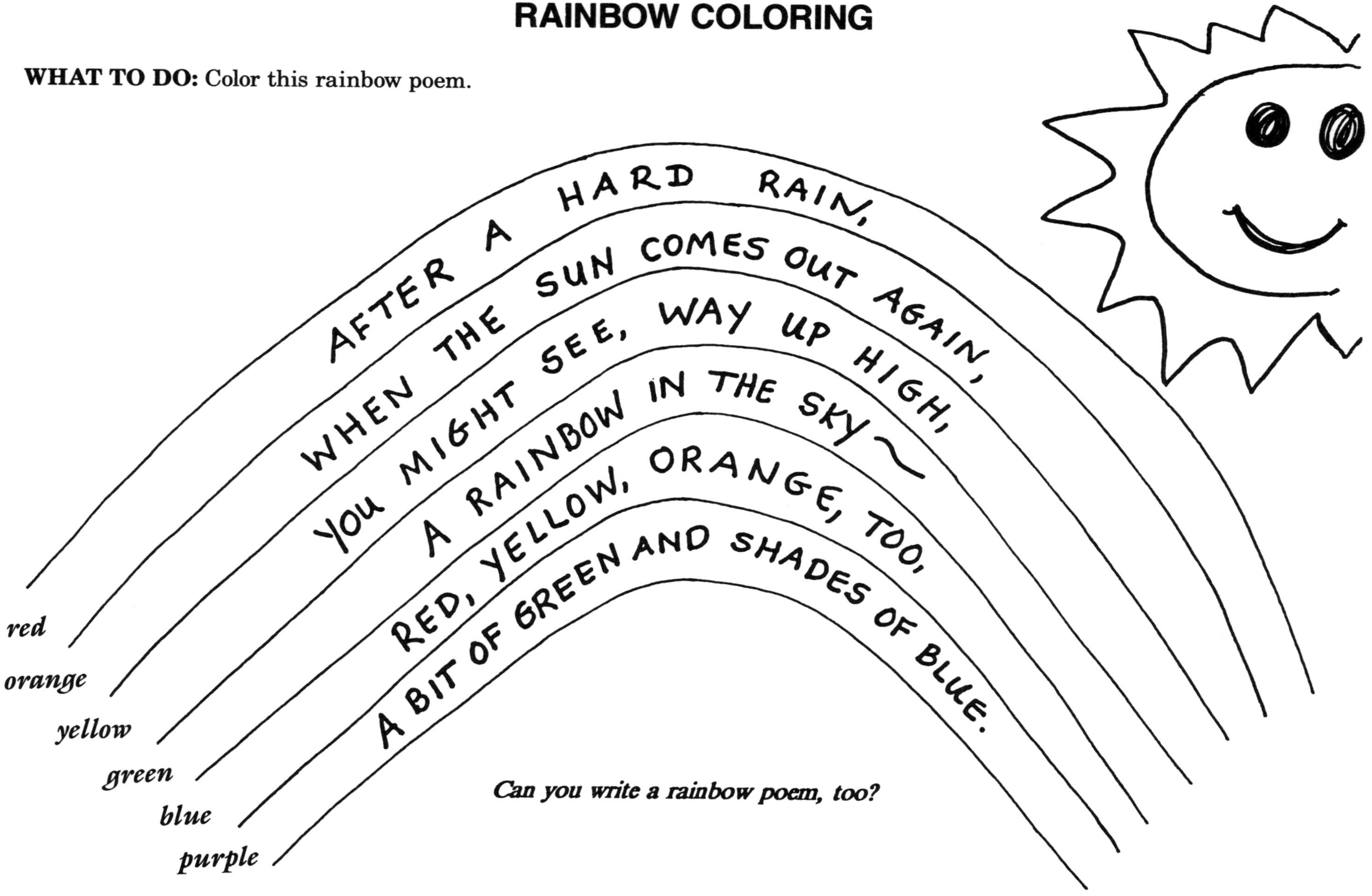

AFTER A HARD RAIN,

THE SUN COMES OUT AGAIN,

WHEN YOU MIGHT SEE, WAY UP HIGH,

A RAINBOW IN THE SKY ~

RED, YELLOW, ORANGE, TOO,

A BIT OF GREEN AND SHADES OF BLUE.

*Can you write a rainbow poem, too?*

red

orange

yellow

green

blue

purple

**Name** _____  **Date** _____

# THE SHAPE OF IT

**Color the shapes:**

rectangle = red

square = green

triangle = yellow

circle = blue

wide oval = orange

narrow oval = brown

square

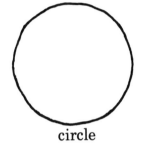

circle

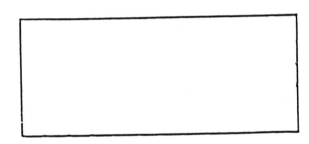

rectangle

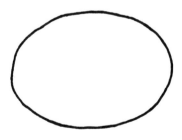

wide oval

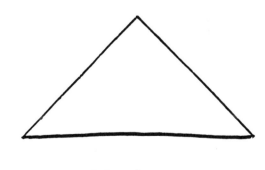

triangle

narrow oval

# SHAPE DRAWING

Add lines to make different objects out of the shapes, as in the examples.

**Name** _____

**Date** _____

# SHAPES AND COLORS

Look at the chart of shapes and colors.
Put your finger on the leaf in the first box.
It shows that I found a red leaf shaped like a triangle.
Now you try it. Look all over your classroom, school, and then outside to find things that match the shapes and colors.

| | RED | GREEN | YELLOW | ORANGE | BLUE | BROWN |
|---|---|---|---|---|---|---|
| ◁ | 🍂 | | | | | |
| ◯ | | | | | | |
| ▯ | | | | | | |
| ▢ | | | | | | |
| ⬭ | | | | | | |
| ⬮ | | | | | | |

# FUN WITH SHAPES

## WHAT DO YOU REALLY SEE?

1. Are these two circles the same size?

   Yes _____    No _____

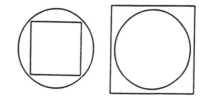

2. Are these two circles the same size?

   Yes _____    No _____

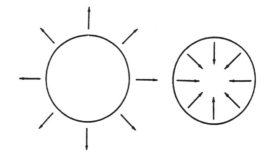

3. Are these two circles the same size?

   Yes _____    No _____

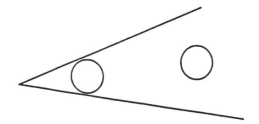

4. Are these two squares the same size?

   Yes _____    No _____

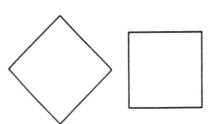

5. Do these lines really bend?

   Yes _____    No _____

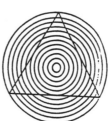 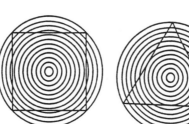 (Ask your teacher!)

© 1994 by The Center for Applied Research in Education

Answers: 1. yes; 2. yes; 3. yes;
4. yes; 5. no

Name _____   Date _____

# THE SHAPE OF MONEY

Coins in the United States look like this.

| NAME OF COIN: | CENTS: | | |
|---|---|---|---|
| penny | = one cent |  | = .01 |
| nickel | = five cents |  | = .05 |
| dime | = ten cents |  | = .10 |
| quarter | = twenty-five cents |  | = .25 |

## NOW TELL HOW MANY . . .

one nickel    = _____ pennies?

one dime    = _____ pennies?

= _____ nickels?

one quarter    = _____ pennies?

= _____ nickels?

= _____ nickels + 2 dimes?

**Answers: 5 pennies; 10 pennies, 2 nickels; 25 pennies, 5 nickels; one nickel**

# THE MONEY TREE

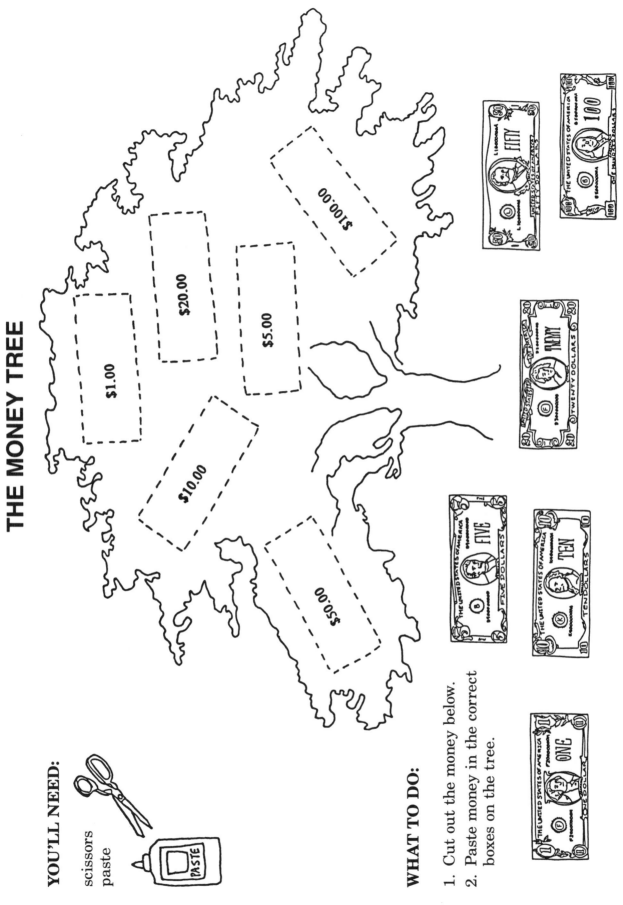

**YOU'LL NEED:**

scissors
paste

PASTE

**WHAT TO DO:**

1. Cut out the money below.
2. Paste money in the correct boxes on the tree.

$1.00

$20.00

$100.00

$5.00

$10.00

$50.00

Name _____    Date _____

**The Major Food Groups:**

# VEGETABLES

Do some coloring!

BEANS
(green)

ONIONS
(skin—orange/brown)
(flesh—white)

BROCCOLI
(dark green)

PEAS
(green)

CARROTS
(orange)

PEPPERS
(dark green)

CELERY
(light green)

POTATOES
(brown)

CORN
(yellow)

RADISHES
(skin—red)
(flesh—white)

CUCUMBERS
(skin—dark green)
(flesh—light green)

SPINACH
(dark green)

LETTUCE
(light green)
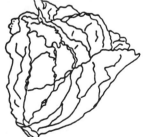

TOMATOES
(red)

**(Eat 3 to 5 servings every day.)**

Circle the vegetables you like.
What is your favorite vegetable? _____

Name _____ Date _____

**The Major Food Groups:**

# FRUITS

Do some coloring!

APPLES
(skin—red)
(flesh—white)

LEMONS
(yellow)

BANANAS
(skin—yellow)
(flesh—white)

ORANGES
(orange)

CANTALOUPE
(skin—tan)
(flesh—orange)

PEACHES
(dark yellow)

CHERRIES
(dark purple)

PEARS
(skin—light green)
(flesh—white)

GRAPES
(light green or purple)

WATERMELON
(skin—green)
(flesh—red)

GRAPEFRUIT
(skin—yellow)
(flesh—white or pink)

PINEAPPLES
(skin—brown/green)
(flesh—yellow)

STRAWBERRIES
(red)

**(Eat 2 to 3 servings every day.)**

Circle the fruits you like.
What is your favorite fruit? _____

Name _____    Date _____

**The Major Food Groups:**

# DAIRY PRODUCTS

Color these mostly white.

MILK

YOGURT

CHEESE

**(Eat 2 to 3 servings every day.)**

What is your favorite dairy product? _____

Name _____   Date _____

**The Major Food Groups:**

# MEATS, POULTRY, FISH, DRY BEANS, EGGS

Do some coloring!

**BEEF:** (brown)

hamburger

steak

roast beef

**POULTRY:** (tan and white)

chicken

turkey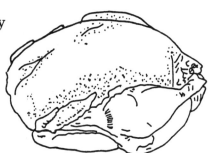

**LAMB:** (brown)

lamb chops

**PORK:**

pork chops (tan)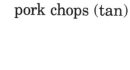

ham (pink)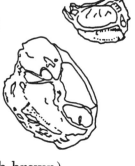

hot dogs (reddish brown)

**FISH:** (skin—gray)
(flesh—white)

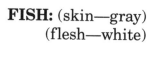

**DRY BEANS:** (tan, green, yellow, brown)

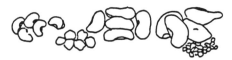

**EGGS:** (white or tan)

**(Eat 2 to 3 servings every day.)**

Circle the foods you like best.

**Name** _____  **Date** _____

**The Major Food Groups:**

# BREADS, CEREALS, RICE, PASTA

Color these all tan or white.

BREAD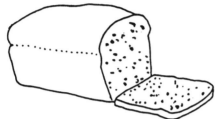

WAFFLES

BAGELS

CEREAL

MUFFINS

RICE

PANCAKES

PASTA—
SPAGHETTI
NOODLES

**(Eat 6 to 11 servings every day.)**

What is your favorite cereal? _____

What other foods do you like on this page? _____

Name _____  Date _____

# UM, UM, GOOD!

Make a check mark beside the foods you like.

FRUITS:

_____ apples

_____ bananas

_____ cantaloupe

_____ cherries

_____ grapes

_____ grapefruit

_____ lemons

_____ oranges

_____ peaches

_____ pears

_____ strawberries

_____ watermelon

VEGETABLES:

_____ beans

_____ broccoli

_____ carrots

_____ celery

_____ corn

VEGETABLES
(continued)

_____ cucumbers

_____ lettuce

_____ onions

_____ peas

_____ peppers

_____ potatoes

_____ radishes

_____ spinach

_____ tomatoes

MEATS, POULTRY,
FISH, EGGS

_____ hamburger

_____ steak

_____ roast beef

_____ chicken

_____ turkey

_____ lamb chops

_____ pork chops

MEATS, POULTRY, FISH,
EGGS (continued)

_____ ham

_____ hot dogs

_____ fish

_____ eggs

DAIRY PRODUCTS:

_____ cheese

_____ milk

_____ yogurt

BREADS, CEREALS,
RICE, PASTA

_____ bread

_____ bagels

_____ muffins

_____ pancakes

_____ waffles

_____ cereal

_____ rice

_____ spaghetti

**Name** _____ **Date** _____

# MEAL PLANNING

Choose from these foods to plan your meals:

| **(2 to 3 servings)** | **(2 to 3 servings)** | **(3 to 5 servings)** | **(2 to 4 servings)** |
|---|---|---|---|
| hamburger | milk | beans | apples |
| steak | cheese | broccoli | bananas |
| roast beef | yogurt | carrots | cantaloupe |
| chicken | | celery | cherries |
| turkey | **(6 to 11 servings)** | corn | grapes |
| lamb chops | bread | cucumbers | grapefruit |
| pork chops | bagels | lettuce | oranges |
| ham | muffins | peas | peaches |
| hot dogs | rolls | peppers | pears |
| fish | pancakes | potatoes | pineapple |
| eggs | waffles | spinach | strawberries |
| | cereal | tomatoes | watermelon |
| | rice | | apple juice |
| | spaghetti | | grape juice |
| | | | lemonade |
| | | | grapefruit juice |

**Breakfast:**

_____

_____

_____

_____

**Lunch:**

_____

_____

_____

_____

**Dinner:**

_____

_____

_____

_____

**Name** _____  **Date** _____

# LET'S GO FOOD SHOPPING!

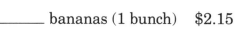

Check off the items you want to buy:

| | | |
|---|---|---|
| _____ bag of potatoes | $3.45 | |
| _____ celery (1 bunch) | $1.39 | |
| _____ broccoli (1 bunch) | $1.59 | |
| _____ bag of carrots | $1.79 | |
| _____ peppers (2) | $1.88 | |
| _____ lettuce (1 head) | $.99 | |
| _____ cucumbers (1) | $.45 | |
| _____ yogurt (1) | $.75 | |
| _____ milk (1 quart) | $.58 | |
| _____ cheese (½ pound) | $1.45 | |
| _____ spaghetti (1 box) | $1.19 | |
| _____ rice (1 box) | $1.99 | |
| _____ cereal (1 box) | $3.59 | |
| _____ bagels (6) | $1.75 | |
| _____ bread (1 loaf) | $1.69 | |

| | |
|---|---|
| _____ bananas (1 bunch) | $2.15 |
| _____ peaches (4) | $.98 |
| _____ pears (4) | $1.34 |
| _____ watermelon (¼) | $1.10 |
| _____ apples (4) | $.95 |
| _____ cantaloupe (1) | $1.49 |
| _____ grapefruit (1) | $.89 |
| _____ grapes (1 bunch) | $1.29 |
| _____ chicken (1 whole) | $12.58 |
| _____ turkey (1 whole) | $19.21 |
| _____ lamb chops (4) | $11.70 |
| _____ pork chops (4) | $10.53 |
| _____ hot dogs (8) | $4.59 |
| _____ steak (1) | $9.76 |

## NOW, ADD IT ALL UP!

I SPENT

$ _____

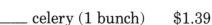

Name _____     Date _____

# FUN WITH FRUIT: INVISIBLE* JUICE INK

**What you'll need to make invisible ink:**

apple or lemon juice

a steel pen or fine brush

white paper

a lamp

**WHAT TO DO:**

1. Dip your brush or pen in the juice.

2. Write a special message to a friend on the paper. You won't be able to see it.

3. Let it dry.

4. Give the paper to your friend.

5. Have your friend hold it over a warm light bulb. Now she or he can read your words!

*invisible—cannot be seen

Name _____ Date _____

# MEASURING WORDS

3 teaspoons  = one tablespoon

4 tablespoons = one-quarter (¼) cup

**4**

16 tablespoons **16** = one cup

one cup  = 8 ounces **8**

2 cups  = 16 ounces

16 ounces  = one pint

1. How many tablespoons are in ½ cup? _____

2. How many ounces are in ½ cup? _____

3. How many ounces are in one pint? _____

Answers: 8; 4; 16

**Name** _____ **Date** _____

# GINGERBREAD-MEN COOKIES

**To make these cookies, you'll need:**

2-¼ cups flour
½ cup sugar
½ cup shortening
½ cup light molasses
1 egg
1 teaspoon double-acting
  baking powder
1 teaspoon ground ginger

1 teaspoon ground cloves
½ teaspoon nutmeg
½ teaspoon baking soda
½ teaspoon salt
raisins
mixer
large bowl

dish towel
rolling pin
cookie sheet
measuring cup
cookie cutters
pancake turner
cooling rack

## NOW, PRE-HEAT THE OVEN TO 350 DEGREES AND . . .

1. Put all ingredients in bowl—except the raisins.

2. With mixer at medium speed, beat until well mixed.

3. Cover and refrigerate.

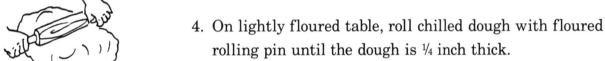

4. On lightly floured table, roll chilled dough with floured rolling pin until the dough is ¼ inch thick.

5. With cookie cutter, cut out gingerbread men.

6. Place gingerbread men on cookie sheet with pancake turner.

7. Give each gingerbread man eyes, a mouth, and buttons with the raisins.

8. Bake for 8 minutes or until brown.

9. Place on rack to cool.

# THE GINGERBREAD MAN

Everyone can help in telling this story.

| | | **Everybody:** |
|---|---|---|
| Narrator: | One day, an old woman made gingerbread dough. (pause) | Kneading and rolling dough motions. |
| Old Woman: | I think I'll make a big gingerbread man with this dough. (pause) | Touch foreheads as if thinking. |
| Narrator: | She gave him a raisin mouth, nose and eyes, and even raisin buttons. | |
| | Then she put him on a cookie sheet. (pause) | Place imaginary raisins. |
| Old Woman: | Into the oven you go, my sweet little gingerbread man. (pause) | Opening oven door and pushing in motions. |
| Narrator: | Suddenly she heard a banging sound. When she opened the oven door, out popped the gingerbread man! (pause) | "Let me out of here!" and snap fingers. |
| | Before she could catch him, he ran outside. (pause) | Pat thighs quickly. |
| Gingerbread Man: | Run, run, as fast as you can, you'll never catch me, I'm the gingerbread man! (pause) | Laughing, pat thighs quickly. |
| Narrator: | The old woman chased him into the garden where her husband was planting seeds. | Digging and planting motions. |
| Old Man: | Stop! Stop! You look good to eat! (pause) | Lick lips and rub bellies. |
| Gingerbread Man: | Run, run, as fast as you can, you'll never catch me, I'm the gingerbread man! (pause) | Laughing pat thighs quickly. |
| Narrator: | Next, he ran past a cow chewing on some grass. (pause) | "Mooo . . . Mooo . . ." and chewing motion. |
| Cow: | Mooo . . . Stop! Stop! You look good to eat. (pause) | Lick lips and rub bellies. |
| Gingerbread Man: | I've run from an old woman; I've run from an old man. Run, run, as fast as you can, you'll never catch me, I'm the gingerbread man! (pause) | Laughing, pat thighs quickly. |

# THE GINGERBREAD MAN (continued)

| | | **Everybody:** |
|---|---|---|
| Narrator: | With the old woman, the old man, and the cow chasing him, the gingerbread man now ran past a horse munching on grass. (pause) | |
| Horse: | Stop! Stop! You look good to eat! (pause) | Neighing sound and chewing motion. |
| Gingerbread Man: | I've run from an old woman; I've run from an old man; I've run from a cow, too. Run, run, as fast as you can, you'll never catch me, I'm the gingerbread man! (pause) | Lick lips and rub bellies. |
| Narrator: | No one could catch the gingerbread man. (pause) | Laughing, pat thighs quickly. |
| | But he had to stop running when he came to a river. (pause) | |
| Everybody: | We'll catch him now! (pause) | "Oh, dear. Oh, dear. He's too fast for us." Pat thighs quickly. Stop suddenly. Place hands on hips. |
| Narrator: | A fox was resting under a tree and saw all of this. (pause) | Get down on all fours |
| Fox: | To himself, he said . . . . | Lick lips and rub bellies. |
| | That little gingerbread man sure would taste good. (pause) | |
| Narrator: | To the gingerbread man, he said . . . . | |
| Fox: | Jump on my back, and I'll take you across the river. (pause) | Pat back/swimming motion. |
| Narrator: | Soon the water got deeper. (pause) | Pat shoulders/swimming motion. |
| Fox: | Stand on my head, so you won't get wet. (pause) | Pat head/swimming motion. |
| Narrator: | Now the water got even deeper. | Pat cheeks/swimming motion |
| Fox: | Sit on my nose. I don't want you to fall in the water. (pause) | Tap nose/swimming motion. |
| Narrator: | The gingerbread man quickly jumped onto the fox's nose. (pause) | Snap fingers/touch nose. |
| | At the same time, the fox opened his mouth very wide and ate the little gingerbread man all up! (pause) | Open mouth wide and make a big gulping sound. |

**Name** _____  **Date** _____

# ANOTHER LOOK

**WHO** made the gingerbread man? _____

**WHO** ran after the gingerbread man?

1. _____

2. _____

3. _____

4. _____

**HOW** did the gingerbread man get across the river? _____
_____

**WHAT** happened to the gingerbread man at the end of the story? _____
_____

Answers: an old woman; the old woman, her husband, a cow,
a horse; on the fox's back; He was eaten by the fox.

# BOX IT!

## LOOK AT THE FIGURE ON THE NEXT PAGE AND THEN:

1. In square #1, write the title, then draw and color the gingerbread man.
2. In square #2, draw and color the old woman running.
3. In square #3, draw and color the old man running.
4. In square #4, draw and color the cow chasing the gingerbread man.
5. In square #5, draw and color the horse galloping.
6. In square #6, draw the fox eating the gingerbread man.

## THEN:

1. Cut out along the solid line.  ✄ _____
2. Fold along dotted lines.  _ _ _ _ _ _
3. Glue as shown. (Glue and fold bottom flap last.)

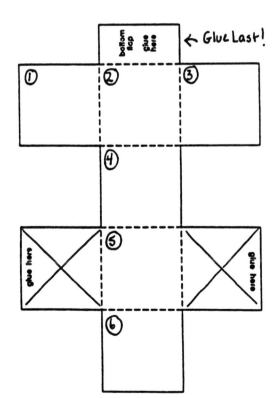

bottom
flap

glue
here

1)

2)

3)

4)

glue here

5)

glue here

6)

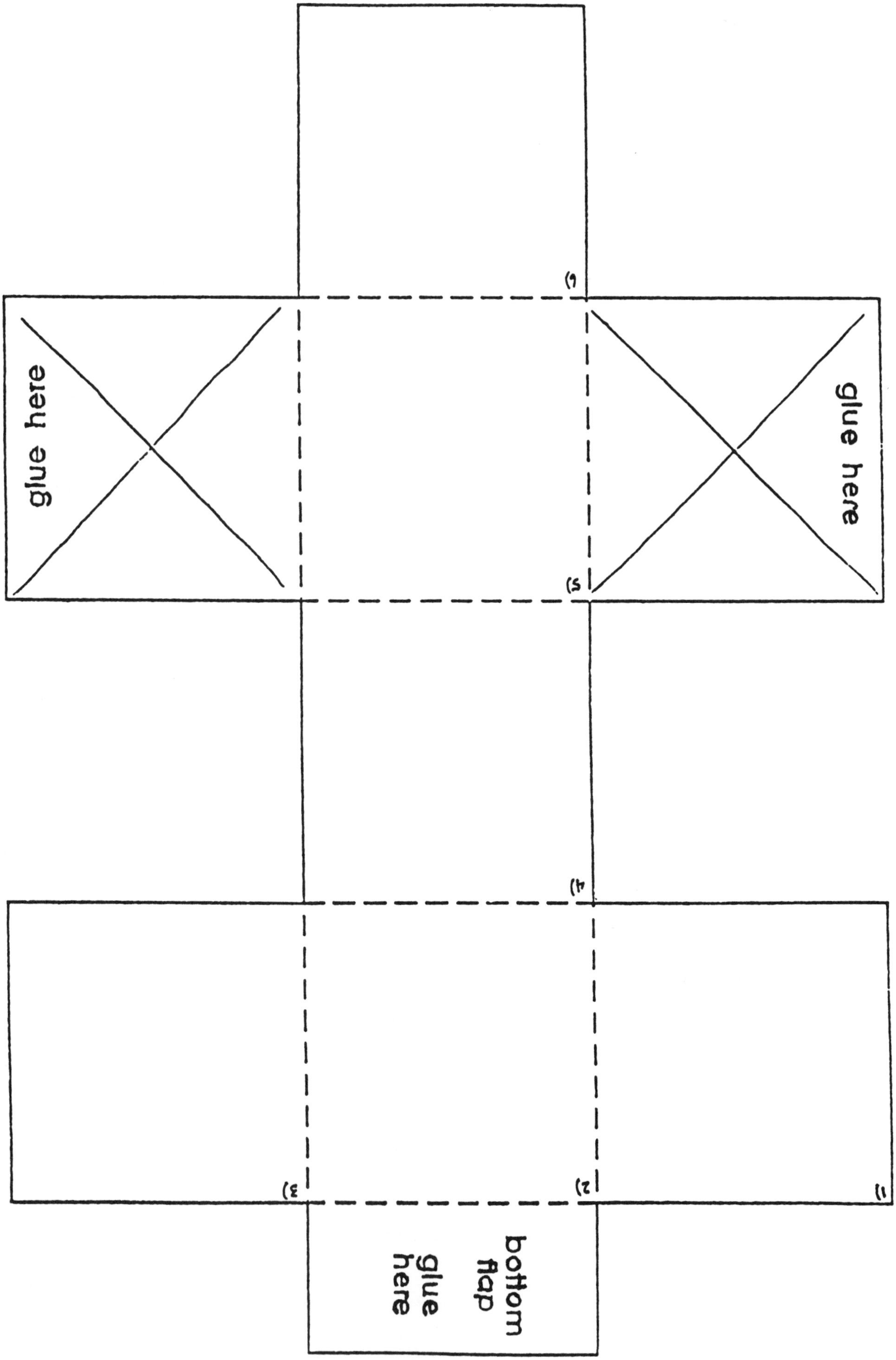

# NOVEMBER

Teacher Notes and Additional Activities
Monthly Activities
Our Bodies and Clothing
Story and Related Activities

# NOVEMBER
# Teacher Notes and Additional Activities

## Calendar

Encourage children to decorate their calendars, noting important dates and birthdays. Make a large classroom calendar, as well, and celebrate birthdays.

Autumn has now changed the landscape considerably. Take the children for a walk and note the changes. Pick up leaves, browned grass, broken twigs, etc. Then, make a large T-Chart for November, noting what the month looks like and feels like. This can also be the basis for a Language Experience Approach Activity, with the students writing about fall and how they feel about leaving summer behind.

## Election Day

The idea of voting may be new to some of your students, so it is important to give them some experience with "choosing." Use the questions I have included as a starting point and add others if you like. Poll their choices and make a large bar graph for each category to reflect their votes. Ask why they voted as they did and generate a list of reasons. If possible, prepare a class lunch based on their favorite meal, vegetable, fruit, and ice cream.

Encourage the children to share how officials are chosen in their native countries and turn into a chart.

Depending on your students, you may also wish to elect class officers, first explaining the responsibilities of those positions.

Using the newspaper, have students follow local, state, and/or national elections. Explain the positions these people are running for and make a list of what each candidate stands for/is promising, as well as their candidates' differences in race and gender. Let them cast ballots and then compare their results with those of the actual elections.

These activities will serve well as the basis for more group writing.

## Thanksgiving

The idea of "giving thanks" needs to be explored. I've given your students a start with home, family, etc. Share their ideas and make a class list of "What We Are Thankful For."

Have each child write a special thank-you sentence to each person in his/her family. These should then be folded and placed on each family member's pillow.

Make Thanksgiving decorations using pine cones, pipe cleaners, and colored paper. Have the children cut tail feathers from the paper and insert these into the pine cones, gluing them in place. Do the same thing with the neck and head. Finally, attach a pipe cleaner for the legs.

Making butter will be fun and easy. Be sure to bring in some bread!

Tell the story of the Pilgrims and how they came to America to find a better life, just as many of their families did. Generate a list of why their families came to this country and what America means to them.

All of these activities can serve as the basis for more group writing.

## Forcing Bulbs

This is a favorite project with most children, and the forced bulbs make wonderful gifts. If there is an unheated storage room in your school, store the plants there, watering them together about once a week, and checking on their progress. They'll be ready just about by Christmas!

Let the children draw sequence pictures starting with the bulb and empty pot and then reflecting what is seen as each week passes until the bulb finally blooms. These can then be labeled.

## Our Bodies

Before doing **Body Parts** and **What Am I?** point to all the parts of your body, letting the children follow your example. Once you are assured of their understanding, play "Simon Says" with commands such as, "Simon says close your eyes!"

Have the students create a "body" using these shapes and directions that you can call out. The children can then use a different color for each body part and then cut their creations out.

| | |
|---|---|
| 1 big circle for the head | 1 small rectangle for the neck |
| 2 small circles for the ears | 1 large square for the body (torso) |
| 1 semicircle for the mouth | 2 rectangles for the arms |
| 2 circles for the eyes | 2 small diamonds for the hands |
| 2 very small semicircles for the eyebrows | 2 long rectangles for the legs |
| 1 small diamond for the nose | 2 small triangles for the feet |

Dictate a "monster" with directions such as, "It has 2 heads; 4 noses; 3 eyes; 1 body; 6 legs; 8 toes; 4 arms; 4 hands; 8 fingers."

"Dem Bones" is a great song to teach your students. You might want to change a few of the lines, such as singing, "Now hear the word of us all!" instead of "Now hear the word of the Lord!" Get the children moving each part of their body at the appropriate time.

Group your students and ask them to think of an action word to go with each body part and put these on index cards, with the body part (lips) on one side, and the verb (smile) on the other. These can then be enacted much like a game of Charades. Later, you can hang the cards in rows with string or you might want to find a fallen branch and put it in a tub filled with sand, suspending the cards from the branches.

Do **All About Me** together as a large-group activity. First read the poem several times for the children, encouraging them to follow along carefully. Some may join you early on. Do all the movements, too. Once most of them are familiar with the words and motions, let them read it, adding all the actions, too.

Have your students go on a "Human Treasure Hunt," going about the room, recording the number of people with blue, brown, or green eyes; red, brown, black, or blonde hair; long/short hair; curly/straight hair. You can follow this up by measuring the height of each child and recording this on a long strip of paper. It will be interesting to remeasure them in June and compare the differences. Charting this information is also suggested.

Engage the children in group writing about the human body and its wonders.

## Clothing

Before beginning this unit, bring in an assortment of clothes and outer wear and label them. To help you find out what they already know, point to each piece of clothing and ask what it is, helping where needed. Then, use commands such as, "Johnny, get the red sweater and give it to Sue," to fully acquaint your students with the various articles of clothing. Hand out the clothes to your students and give such commands for buttoning, unbuttoning, zipping, unzipping, putting on, and taking off.

Later, have the children group the clothing and outer wear according to their appropriate season and/or activity, such as beach wear, school clothes, etc., and tell why. Develop this into a class chart.

For the paper-doll activity, have your students cut out and color everything. Then, with the whole group, give directions such as, "Take off her dress and put on her blouse and skirt," etc. Later, working in small groups, have the children create mobiles with these materials.

Move all the desks and chairs out of the way and have your students line up across the back of the room. Say such things as, "If you're wearing slacks, take one giant step forward," etc. Give the winner some kind of reward, perhaps an ice cream coupon redeemable in the cafeteria, some bonus points, or a lollipop.

## All of Me

For this review activity, be sure to pair up your students so they can trace each other's bodies on brown wrapping paper or shelving paper. Before coloring in both the body parts and the clothing they happen to be wearing they should label them.

## Print People

Before involving your students in this activity, you might want to bring in lots of newspaper comics. These can then be put on the overhead and read together. The words can also be whited out and filled in by your students. You can also give a comic to groups of children to be acted out.

Another fun activity is to let the children cut out pictures of people from magazines and paste on paper. They can then draw balloons and make them "talk."

When you feel they are ready for **Print People,** make sure that you have enough stamp pads to go around. After they complete this activity, have them share their creations. You can follow this up by having the children fold a sheet of white paper in quarters, so that they can develop their own "print people" comic strip.

**Remember that many of these activities lend themselves well to Language Experience Approach (LEA) activities.**

## "Little Red Riding Hood"

This classic tale is full of action, with a predictable plot and happy ending. I have rewritten it as a play, but first be sure to read it several times so that your students become fully acquainted with the story before trying it themselves. Add lots of actions and sound effects in your telling. Once that has been accomplished, let your students volunteer for the various parts. Some may feel more comfortable working in pairs. Your less fluent readers will, of course, participate in the "Everybody" parts. If you can, bring in some props, such as a cape (very large scarf) for Little Red Riding Hood, an apron for her mother, a nightcap (shower cap) for the grandma and wolf, oversized Halloween teeth for the wolf, and a large stick to serve as the ax for the woodcutter.

**Tell It Again** can be done individually, in groups, or all together using an overhead, filling in the blanks as they summarize the story and then describe the ending. This can also be turned into a Language Experience Approach (LEA)/big book activity.

**What's Happening** asks the students to recall the story and do some writing. If need be, you can do this as a whole group activity using an overhead.

# IT'S NOVEMBER!

Autumn

30 days

Election Day

"Vote for me!"

Thanksgiving

"Gobble, Gobble!"

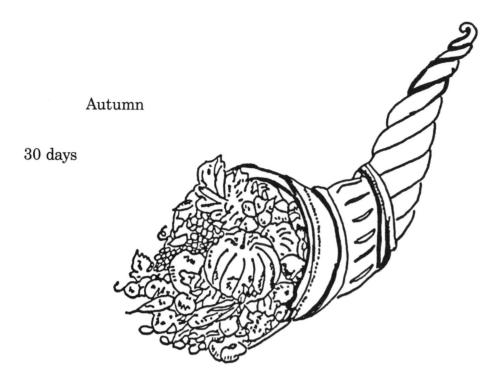

**Look at the November calendar on the next page and . . .**

1. Number the days on your calendar.

2. Cut and paste  on the first Tuesday of the month—after the first Monday—for Election Day.

3. Cut and paste  on the fourth Thursday of the month for Thanksgiving.

4. Cut and paste    on special birthdays.

Name _____

Date _____

# NOVEMBER

| SUNDAY | MONDAY | TUESDAY | WEDNESDAY | THURSDAY | FRIDAY | SATURDAY |
|--------|--------|---------|-----------|----------|--------|----------|
|        |        |         |           |          |        |          |
|        |        |         |           |          |        |          |
|        |        |         |           |          |        |          |
|        |        |         |           |          |        |          |
|        |        |         |           |          |        |          |

Name _____  Date _____

# ELECTION DAY

On Election Day, Americans choose (elect) the people they want to lead them in their towns, states, and country. Every four years, we also vote for our president and vice-president to be our national leaders.

Who is the president of the United States? _____

Who is our vice-president? _____

## ANOTHER KIND OF VOTING:

1. Vote for your favorite fruit:

_____ apples

_____ bananas

_____ oranges

_____ grapes

2. Vote for your favorite vegetable:

_____ broccoli

_____ carrots

_____ potatoes

_____ celery

3. Vote for your favorite season:

_____ autumn

_____ winter

_____ spring

_____ summer

4. Vote for your favorite meal:

_____ hamburgers

_____ pizza

_____ spaghetti

_____ chicken

_____ steak

_____ hot dogs

5. Vote for your favorite ice cream flavor:

_____ chocolate

_____ vanilla

_____ strawberry

_____ chocolate chip

6. Vote for your favorite school subject:

_____ reading/English

_____ math

_____ science

_____ social studies/history

## CLASS FAVORITES:

FRUIT: _____  VEGETABLE: _____

SEASON: _____  MEAL: _____

ICE CREAM: _____  SUBJECT: _____

# HAPPY THANKSGIVING!

On Thanksgiving Day, families get together to give thanks for all they have. Then they share a big turkey dinner.

I am thankful for my: home    _____     _____

friends    _____     _____

family    _____     _____

school    _____     _____

At the first Thanksgiving dinner, the Pilgrims sat down with the Indians and ate for three days. One of the things they ate was homemade butter. Now you can make it, too!

**WHAT YOU NEED:** ½ pint of heavy cream

an egg beater

a mixing bowl

**WHAT TO DO:**

1. Pour the cream into the bowl.
2. Beat the cream until the cream stiffens into butter. (This will take some time.)
3. Put on some bread and enjoy!

**Name** _____   **Date** _____

# SPRING INTO WINTER!

**To enjoy spring flowers this winter, this is what you will need:**

hardy bulbs, such as:     tulip     crocus     hyacinth     daffodil

clay pot or coffee can that is at least 2 times as high as the bulb
potting soil
a large box with a cover
water
a cool garage or basement

## NOW:

1. If using a clay pot, cover the drainage hole with a stone.
2. Fill the container about halfway up with soil.
3. Gently press the bulb(s) into the soil.
4. Add more soil so only the tips of the bulb show.
5. Water well.

## THEN:

1. Place your container in the large box and cover.
2. Place the box in a cool basement or garage.
3. Water once a week.

## 12 WEEKS LATER:

Now the sprouts will be about 2" tall, so you can take your container
out of the box and bring it into your house. Let it rest away from the
light for a few days. Then put it in a sunny window and watch your
flowers bloom!

**Name** _____  **Date** _____

# BODY PARTS

Let's start with my  head. On top, you see, it is covered with

 hair. On each side of my head, I have an  ear, so I can hear you. I

also have two big  eyes. They let me see you. My  nose is for

smelling. My mouth has two  lips for kissing and licking. Inside it has

 teeth for chewing and a  tongue for tasting my food. It lets me talk,

too. My head sits on my  neck. It lets me look to my  left and

 right and up and  down.

Inside my  chest, my  heart beats  day and

 night. When I eat, my  stomach fills with food. My two

 arms can hug you, and with my two  hands and ten

 fingers, I can catch a ball and write my name! And down

below, with those two  legs, two  feet, and ten

 toes of mine, I sure do get around!

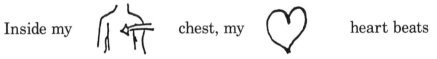

Name _____ Date _____

# WHAT AM I?

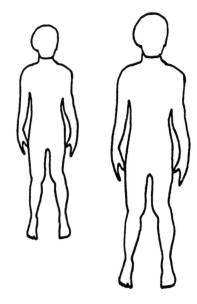

**WORD BANK:**

| | | | |
|---|---|---|---|
| teeth | hair | toes | neck |
| nose | legs | tongue | eyes |
| heart | fingers | stomach | lips |
| ears | feet | | |

**DIRECTIONS:** Find the right answers, using the words listed above.

1. Curly ⦃ or straight ⧸ , I'm on top of it all. _____

2. You see with me. _____

3. My job is smelling. _____

4. I hear every sound. _____

5. I smile and frown and can kiss you, too! _____

6. I like to chew. _____

7. I taste your food and help you talk. _____

8. Your head sits on me. _____

9. Inside your chest, I beat all the time. _____

10. I tell you when you are hungry. _____

11. There are ten of me, five on each hand. _____

12. You need me to walk and run. We are your _____.

   We each have one _____ and five _____.

© 1994 by The Center for Applied Research in Education

**Answers: 1. hair; 2. eyes; 3. nose; 4. ears; 5. lips; 6. teeth; 7. tongue; 8. neck; 9. heart; 10. stomach; 11. fingers; 12. legs, foot, toes**

# ALL ABOUT ME!
## (A Class Activity)

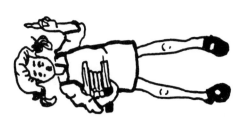

**Everybody:**

Open your mouth wide. Laugh and chew.
Sniff the air.

"No, No!" and shake your head.

Touch both ears; clap loudly and softly.
Roll your eyes around.

"No, No!" and shake your head.

Hugging motion
Put both hands up and wiggle fingers.
Pretend to write and carry something. Wave.

"No, No!" and shake your head.

"Thump, thump!"
Rub your stomach.

"No, No!" and shake your head.

Look down at your legs and feet.
Shake legs and wiggle toes.
Run, hop, and walk around the room.

---

I use my mouth to open wide, talk and laugh and eat my food.
And with my nose, I sniff the air—oh, everything smells so good!

    BUT THAT'S NOT ALL!

I listen very carefully, so my two ears can hear every sound,
While my two shining eyes go round and round.

    BUT THAT'S NOT ALL!

My two arms reach out to hug and hold,
But they need my two hands and ten fingers, too,
So I can write and carry things, and wave to you.

    BUT THAT'S NOT ALL!

Inside my chest, my heart beats day and night.
And right below, my stomach growls for food to make it feel right.

    BUT THAT'S NOT ALL!

There's more of me, as you can see, if you just look straight down.
I have two legs, two feet, and ten little toes,
So I can run, and jump, and walk around!

**Name** _____  **Date** _____

# THE CLOTHES WE WEAR

When I get dressed for school in the morning, I like to wear a  skirt and

a  blouse. Sometimes, I wear a pretty  dress. On my feet, I wear

 socks and a pair of  shoes. My brother wears  slacks

and a  shirt. He almost never wears a  suit. If it is cool outside, we

put on a  sweater or a  jacket.

When it's raining, I wear my  raincoat and carry my

umbrella. In the winter, I always have to wear my  coat and

 gloves. I tie a  scarf around my neck to keep it warm. We wear

 boots, so we can walk in the snow.

In the summer, we love to play outside. I wear just my  shorts and a

 T-shirt. Sometimes we go to the beach. That's when I wear my green and

pink bathing suit.

# PAPER-DOLL MOBILES

## WHAT YOU NEED:

crayons     needle and thread
scissors     hangers

## WHAT TO DO:

1. Color the paper dolls and their clothes on the following pages.
2. Cut them out.
3. Label each article of clothing on the back.
4. Dress the dolls up, putting on and taking off their clothes.
5. Make a mobile.

CONTINUED . . .

# PAPER-DOLL MOBILES (continued)

COLOR AND CUT OUT . . .

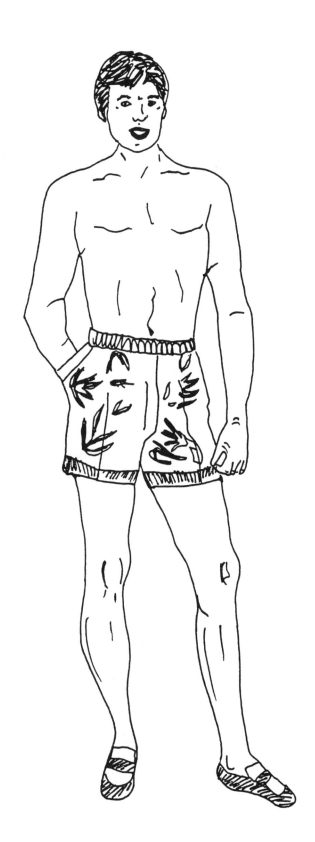

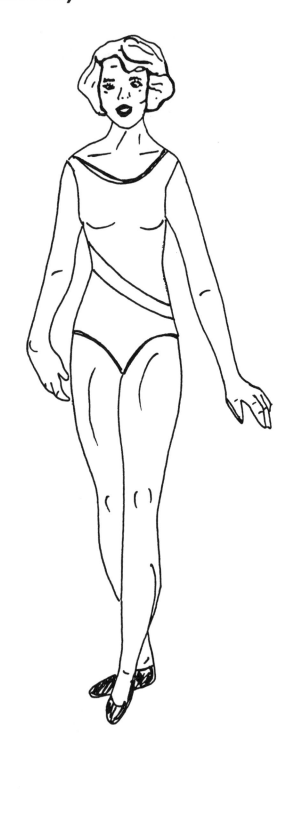

# PAPER-DOLL MOBILES (continued)

## COLOR AND CUT OUT . . .

# PAPER-DOLL MOBILES (continued)

**COLOR AND CUT OUT . . .**

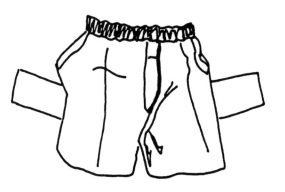

# PAPER-DOLL MOBILES (continued)

COLOR AND CUT OUT . . .

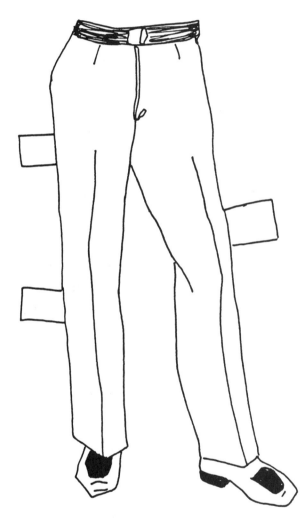

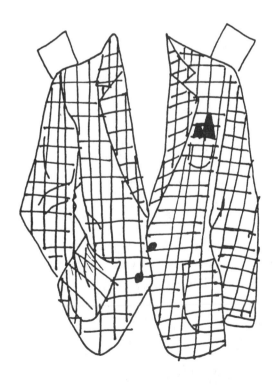

# ALL OF ME

**To draw a picture of yourself, you will need a partner and:**

1. A long sheet of butcher block paper or white shelving paper
2. A pencil and crayons

**NOW:**

1. Lie on the paper while your friend traces around your body.

2. Switch and do the same thing for your friend on another piece of paper.

3. Color yourself in to look just the way you do today, right down to your shoes!

4. Label all the parts of your body that you can and all the clothes you're wearing.

5. Put your name on the very top.

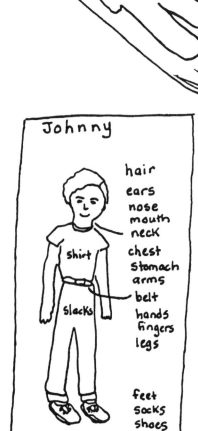

Name _____ Date _____

# PRINT PEOPLE

**To create fingerprint people, you will need:**
a black, felt-tip pen,
crayons or colored pencils

"PLEASE, FIX US UP AND MAKE US TALK!"

With a stamp pad, you can make your own print people!

# LITTLE RED RIDING HOOD
## (A Class Activity)

CHARACTERS:    Little Red Riding Hood    Grandma
    Mother    Woodcutter
    Wolf

| | |
|---|---|
| Narrator: | Once upon a time, in the middle of the forest, a little girl lived with her mother in a small house. Instead of a jacket, she always wore a red cape. It had a nice, warm hood, and she loved it very much—especially since it was red! |
| Everybody: | Ooh, how that girl loved the color red! That's why we call her Little Red Riding Hood. |
| Narrator: | Everyone loved the little girl, especially her grandmother who lived on the other side of the forest. |
| Everybody: | She loved her so much! |
| Narrator: | Little Red Riding Hood's grandma visited her every day. But one day, Grandma got very sick and had to stay in bed. |
| Everybody: | What a shame! |
| Mother: | Grandma is sick in bed, Little Red Riding Hood. |
| Little Red Riding Hood: | Then I will go and visit her. |
| Mother: | Take this basket with you, dear. I've made some chicken soup and juice for her. But you must promise to stay on the path and don't talk to strangers. |
| Everybody: | No, no! Don't talk to strangers! |
| Little Red Riding Hood: | I promise, mother. |

| | |
|---|---|
| Narrator: | Little Red Riding Hood took the basket, waved goodbye, and started down the path. Before long, she met a wolf. |
| Everybody: | Oh, dear! Oh, dear! |
| Wolf: | Good morning, Little Red Riding Hood! And where are you going this fine day? |
| Everybody: | What a polite wolf! |
| Little Red Riding Hood: | I'm taking some chicken soup and juice to my grandmother. She is not feeling well. |
| Wolf: | What a nice child you are! Now tell me, where does your grandma live? |

# LITTLE RED RIDING HOOD (continued)

| | |
|---|---|
| Everybody: | What a smart wolf! |
| Little Red Riding Hood: | She lives near the end of the path. I must go now and take care of her. |
| Wolf: | Yes, yes, but first, why not pick some flowers for her? |
| Little Red Riding Hood: | I promised my mother I would stay on the path. |
| Wolf: | Yes, but flowers are so pretty. Your grandma will love them. |
| Everybody: | Don't listen to him, Little Red Riding Hood. Hurry to your grandma's house! |
| Narrator: | The wolf ran off to Grandma's house, and Little Red Riding Hood started picking flowers. |

| | |
|---|---|
| Everybody: | Knock! Knock! |
| Grandma: | Who is knocking at my door? |
| Wolf: (in a high voice) | Grandma, it's me, Little Red Riding Hood. |
| Grandma: | Come in, my sweet girl. Come in. |
| Everybody: | No, No! |
| Narrator: | The wolf went in, licking his lips and rubbing his belly. |
| Everybody: | (*Lick lips and rub bellies.*) |
| Wolf: | I'm putting you in the closet for now, Grandma. She'll be here soon. What a dinner I'll have tonight! |
| Narrator: | Quickly, the wolf put on a nightgown and night cap and jumped into bed. Then he pulled the blanket up over his nose and waited. |

| | |
|---|---|
| Everybody: | Knock! Knock! |
| Little Red Riding Hood: | It's me, Grandma. |
| Wolf: | Come in, my sweet child. |
| Everybody: | Run away, Little Red Riding Hood! |
| Narrator: | When Little Red Riding Hood looked at her grandma, she couldn't believe her eyes. |
| Little Red Riding Hood: | Oh, Grandma! What big ears you have! |
| Wolf: | All the better to hear you with, my dear. |
| Everybody: | (*Touch ears and rub bellies.*) |

# LITTLE RED RIDING HOOD (continued)

Little Red Riding Hood:    Oh, Grandma! What big eyes you have!

Wolf:    All the better to see you with, my dear.

Everybody:    (*Roll eyes and rub bellies.*)

Little Red Riding Hood:    Oh, Grandma! What big teeth you have!

Wolf:    All the better to eat you with, my dear!

Narrator:    The wolf jumped from the bed and chased Little Red Riding Hood around the room.

Little Red Riding Hood:    Help! Help!

Narrator:    A woodcutter heard her cries and ran into the house.

Woodcutter:    You nasty wolf! You'll not eat again!

Narrator:    The woodcutter lifted his ax and killed the wolf.

Everybody:    Yes! Yes! The mean, old wolf is dead!

Narrator:    The woodcutter and Little Red Riding Hood took Grandma out of the closet. Then Little Red Riding Hood opened up her basket and they all sat down and ate some chicken soup and juice.

Everybody:    Slurp! Slurp!

**Name** _____  **Date** _____

# WHAT'S HAPPENING?

**DIRECTIONS:** Tell what's happening in each picture.

1.  _____

_____

_____

2.  _____

_____

_____

3.  _____

_____

_____

4.  _____

_____

_____

5.  _____

_____

_____

6.  _____

_____

_____

7.  _____

_____

_____

**Name** _____  **Date** _____

# TELL IT AGAIN!

**DIRECTIONS:** Fill in the blanks.

Little Red Riding Hood's _____ got sick, so her mother

asked her to take a _____ with her when she visited her grandma.

Inside the basket, her mother had packed _____ and _____.

Little Red Riding Hood promised her mother that she would _____

and not _____. But, on the path, Little Red Riding Hood met a

_____. He was very polite. After he left, she picked some _____

to take to her grandma. Where did the wolf go? _____

_____. After the wolf put Grandma in the _____, he put on her

_____ and _____. Then he jumped into her _____

and waited for _____ to arrive. When Little Red

Riding Hood saw her grandma, she said: "Oh, what big _____, _____,

and _____ you have, Grandma! Then the wolf tried to _____

_____. The story ends when _____

_____

_____

_____

_____

_____

© 1994 by The Center for Applied Research in Education

**Answers: grandmother; basket; chicken soup and juice; not talk to strangers; wolf; flowers; to Grandma's house; closet; nightgown and night cap; bed; Little Red Riding Hood; ears, eyes, teeth; catch and eat Little Red Riding Hood; the woodcutter kills the wolf, saves Grandma, and they eat.**

# DECEMBER

# DECEMBER
# Teacher Notes and Additional Activities

## December and December Calendar

Besides special holidays, December ushers in the first day of winter—the shortest day of the year. To start, put **December** on an overhead, going through the statements together. As a group, brainstorm the holidays and talk about the coming season. Have the children color and cut out the small pictures, pasting them onto the calendar. Note and celebrate December birthdays.

Read books such as *The Penguin That Hated the Cold* by Barbara Brenner and *The Snowy Day* by Ezra Jack Keats to the class.

A Venn diagram would work very well here, comparing and contrasting autumn and winter.

A T-Chart will allow your students to talk about what winter feels like and looks like.

Your children can make snowman pins by gluing 3 cotton balls on a strip of felt and then adding felt or paper details. Attach a safety pin to the back.

Using black construction paper and white chalk, have your students draw winter scenes.

You can show the children how and why the seasons change by showing how the earth turns on its axis, while revolving around the sun. Painted Styrofoam balls and a flashlight will do the trick!

How short is the shortest day of the year? Take the children to the library and check the newspaper for the time the sun rose and when it will set each day this month. Record their findings on a chart drawn on butcher block paper, adding up the hours and minutes of daylight for each day. Continue this project for some time, watching the days slowly grow longer. If you prefer, tape nightly TV forecasts that include the time of the rising and setting of the sun.

## Hanukkah

First, list the major religions of the world and explain that a temple or synagogue is a place of worship for Jews. Then briefly tell the story of Hanukkah, using a map to show the Middle East as an aid: 2000 years ago, the Jews were ruled by a mean Syrian king named Antiochus. He made the Jews leave their Temple in Jerusalem and told them they had to worship Greek gods. If they said no, he killed them. Finally, the Jews fought back. Judah Maccabee was their leader, along with his five sons. At last, the Jews took back their city of Jerusalem. After they cleaned their Temple, they could find only one small jar of oil, enough to burn for only one night. But something wonderful happened—a miracle. The oil burned for eight days, giving the Jews time to find more oil. That is why Jews today celebrate Hanukkah for eight days, and light a candle for each of those eight days.

Children can make a simple memorah by making 9 small candle holders out of clay. These can then be placed on a metal tray. Birthday candles will do fine. Insert first one, then two, then three candles, etc., for each of the eight days, always using the ninth candle to light the others.

You will very likely find children of different faiths in your classroom. You might want to encourage them to share one or two of their customs with the class.

The dreidel game is easy and fun to play. Directions are provided on page 113.

## Christmas: A Wreath of Hands; Holly Place Cards

"A Wreath of Hands" works well with small groups, setting the tone for the holiday. Afterward, you might want to make a class wreath.

Read Clement C. Moore's *The Night Before Christmas* and Patricia Scarry's *The Sweet Smell of Christmas* to the class.

Bring in a bag filled with cards noting different gifts. Hand one to each child who pretends to unwrap it and then describe it, such as "It has 2 wheels, 2 handlebars, 1 seat." The class guesses what it is.

Recycle old Christmas cards, giving some to each child to make "new" ones for sending this year.

Children can make their own wrapping paper using sponges or potato halves cut with a design dipped into colorful tempera paint.

Bring in lots of catalogs and have the children cut out gifts they want either for themselves or to buy for someone else. These can then be pasted on a large red paper boot and displayed.

Have each child bring in their favorite toy. Do a group writing activity with each child describing his or her toy and why it is so special to him or her.

Plan a party and have the children make their holly place cards. Invite parents, too. Ask them to bring in cookies and juice. Children can swap small gifts, but this isn't necessary.

At the party: Play such games as **Musical Chairs** using (nonreligious) Christmas music.

Play **Button Button**: everyone—except IT—sits in a circle. IT sits in the center. The button is passed from one child to the next but all hands remain in motion so it looks as if everyone is passing along the button. When IT guesses who has the button, the two trade places.

Play **Solemn Action** (Iran): Everyone sits in a circle and one player begins by making some motion, such as tickling the chin of the next player. Each player repeats that motion with the person to his or her right, and so on, around the circle. Anyone who laughs or speaks is out of the game, and the last one left is the winner.

## Transportation: What Am I?, Getting There, Reading a Train Schedule

Make a group list of traveling words, everything from walk and crawl to fly. Then let the children enact the words. Add a few of your own to the list and act them out for the class.

Generate a list of the different ways of getting from one place to another, from feet to planes. Then, let the children role-play the vehicles, complete with sound effects. Then, using magazines, newspapers, and original drawings, have the class make transportation mobiles. (Be sure that the children understand that more than people are transported from one place to another.) This can be done in groups, with each choosing between water, land, and air travel.

On the board, write **slow, fast, faster, fastest**. Together, categorize the various means of getting from one place to another, including walking and biking.

Enlarge and put the map from "Getting There" on the overhead. Identify the states and show their location on a full map of the country. Explain what is meant by a legend and go over the symbols used in this activity. Next, make cards for each city and the different modes of transportation. Hand these out so that each child has a destination and a way of getting there. Clear an area of the room and let a chair represent each city and label it. Spread the children across the front of the "map" area and let them move to their destination at the appropriate speed. Then complete the questions together.

Learning to read schedules is not only practical but reinforces such concepts as time, sequence, distance, relationships, and numbers. Put the schedule on an overhead, explaining how to read both across and down the columns. Ask a few questions, such as "If you miss a train, how long do you have to wait for the next one?" Then work through the activity together. As a follow-up, divide the class into groups and have the children create train and/or bus schedules of their own, together with some questions. Then the groups swap schedules and answer those questions. Bring in various schedules for display and study.

## Travel: A December Vacation, Pick Your Vacation Spot, Write Home

Write to the tourist bureaus in Orlando, New Orleans, Niagara Falls, and San Francisco, asking them to send enough brochures for your class, or duplicate them on a copier.

Make a group list of vacation words, everything from money to seashore, clustering the responses and continuously adding to the various lists as you proceed. Find out what some of the students' favorite places are and the influence weather has on their choices. Poll the class and see how many prefer warm/hot or cool/cold weather.

Using newspapers and magazines, have the children make a class collage about traveling/vacationing.

Such pictures can also be used in a noun chart by writing: "People," "Places," "Things" on butcher-block paper and letting the children fill them in.

Talk about one-way and round-trip. This can be easily demonstrated by asking the children to go out the door and then come back in.

Using a large map of the United States, show the children where Philadelphia is and insert a thumbtack. Do the same with Niagara Falls, New Orleans, Orlando, and San Francisco. Link these cities to Philadelphia with string. Then talk about the following with the children:

**Distance:** Show how far each city is from Philadelphia by using string and thumbtacks; write the distance on a card and attach to map.

**Temperature:** Draw a picture of a thermometer on the board. Have the children group and label the temperatures with the words: cold, cool, warm, hot.

Have the children role play temperature, shivering, sweating, etc. Then group the children: cold, cool, warm, hot, with each generating a list of suitable clothes to pack for their climate.

**Speed:** Have one child crawl across the floor, another walk, another jog slowly, and another run to reinforce the concept of speed and time.

**Cost:** Use Monopoly money or have the children make their own using index cards, so that each child ends up with $1,000. Let them role-play buying a ticket, ordering and paying for a meal, etc. Words such as "expensive" and "cheap" can be introduced here.

Put **Pick Your Vacation Spot** on an overhead and go over it carefully, talking about one-way travel time for cars/buses, trains, planes, together with round-trip fares and hotel costs, climate, and the main tourist attraction. Share the tourist bureau brochures and then let the children pick their spot and complete pages 119 and 120, figuring out how they will get to their vacation spot, how many days they can afford to stay, etc. Remind them not to forget a food allowance—at least $20 per day.

Take the children to the library to look up their vacation spot in an encyclopedia and write down at least five things of interest to them, adding this information to what they have already learned about their chosen city. When they write home (p. 121), they will include some of these facts as they tell about their holiday and then draw a picture on the front of their "postcard." You might want to have the children first cut these out and paste them on a 4" × 6" index card. These make great mobiles!

Group the children according to vacation spots and let them make a travel poster.

## Travel Through Time

Now the children travel through their own personal histories, first listing and then ordering events and experiences that are important to them. Finally, using adding-machine tape, help the children create time lines. Add their photos to the top of these strips and display.

## Idioms

Taken for granted by most of us, idioms can be a source of confusion for novice speakers of English who tend to take their meaning literally. Here are two activities to introduce your children to these sayings. "Idiom Match-Up" asks them to match the idiom with its actual meaning; "Acting Out" gives these meanings but allows the children to act out their literal meanings for others to guess, much like Charades. A useful reference book is *Heavens to Betsy and Other Curious Sayings,* by Charles Earle Funk, Harper & Row Publishers, 1983. You might want to include idioms from time to time in your lessons. Here are a few more you might want to include:

| | | |
|---|---|---|
| crying wolf | having something up my sleeve | left holding the bag |
| crying over spilled milk | keeping it under your hat | white/blue collar worker |
| skeletons in the closet | not worth a hill of beans | getting into hot water |
| being a good/bad egg | be at the end of your rope | go out on a limb |
| letting the cat out of the bag | burning the candle at both ends | turning over a new leaf |

## Giving Gifts

This brings us back to the idea of giving and thanking, asking the children to think about different kinds of gifts, helping them see that not all gifts come in store boxes. This can be done in small groups, followed by whole-class sharing using an overhead, setting the stage for "The Elves and the Shoemaker."

Read to the class Shel Silverstein's *The Giving Tree*.

Have each child develop a list of gifts that can't be bought for classmates/friends, teachers, family. These lists can then be transferred to adding-machine tape, illustrated, and then displayed. Or they can be combined and placed on butcher-block paper, cut out in the shape of a tree.

These activities lend themselves well to a whole-class sharing/writing Language Experience Approach (LEA) activity, including favorite gifts and illustrations. This could then be made into a classroom book about giving.

## "The Elves and the Shoemaker"

First, be sure to talk about elves, who also play a role in our Christmas stories. Be sure that they also understand the concept of "shoemaker," talking about how shoes were made a long time ago and now.

This version differs somewhat from the original story and includes a Silent Directed Reading-Thinking Activity component that encourages your students to make predictions based on the title and each section, and then reading further to either verify or change those predictions.

You can either read the story to the class, pausing long enough for the children to write and/or tell you their predictions, or let the children read the story silently, working at their own pace.

## Story Tree

Serving as a follow-up to the story, this activity allows your children to rethink the story. Start by asking who, what, where, when, why and how questions and put the responses on the board. Then, using the accompanying pictures as a guide, let them fill in the tree, either individually or as a group using an overhead. Once completed, these can then be colored and displayed on a large butcher-block paper tree.

## Beginning, Middle, and End

This follow-up activity encourages the children to both sequence and summarize the beginning, middle, and end of the story and do some illustrating of their own. Once completed, the booklets should be cut, stapled together, and displayed.

# DECEMBER

**Look at December's calendar on the next page, and do the following:**

1. Number the days on your calendar. December has 31 days.

2. Cut and paste  on December 21st. This is the first day of winter.

3. On December 25th, cut and paste  . This is Christmas day.

4. Cut and paste  on the first day of the Jewish holiday, Hanukkah.

5. Cut and paste   on special December birthdays.

Name _____

Date _____

## DECEMBER

| SUNDAY | MONDAY | TUESDAY | WEDNESDAY | THURSDAY | FRIDAY | SATURDAY |
|--------|--------|---------|-----------|----------|--------|----------|
|        |        |         |           |          |        |          |
|        |        |         |           |          |        |          |
|        |        |         |           |          |        |          |
|        |        |         |           |          |        |          |
|        |        |         |           |          |        |          |

# MAKE AND PLAY: THE DREIDEL GAME

**YOU'LL NEED:**     scissors     tape
                    pencil       15 markers (beans, buttons, peanuts, etc.)

## TO MAKE A DREIDEL:

1. Cut out the dreidel.
2. Fold along the – – – dashed lines and tape in place.
3. Snip off a small piece of the top and bottom points of the dreidel.
4. Put a pencil through the holes, with the point down.

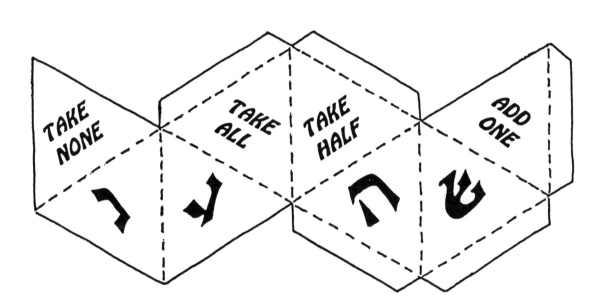

## TO PLAY THE DREIDEL GAME:

1. Each player puts a marker in the middle. This is called the Pot.
2. Players take turns spinning the dreidel.

   If the TAKE NONE  is on top, the player takes nothing.
   If the TAKE ALL   is on top, the player takes the whole Pot.
   If the TAKE HALF  is on top, the player takes one half the Pot.
   If the ADD ONE    is on top, all players add one marker to the Pot.

# A WREATH OF HANDS

**GATHER:**

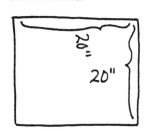

NEWSPAPER
GREEN AND RED TEMPERA PAINT
20-INCH SQUARE OF WHITE PAPER
PAINTBRUSHES
RIBBON
TAPE

**NOW:**

1. SPREAD NEWSPAPER OVER YOUR WORK AREA.

2. PAINT YOUR PALM WITH GREEN TEMPERA PAINT.

3. TAKING TURNS, EACH STUDENT ADDS HIS OR HER HAND PRINT TO MAKE A CIRCLE OF HAND PRINTS ON ONE OF THE PAPER SQUARES.

4. WHEN THE PRINTS ARE DRY, DIP A FINGERTIP INTO RED PAINT AND PRINT BERRIES ON THE WREATHS.

5. TIE RIBBON INTO A BOW AND TAPE IT TO THE BOTTOM OF THE WREATH.

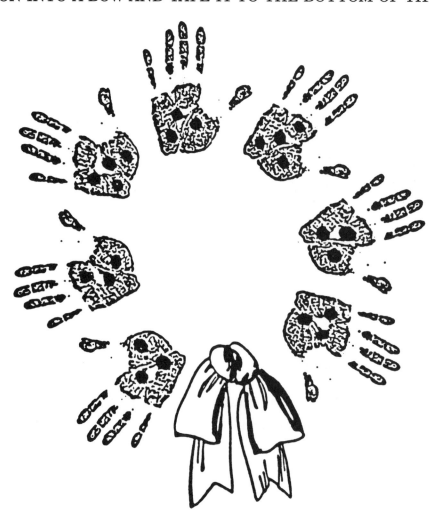

# HOLLY PLACE CARDS

**YOU'LL NEED:** green and red construction paper
scissors
glue

1. Trace the leaves and base on green construction paper and cut out.

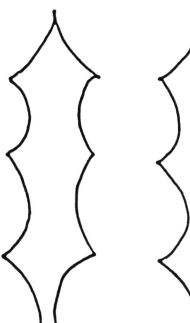

2. Trace the berries on red construction paper and cut out.

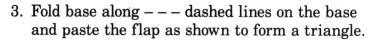

3. Fold base along – – – dashed lines on the base
and paste the flap as shown to form a triangle.

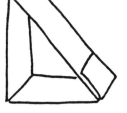

4. Write your name on one leaf and paste on one side of triangle.

5. Paste the two other leaves to each side of the first leaf.

6. Paste berries over the three leaf ends.

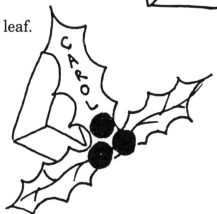

**Name** _____ **Date** _____

# WHAT AM I?

## DRAW A LINE TO THE RIGHT ANSWER:

1. I have two tires and a motor. I travel quickly on roads. I can carry only one or two people.

    train

2. I have two tires, and you must pedal me to make me move.

    ship

3. I can travel a few miles without any help at all!

    bus

4. I need water to travel on, moving people and goods from one port to another.

    motorcycle

5. I have many tires and am very big. I travel on roads. My job is to carry goods from one town to another.

    airplane

6. I have many tires and am very big. I travel on roads. My job is to carry many people from one place to another.

    car

7. My wheels run only on tracks. I can carry people and goods from one town to another.

    bicycle

8. My wheels are only for landing and taking off. Most of the time, I am up in the air.

    legs

9. I can take you near and far on my four tires. I travel on roads and lots of people own me.

    truck

© 1994 by The Center for Applied Research in Education

**Answers:** 1. motorcycle; 2. bicycle; 3. legs; 4. ship; 5. truck; 6. bus; 7. train; 8. airplane; 9. car.

Name _____     Date _____

# GETTING THERE!

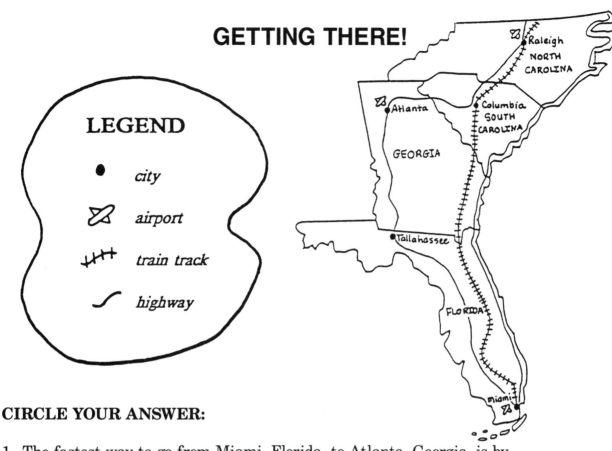

LEGEND

•     city

✈     airport

ⱵⱵ     train track

∫     highway

## CIRCLE YOUR ANSWER:

1. The fastest way to go from Miami, Florida, to Atlanta, Georgia, is by

      car/bus            train            airplane

2. To go from Columbia, South Carolina, to Raleigh, North Carolina, you *cannot* take a

      car/bus            train            airplane

3. The best way to travel from Miami, Florida, to Columbia, South Carolina, is by

      car/bus            train            airplane

4. The only way to travel from Miami, Florida, to Tallahassee, Florida, is by

      bus/car            train            airplane

5. The slowest way to go from Atlanta, Georgia, to Raleigh, North Carolina, is by

      bus/car            train            airplane

6. The only way to travel from Tallahassee, Florida, to Raleigh, North Carolina, is by

      bus/car            train            airplane

**Answers: 1. airplane; 2. airplane; 3. train;
4. bus/car; 5. bus/car; 6. bus/car**

# READING A TRAIN SCHEDULE

| Market East | North Broad | Melrose Park | Elkins Park | Glenside | North Hills | Ambler |
|---|---|---|---|---|---|---|
| 6:15 A.M. | 6:32 A.M. | 6:43 A.M. | 6:50 A.M. | 7:00 A.M. | 7:12 A.M. | 7:20 A.M. |
| 8:15 A.M. | 8:32 A.M. | 8:43 A.M. | 8:50 A.M. | 9:00 A.M. | 9:12 A.M. | 9:20 A.M. |
| 10:15 A.M. | 10:32 A.M. | 10:43 A.M. | 10:50 A.M. | 11:00 A.M. | 11:12 A.M. | 11:20 A.M. |
| 12:15 P.M. | 12:32 P.M. | 12:43 P.M. | 12:50 P.M. | 1:00 P.M. | 1:12 P.M. | 1:20 P.M. |
| 2:15 P.M. | 2:32 P.M. | 2:43 P.M. | 2:50 P.M. | 3:00 P.M. | 3:12 P.M. | 3:20 P.M. |
| 4:15 P.M. | 4:32 P.M. | 4:43 P.M. | 4:50 P.M. | 5:00 P.M. | 5:12 P.M. | 5:20 P.M. |
| 6:15 P.M. | 6:32 P.M. | 6:43 P.M. | 6:50 P.M. | 7:00 P.M. | 7:12 P.M. | 7:20 P.M. |
| 8:15 P.M. | 8:32 P.M. | 8:43 P.M. | 8:50 P.M. | 9:00 P.M. | 9:12 P.M. | 9:20 P.M. |

1. You left Market East at 8:15 in the morning. What time do you arrive in Ambler? _____

2. The last train from Melrose Park leaves at what time? _____

3. The first train from Glenside leaves at what time? _____

4. I will leave Elkins Park at 10:50 in the morning. When will I arrive in North Hills? _____

5. The earliest train leaves from _____. What time does it leave? _____

6. I have to be in Ambler by 9:20 tonight. What time must I leave North Broad? _____

7. How long will it take you to travel from Market East to Elkins Park? _____

8. How long will it take me to travel from Glenside to Ambler? _____

© 1994 by The Center for Applied Research in Education

# A DECEMBER VACATION!

## WHAT YOU NEED TO KNOW:

1. You live in Philadelphia, Pennsylvania.
2. You have $1,000 to spend on your vacation.
3. There are 24 hours in one day and night.
4. You have 7 days (one week) for your trip.

## WHAT TO DO:

1. Look carefully at the information on the next page.

2. Decide:

   a. How far do you want to travel? _____

   b. Do you want to be warm or cold? _____

   c. Will you travel by bus, car, train, or plane? _____

   That will cost you: $_____

   d. How many days and nights will you stay? _____

   The hotel will cost you: $_____

   e. If you spend $50.00 every day for food, eating will cost you: $_____

CONTINUED . . .

**Name** _____  **Date** _____

# PICK YOUR VACATION SPOT

Use the postcard on the next page to write to someone about your vacation.

**Niagara Falls, New York: 360 miles**
One-way Travel time/Round-trip costs:
| | | |
|---|---|---|
| bus: | 9 hours/ | $150.00 |
| car: | 9 hours/ | $ 60.00 |
| train: | 8 hours/ | $180.00 |
| plane: | 2 hours/ | $220.00 |

Spot hotel daily rates: $55.00
December temperatures: 20–35 degrees
What to see: The Falls

**San Francisco, California: 2900 miles**
One-way Travel time/Round-trip costs:
| | | |
|---|---|---|
| bus: | 65 hours/ | $450.00 |
| car: | 65 hours/ | $400.00 |
| train: | 62 hours/ | $460.00 |
| plane: | 6 hours/ | $530.00 |

Spot hotel daily rates: $75.00
December temperatures: 40–65 degrees
What to see: The Golden Gate Bridge

**New Orleans, Louisiana: 1,229 miles**
One-way Travel time/Round-trip costs:
| | | |
|---|---|---|
| bus: | 28 hours/ | $185.00 |
| car: | 28 hours/ | $170.00 |
| train: | 26 hours/ | $160.00 |
| plane: | 4 hours/ | $300.00 |

Spot hotel daily rates: $70.00
December temperatures: 50–70 degrees
What to do: Take a steamboat up the
            Mississippi River

**Orlando, Florida: 986 miles**
One-way Travel time/Round-trip costs:
| | | |
|---|---|---|
| bus: | 18 hours/ | $280.00 |
| car: | 18 hours/ | $130.00 |
| train: | 16 hours/ | $275.00 |
| plane: | 3 hours/ | $350.00 |

Spot hotel daily rates: $90.00
December temperatures: 60–80 degrees
What to see: Disney World

# WRITE HOME

**TELL US:**

WHERE DID YOU GO?

HOW DID YOU GET THERE?

HOW LONG DID YOU STAY?

HOW WAS THE WEATHER?

WHAT DID YOU DO AND SEE?

Post Card

**Name** _____ **Date** _____

# TRAVEL THROUGH TIME

**YOU WILL NEED:** adding-machine tape
pencil
black felt-tip pen
crayons or colored pencils

## LIST IMPORTANT EVENTS AND DATES IN YOUR LIFE:

1.

2.

3.

4.

5.

## PUT THEM IN ORDER:

1st:

2nd:

3rd:

4th:

5th:

Birth :
December 12, 1982

First Steps:
November 2, 1983

To America:
August 15, 1988

Start School:
September 7, 1988

10th Birthday:
December 12, 1992

## AND NOW . . .

1. Put these dates and events on a strip of adding-machine tape.
2. Draw a picture to go with each date and event.*

*Ask your teacher to take your photograph and tape it to the top of your strip.

# IDIOM MATCH-UP

An *idiom* is a phrase whose meaning can't be understood from the meanings of the words in it.

>   Example: **It's raining cats and dogs.**
>
>   Are cats and dogs really falling from the sky? No, of course not!
>   It just means that it's raining very hard!

## NOW, MATCH THESE IDIOMS WITH WHAT THEY REALLY MEAN:

_____ 1. to keep it under your hat        a. to slow down; take it easy

_____ 2. Time flies.       b. to show your feelings

_____ 3. to blow your top       c. to agree

_____ 4. to wear your heart on your sleeve    d. to get angry

_____ 5. to hold your horses       e. Time passes quickly.

_____ 6. to see eye to eye       f. to keep a secret

**Answers: 1. f; 2. e; 3. d; 4. b; 5. a; 6. c**

# ACTING OUT!

Study these idioms and their true meanings. Then choose one and act it out for your classmates. See if they can guess your idiom.

to throw in the towel  = to give up; stop trying

to pull someone's leg  = to fool someone

to stick your neck out 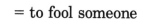 = to take a chance

to cry uncle  = to give up

to cross your heart 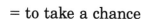 = to make a promise

to kick the bucket  = to die

to hold your tongue  = to stop talking

**Name** _____  **Date** _____

# GIVING GIFTS!

1. Are any of these gifts? Check the ones that are:

_____ I bought you a bicycle.

 _____ I made your favorite dinner.

_____ I called you on the phone.

 _____ I baked a cake for you.

_____ I let you wear my sweater.

 _____ I gave you $10.00 for no reason.

_____ I killed a spider for you.

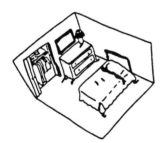 _____ I cleaned your room for you.

2. What is the best present you ever received? _____

3. Who gave it to you? _____

4. Was it bought in a store? _____

   Was it handmade? _____

5. Did you ask for it? _____

6. What did you give in return? _____

**The story that begins on the next page is about giving presents . . .**

# THE ELVES AND THE SHOEMAKER

Read the story and answer the questions.

"Bread! Bread! That's all we eat—morning, noon and night!"
"What are we going to do, Samuel?"
"I don't know, dear wife. I don't know. I have only enough leather to make one more pair of shoes."
"And tomorrow, someone will buy them. You'll see."
"Yes, yes, of course, Rachel. First thing in the morning, I will cut and sew them. Now, let's just go to sleep."

What do you think will happen next? _____

_____

In the morning, Samuel went down to his workbench to make one last pair of shoes. He couldn't believe what he saw!
"Rachel! Rachel! Come quickly!" he shouted.
"What's wrong, Samuel?" she asked, running into the shop.
"Look for yourself!" he cried. "Look at these shoes! They were sitting here on the workbench, all made. Every stitch is perfect!"
"I don't understand," said Rachel. "Are you saying someone came and made them while we were sleeping?"
"I don't know!" said the shoemaker. "I don't know."

Who do you think made the shoes for the shoemaker? _____

_____

Just then a customer entered the shop. "Good morning, sir," said the shoemaker. "What can I do for you today?"
"How much do you want for those beautiful shoes in your hand?"
"Well, I'm not sure yet. I was thinking perhaps $10."
"Then I will pay you $20 for them!"
After he left, Rachel and Samuel danced about the room like two children.
"Now we can eat a good meal and still have enough money left to buy leather for two pairs of shoes!" laughed the shoemaker.
That evening after supper, the shoemaker left the new piece of leather on his workbench. Smiling at his wife, he said, "In the morning, I will cut and sew two fine-looking pairs of shoes!"

What do you think will happen next? _____

_____

_____

© 1994 by The Center for Applied Research in Education

# THE ELVES AND THE SHOEMAKER (continued)

"Rachel! Rachel! Come quickly! It's happened again!" cried the shoemaker the next morning.

"What's happened again, Samuel?" she asked, running into the workshop.

"The shoes, Rachel. Look at the shoes! They were sitting here on the workbench, all made. Again every stitch is perfect!"

"What's going on, Samuel? Why would someone make beautiful shoes for us to sell?" she asked, scratching her head.

"I don't know!" said the shoemaker. "I don't know."

Who do you think is making the shoes for the shoemaker? _____

_____

© 1994 by The Center for Applied Research in Education

Just then two customers entered the shop. "Good morning, gentlemen," said the shoemaker. "How can I help you?"

"How much are these shoes?" asked the first customer.

"Yes, how much do you want?" asked the second.

"Well, I'm not sure yet. I was thinking perhaps $10."

"Then I will pay you $20," said the first customer.

"I will, too," said the second. "The shoes are perfect!"

After they left, Rachel and Samuel danced about the shop like two children.

"We can eat like kings tonight, and still have enough money left to buy leather for four pairs of shoes," laughed the shoemaker.

That evening after supper, the shoemaker left the new pieces of leather on his workbench. Smiling at his wife, he said, "In the morning, I will cut and sew four pairs of fine-looking shoes."

What do you think will happen that night? _____

_____

The next morning, and every day after that, the shoemaker found perfectly made shoes on the workbench. Customers filled the shop.

"Someone is making us rich, and asking nothing in return. I must know who it is," said the good shoemaker one morning.

"You're right, Samuel. Tonight, let's hide by the door and find out."

That night, they hid behind the door and waited.

Whom do you think they'll see? _____

# THE ELVES AND THE SHOEMAKER (continued)

At midnight, two little men appeared. They said nothing, but went right to work. Tiny fingers flew through the air, cutting and stitching beautiful shoes.

"They're dressed in nothing but rags, Rachel," whispered the shoemaker.

"And they have no shoes! They must be so cold!"

As they spoke, the two little men finished working. In a blink of an eye, they were gone.

What do you think will happen now? _____

_____

"I can't believe it!" exclaimed the shoemaker.

"What strange, little men!"

"Whoever they are, we must thank them."

"I know! I'll make them some clothes." she said.

"And I'll make them shoes!" shouted the shoemaker.

What will the elves do when they see the clothes and shoes?

_____

_____

Again the shoemaker and his wife hid behind the shop door. Exactly at midnight, the elves returned. When they saw the clothes, they held them up and began to giggle.

"Look, look," whispered Rachel. "They like our presents!"

In a minute the elves were dressed and dancing around the shop. Then ever so quickly, they danced right out the door, and they never came back!

What will happen to the shoemaker and his wife now?

_____

_____

_____

_____

# STORY TREE

Complete this page after you've read "The Elves and the Shoemaker."

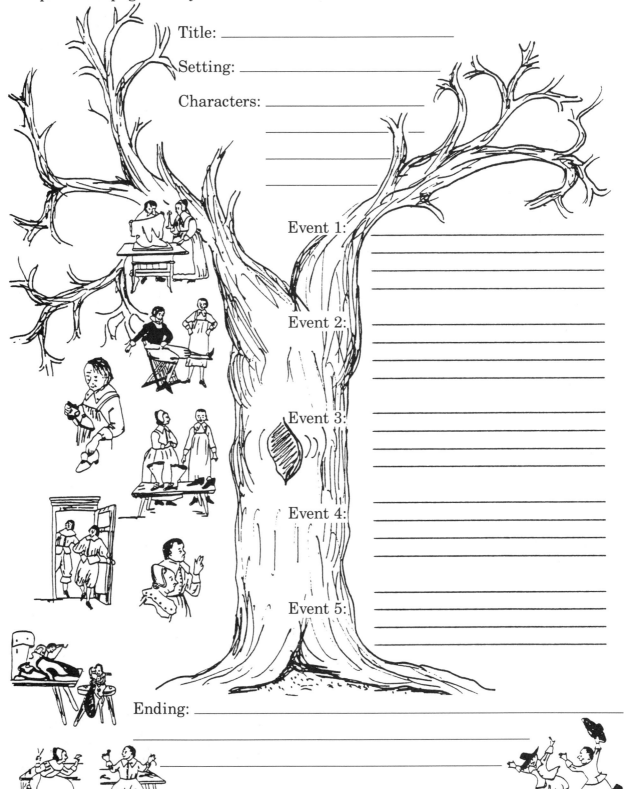

Title: _____

Setting: _____

Characters: _____

_____

_____

_____

Event 1: _____

_____

_____

_____

Event 2: _____

_____

_____

_____

Event 3: _____

_____

_____

_____

Event 4: _____

_____

_____

_____

Event 5: _____

_____

_____

Ending: _____

_____

_____

# IN THE BEGINNING, MIDDLE, AND END

Draw a picture and write what happened
in "The Elves and the Shoemaker."
Then cut out along the dark, solid lines.
Staple the parts into a booklet.

| | At the beginning . . . |
|---|---|
| | _____ |
| | _____ |
| | _____ |
| | _____ |
| | _____ |
| | _____ |
| | In the middle . . . |
| | _____ |
| | _____ |
| | _____ |
| | _____ |
| | _____ |
| | _____ |
| | At the end . . . |
| | _____ |
| | _____ |
| | _____ |
| | _____ |
| | _____ |
| | _____ |

# JANUARY

Teacher Notes and Additional Activities
Monthly Activities
Friendship
Animal Friends
Story and Related Activities

# JANUARY
# Teacher Notes and Additional Activities

## It's January, January Calendar

Encourage children to decorate their calendars, noting important dates and birthdays. Make a large classroom calendar, as well, and celebrate January birthdays.

## Promises to Keep

Talk about the concepts of "new," "beginning over," and "fresh start." Bring in new/unused items. Also, write all over the board until there's hardly any room left at all. Then erase it all for a fresh start.

Find out what the children know about promises and make a class list of promises they've made to others and categorize them. Then move onto those we make to ourselves, our resolutions, and share a few. Next, complete **Promises to Keep**, and then, if you like, ask the children to rank their resolutions in order of importance and turn this into a writing activity.

Explain our custom of celebrating the new year at midnight and find out how the holiday is celebrated in the children's native countries.

Teach "Auld Lang Syne" to the children, perhaps simplifying the words to, "Should old friends be forgotten and never brought to mind? Should old friends be forgotten and days of old long ago. For old long ago, my dear, for old long ago; we'll take a cup of kindness yet for old long ago."

You might also want to celebrate the Chinese New Year, which falls between January 21 and February 19 and is considered the most important Chinese holiday and culminates in the Festival of Lanterns when huge paper dragons are paraded through the streets. Your class will enjoy making dragon masks of their own using large grocery bags. After their parade, fortune cookies make a fine treat as they share their New Year's fortunes.

## Martin Luther King, Jr.

Start by bringing in a few Superman, etc., comics to help the children understand the concept of hero. Bring in pictures of real heroes, too, such as Neil Armstrong, the President, etc. Then have the children list their own heroes/heroines and categorize their choices.

Make a large chart on the board, labeling one side, "How We Are the Same" and the other with "How We Are Different." Then let the children do some brainstorming and record their responses. Let the children talk about their own experiences. Follow this up by inviting the children to write about their experiences and their feelings.

Ask the children how we usually ask someone to do something for us, talking about the words *please* and *thank you*. Then demonstrate the concept of slavery by explaining to the class that for the next few minutes or so, you will play the role of the landowner/

master and they will be your slaves. Then order them to do some chores for you, such as erase the board, wipe the desks, empty the trash can. Explain how we once captured and then used slaves in this country and then fought a war to free black slaves—but not make them equal. Give examples. Explain that King was devoted to helping his people and is an American hero. Then put the activity on an overhead and read his story to the class. Ask the children why they think he is a hero, why he was killed, and why his birthday is a national holiday. As a follow-up, the children can read books about King and other black leaders. Then ask the children to write a letter to the person they've just read about.

## Winter Wonderland

This paper-folding activity will help your students follow directions while decorating your room. Be sure, though, to model the steps first a few times.

Take the children outside for a walk on a cold winter day. As you walk, talk about what they see (snow, frozen puddles, etc.), what they don't see (lots of birds, leaves, etc.), and how they feel (cold, chilly, etc.). Once inside, serving hot cocoa is a nice touch. Then, on the board, make a large "T." On one side, write "Winter Looks Like," and on the other, "Winter Feels Like," and generate class lists.

Bring in a good-sized fallen branch, and, if you like, paint it white before inserting it in a bucket of sand. Next, write *nouns, verbs,* and *adjectives* on the board, with an example under each heading, such as *snow, skate, cold.* Then let the children add words of their own and record them under the proper heading. Next, divide the class into three groups, one for each part of speech, giving each group a stack of index cards for recording their words. Then hang these cards on the branch.

As a follow-up, let the children make a winter vocabulary book, complete with illustrations.

## Winter Doodling

This can be done as a whole-class or a small-group activity, generating lists of winter clothing, activities, and weather. Then, gather the children together on the floor around an old sheet or tablecloth, with plenty of crayons or markers, and let the children draw their winter words.

## Coconut Ice

A delicious "winter" treat, this no-bake recipe is perfect for eating right away, gift-giving, or setting aside for another day.

## It Takes Two

Generate and record lists of activities your students like to do alone and with others.

**It Takes Two** introduces the theme of friendship, and ties in well with the sentiments of "Auld Lang Syne." Read it aloud several times, modeling the accompanying motions. Then, either assign the stanzas or recite and act it out all together.

Brainstorm the idea of friends and friendship. Then have the children transfer and illustrate these associated words onto a large sheet of bulletin-board paper, adding to it as time goes along.

Teach the song, "Side by Side," by Harry Woods. Then let the children write their own lyrics.

Make a friendship salad by cutting out shapes of salad vegetables and handing out an assortment to each child. Then have them write a "friendship" word on each vegetable before dropping it into a large salad bowl. When done, each child can come up and pick a vegetable or two from the bowl and read what is written. A discussion is sure to follow— maybe even some disagreements!

Put a simple recipe on the board so everyone understands how to write one. Then hand out a large index card to each child so they can write "Friendship Recipe," complete with ingredients and cooking instructions. These can then be displayed or compiled into a friendship cookbook.

## A Secret Code

With everyone in a circle, whisper the same secret message into each child's ear, cupping your hand as you do so. When done, ask if they know what you were doing and why. Then write *secret* on the board, asking what it means. Don't forget to ask them to repeat your message.

Next, put a simple code such as "A = 1; B = 2; C = 3," etc., on the board. Then add a simple secret message using the code. Ask the children to decode it.

Finally, display the secret-code activity on the overhead, explaining that they are to figure out the message using the given code. Then, using the same code, let them each write a message on a slip of paper for another student to decode.

A related activity is playing "Whistling Down the Lane." Make up a fairly short message and jot it down on a slip of paper. Then, with everyone in a circle, whisper your message to the child next to you, who passes it to the next child, and so on. The last child tells what they just heard, to be compared with the original message.

## Our Pet Friends

Brainstorm *pet* and make a list of their pets.

Next, put **Our Pet Friends** on an overhead, reading the descriptors before the children complete the activity on their own. Record their responses on the overhead. Make any needed additions. You can then use this as the basis for a Language Experience Approach (LEA) activity that can later be turned into an illustrated big book. Put each pet's name on an index card and give one to each child. In turn, she/he must imitate the sounds and movements of their pet while the rest of the class guesses what they are.

Ask the children to paste a picture of their pet (or a magazine picture of one they wouldn't mind owning), and then write an accompanying description.

## I Have and Don't Have . . .

This semantic feature-analysis chart continues the pet theme by examining their similarities and differences. Place the chart on an overhead and carefully model the directions by redoing the cat and explaining how to use the positive and negative signs.

Have each child find pictures of pets in magazines and make a pet collage.

As a follow-up activity, let your children create their own pets—pet rocks! Once a suitable rock has been found, faces can be made using either markers and/or pieces of felt and glue. Then let the children create a "bio" of their pet.

## Our Feathered Friends

Although not pets, we need to remember birds that winter over with us. First explore the reasons birds cannot always find food in the winter and jot these down. Explain that we can help, showing a pine cone already covered with peanut butter and bird seed. If possible, collect the pine cones together. Once done, hang them from trees around your school and let your students enjoy watching the feasting birds.

## The Farm Friends Rap

First, brainstorm *farm*—what belongs on a farm and the types of work done there. Then do the same thing for each of the listed animals. (Be sure to stock the room with lots of farm and animal books.)

Next, teach the children "Old Macdonald Had a Farm," showing pictures of each animal referred to.

Find out what is known about rap music, bringing in a sample or two and keeping time with hands and/or feet. Keep the beat, but now "rap" the words to "Our Farm Friends Rap" for the class, repeating it until all the children have joined in. You can also assign different parts.

Make a Venn diagram for pets and farm animals to help the children see the similarities and differences between them.

Divide the class into three groups: one group gets a pair of earmuffs, so they'll be the class's "ears"; the second group receives a pair of glasses and will act as the class's "eyes"; and the last group is given a can of air freshener, so they can be everyone's "nose." Then visit a farm, with the groups recording the sounds, sights, and smells they encounter, to be shared upon returning. If a field trip is impossible, just act as their guide through an imaginary farm.

Such visits make ideal subjects for a Language Experience Approach (LEA) activity, with the children writing about their experiences and impressions of farms and farm life.

## What Am I?

This activity can serve as a follow-up, with the children completing it on their own.

Let each child "adopt" a farm animal, looking for pictures and information, to be written up and shared with the rest of the class. These reports can then be bound together in a class book.

Give each child a sheet of white construction paper. Have them fold it in half lengthwise, and then in thirds. Then give the directions that follow. The results are always fun!

a. On the first third, draw the head of a cow.

b. On the second third, draw the body of a cat, with the legs of a turkey.

c. On the last third, draw the tail of a fish.

As a follow-up to both pet and farm animals, draw a 4" × 4" grid on a sheet of construction paper, similar to the sample. With the children's help, fill in each square with directions, such as "Meow three times like a cat." To play, each student takes a turn tossing the coin or chip on the game board and complying with the directions on the square she/he has landed on.

Read *Charlotte's Web,* by E. B. White, to the class.

## "The Three Little Pigs"

This version enables the children to participate in both the telling and acting out of the story. However, first read it to them several times, modeling the actions as you go along and changing the tone of your voice for each character. Once they are familiar with the story line, assign parts to volunteers, with all students participating in the "everybody" parts. Doubling up pairs can ease anxiety. Repeat lots of times.

Teach and dance to the Disney song, "Who's Afraid of the Big, Bad Wolf?"

Turn the story into a "hand" play, by having the children draw their character on their palm.

Divide the class into groups and let each come up with a sequel to the story. Start them off with questions, such as "Will the wolf ever become a friend?" and "Do Porker and Hammer live on with Baco?"

Make "Wanted" posters, including a detailed description of the wolf, his crime, where he was last seen, and an award for his capture.

The children have now read three stories with either a villainous fox or wolf: "The Gingerbread Man," "Little Red Riding Hood," and this story. Write these titles and animals on the board, asking for similarities and differences among the three. Then ask the children to write a story where such an animal is the hero. This can be done individually or in groups.

## Who Did That?

Allow the children to go back to the story whenever they need to in order to answer the questions.

## Making a Book Cover

Show and explain several covers from hard-bound books. Then model the directions in this activity, cutting off the lined panels, gluing them onto the construction paper, and folding them down, etc.

## The Baco Award

Talk about the fact that here the hero is, in fact, the heroine. Remind the children of what was said about heroes when you studied Martin Luther King, Jr. Can we make any comparisons? One thing they both have in common is their willingness to work hard. Start off this discussion by demonstrating several meanings of the word *hard:* raining hard, squeezing hard, a hard winter, hard work. Once assured that there is no confusion, ask the children to share examples of their own hard work, such as doing chores or studying. Then talk about the word *award* and how we applaud hard work and a job well done. Afterward, put "The Baco Award" activity on an overhead and answer the questions together. Be sure that everyone understands that Baco did more than her brothers. Finally, let each child make his own award, cutting it out and wearing it proudly.

# IT'S JANUARY!

Look at January's calendar on the next page and do the following:

1. Number the days on your calendar. January has 31 days.

2. Cut and paste  on January 1st. This is New Year's Day.

3. Cut and paste  on January 15th. This is Martin Luther King Jr.'s birthday.

4. Cut and paste  on special January birthdays.

Name _____

Date _____

## JANUARY

| SUNDAY | MONDAY | TUESDAY | WEDNESDAY | THURSDAY | FRIDAY | SATURDAY |
|--------|--------|---------|-----------|----------|--------|----------|
|        |        |         |           |          |        |          |
|        |        |         |           |          |        |          |
|        |        |         |           |          |        |          |
|        |        |         |           |          |        |          |
|        |        |         |           |          |        |          |

# PROMISES TO KEEP

A RESOLUTION IS A PROMISE YOU MAKE TO YOURSELF.
HERE IS MY LIST OF NEW YEAR'S RESOLUTIONS:

1. DO ALL MY HOMEWORK.

2. EAT ALL MY SPINACH.

3. READ TWO BOOKS EVERY MONTH.

4. BE NICE TO EVERYONE.

WHAT DO YOU PROMISE FOR THIS NEW YEAR?

1.

2.

3.

4.

5.

6.

7.

# MARTIN LUTHER KING, JR.

To be **equal** means to be the same. No two people are ever the same. But all people should be treated the same. All people should be treated fairly.

When Martin was growing up in the south, blacks were not treated the same as white people. They were not treated fairly. For example:

Black people could not eat in the same restaurants as white people.

Black children could not go to school with white children.

Black people had to give their seats to white people on buses and trains.

Black people could not vote.

Martin Luther King, Jr., spent his whole life trying to make things better for his people. Slowly, the laws changed. That made some white people very angry. He was even put in jail. But he never stopped working.

Then, in 1968, he went to Memphis, Tennessee, to march with underpaid workers. When he stepped out onto the balcony of his motel room, James Earl Ray saw him and fired his gun. Martin Luther King, Jr., died that day. It was April 4th.

His birthday, January 15th, is now a national holiday. On that day every year, we celebrate him and all he did for Americans, both black and white. He hoped that someday all people would be treated equally in this country. We must continue his work and make that dream come true.

# A WINTER WONDERLAND

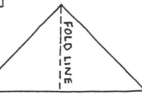

## WHAT YOU NEED:

1. a 6-inch square piece of white paper
2. string
3. scissors

## WHAT TO DO:

1. Fold your square in half to form a triangle.

FOLD LINE

2. Fold the paper in half again, forming a smaller triangle.

FOLD LINE

3. With scissors, snip (cut) different shapes from the three sides of the triangle. Work on one side at a time.

4. When you are finished, open the folded paper carefully.
5. Tie a piece of string to one end of your snowflake and hang.

**Name** _____ **Date** _____

# WINTER DOODLING

## WHAT YOU WILL NEED:

an old sheet or tablecloth
marking pens and/or crayons

## WHAT TO DO:

1. Lay the sheet or tablecloth on the floor.
2. Close your eyes and think about winter.
3. Make a list of winter activities, clothing, weather.

| Activities: | Clothing: | Weather: |
|---|---|---|
| 1. | 1. | 1. |
| 2. | 2. | 2. |
| 3. | 3. | 3. |
| 4. | 4. | 4. |
| 5. | 5. | 5. |

4. Now draw and write all about winter on your sheet or tablecloth.

# COCONUT ICE

## YOU'LL NEED:

1 cup of dried coconut
1 heaping cup of powdered sugar
½ can of condensed milk
a large mixing bowl
a sieve

a measuring cup
a wooden spoon
a knife
a rolling pin
waxed paper

## NOW:

1. Put the coconut into a large bowl.

2. Sieve sugar on top of coconut.

3. Add a bit of condensed milk a little at a time until it's all finished, while pounding the mixture with a wooden spoon.

4. Sprinkle some powdered sugar on a tabletop, as well as on the rolling pin.

5. Roll out the coconut ice into a thick slab.

6. Cut the coconut ice into chunks.

7. Wrap each piece in waxed paper and . . . .

SHARE WITH A FRIEND!

# IT TAKES TWO
## (A Class Activity)

| | **Everybody:** |
| --- | --- |
| | (Follow the directions.) |
| One alone is fine and dandy (pause) | Hold up one finger and smile. |
| For reading a book, (pause) | Pretend to read a book. |
| Or taking a walk. (pause) | Walk around the room. |
| | |
| And one alone is fine and dandy (pause) | Hold up one finger and smile. |
| For taking a nap, (pause) | Close your eyes and pretend to sleep. |
| Or drawing a picture. (pause) | Pretend to draw. |
| | |
| But one alone is never enough (pause) | Hold up one finger; shake head and say, "No, no!" |
| For playing a game, (pause) | With a partner, pretend to play a game. |
| Or talking on the phone. (pause) | With a partner, pretend to talk on the phone. |
| | |
| And one alone is never enough (pause) | Hold up one finger; shake head and say, "No, no!" |
| For sharing secrets, (pause) | Whisper into your partner's ear. |
| Or saying "I love you." (pause) | Hug each other. |
| | |
| That takes two; it always takes two. (pause) | Hold up two fingers and smile. |
| For that, I need a friend like you. (pause) | Reach out and hold your partner's hand. |

Name ______________________ Date ______________________

# A SECRET CODE

Using this code, fill in the blanks below to finish the poem:

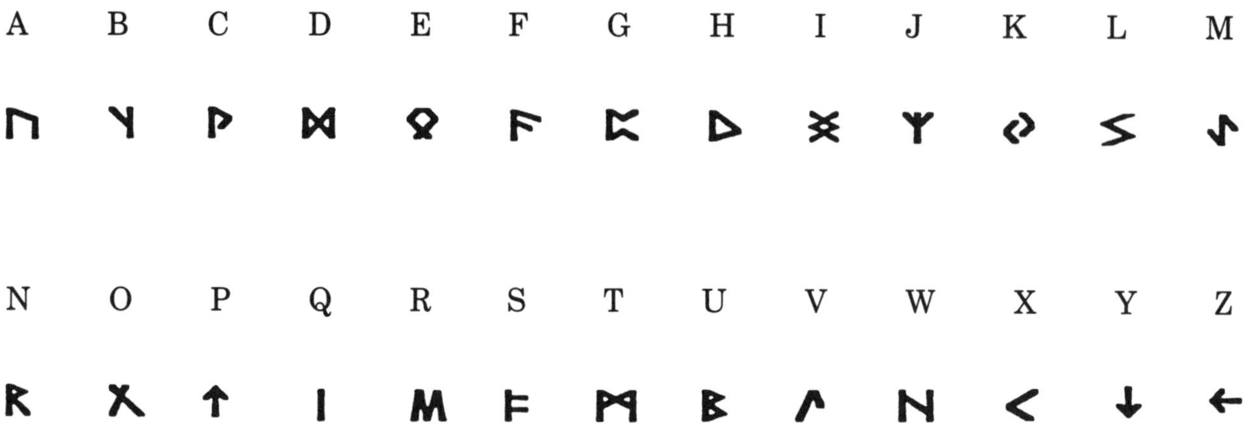
A B C D E F G H I J K L M
N O P Q R S T U V W X Y Z

Wherever I go,
Whatever I do,

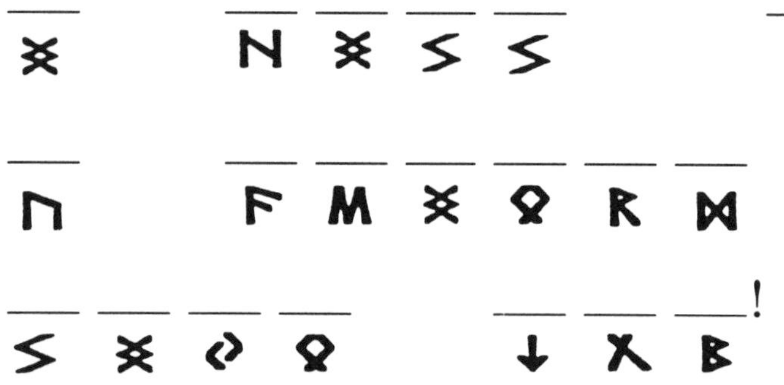

Now, in the space below, write a secret message to a friend:

Answers: I will need
A friend
Like You!

© 1994 by The Center for Applied Research in Education

# OUR PET FRIENDS

**DO YOU KNOW ME?** Write the number of the correct animal in the blank.

_____ My feathers come in many colors, and
I can even learn to say a few words.

1. cat

_____ I'm furry and small, and you'll
often hear me purr and say "meow."

2. dog

_____ On my back I carry a shell and am at
home both on land and in the water.

3. rabbit

_____ I'm man's best friend, and whether I'm
big or small, you'll know me by my bark.

4. parrot

_____ I am the color of the sun and in the
water is where I belong.

5. canary

_____ I have long ears and a fluffy tail,
and I nibble all day long.

6. turtle

_____ I am a little yellow bird, and all
I want to do is sing for you.

7. goldfish

**Answers: 4, 1, 6, 2, 7, 3, 5**

# I HAVE AND DON'T HAVE . . .

**DIRECTIONS:** Does the animal have wings? If yes, put a (+); if not, put a (−). Do that for all the animals and all the features. The cat is done for you.

| | wings | fins | 4-legs | 2-legs | fur | feathers |
|---|---|---|---|---|---|---|
| cat | − | − | + | − | + | − |
| goldfish | | | | | | |
| parrot | | | | | | |
| dog | | | | | | |
| turtle | | | | | | |
| canary | | | | | | |
| rabbit | | | | | | |

# FOR OUR FEATHERED FRIENDS

**DIRECTIONS:** Follow the directions below to make a bird feeder to help our feathered friends this winter.

## YOU WILL NEED:

a pine cone
a jar of peanut butter
a knife
string
bird seed

## WHAT TO DO:

1. Tie a piece of string around the pine cone.

2. Spread peanut butter all over the pine cone.

3. Now roll the pine cone in the bird seed, making sure it sticks.

4. Hang your pine cone on a tree—and watch all the hungry birds!!!

# THE FARM FRIENDS RAP
## (A Class Activity)

**Everybody:**

Broilers, fryers, cutlets, too,
All my meat is good for you.
And it's no wonder that I peck all day,
'Cause I've got lots of eggs to lay—
    What a great chick I am!

I moo and moo
The whole day through,
Making beef and milk just for you—
    What a great cow I am!!!

With a "quack, quack," my day begins;
My eggs and meat will make you grin,
Put me in a pond and watch me swim—
    What a great duck I am!!!

"Oink, oink," is how I talk.
Now go ahead and grab your fork
And enjoy my bacon, ham, and pork—
    What a great pig I am!!!

Talk to me and I'll neigh right back.
Then I'll take you for a ride,
If you'll hop up on my back—
    What a great horse I am!!!

I gobble, gobble, but never wobble,
'Cause my two legs are fitted with claws,
And I bring lots of Thanksgiving applause—
    What a great turkey I am!!!

"Bah, bah," I repeat.
So does my baby lamb.
With my warm, woolly coat,
My sweaters really can't be beat—
    What a great sheep I am!!!

© 1994 by The Center for Applied Research in Education

Name _____     Date _____

# WHAT AM I?

**DIRECTIONS:** Read each item below and tell what animal is "talking."

1. What am I? _____
   a. I'm covered with feathers.
   b. People love to eat my meat.
   c. I'm usually served on Thanksgiving

2. What am I? _____
   a. I'm covered with feathers.
   b. I do a lot of pecking.
   c. I'm known for my meat and eggs.

3. What am I? _____
   a. My legs are long and strong.
   b. People love to ride on my back.
   c. Instead of talking, I just neigh.

4. What am I? _____
   a. All I can say is "bah, bah."
   b. I'm covered with wool.
   c. My baby is called a lamb.

5. What am I? _____
   a. I'm big and fat.
   b. I make bacon, ham, and pork.
   c. "Oink, oink," is all I can say.

6. What am I? _____
   a. Quacking is the way I talk.
   b. I've got feathers and love to swim.
   c. I can give you meat and eggs.

7. What am I? _____
   a. When I call you, I'll just moo.
   b. You love my beef.
   c. You love my milk.

© 1994 by The Center for Applied Research in Education

**Answers: 1. turkey; 2. chicken; 3. horse; 4. sheep; 5. pig; 6. duck; 7. cow**

# THE THREE LITTLE PIGS
## (A Class Activity)

**CHARACTERS:** Porker (1st little pig) 1     Seller of straw 4     Mama Pig 4
                Hammy (2nd little pig) 2   Seller of sticks      Wolf 5
                Baco (3rd little pig) 3     Seller of bricks      N 6

| | | **Everybody:** |
| --- | --- | --- |
| | | (Follow the directions.) |
| Mama Pig: | Before you say goodbye and leave home, (pause) | Put hands on hips. |
| | Promise to remember a few things for me. | |
| The three pigs: | We promise, Mama. (pause) | Nod head up and down. |
| Mama Pig: | Eat well, work hard, and build good, strong houses. (pause) | Point finger and shake it. |
| | And keep away from that big, bad wolf! Do you understand? | |
| The three pigs: | Yes, Mama. (pause) | Nod head up and down. |
| Mama Pig: | Now kiss me goodbye and be on your way. (pause) | Wipe a tear away. |
| | And don't forget what I told you. | |
| The three pigs: | Bye, Mama. We won't forget. (pause) | Wave/kissing sounds. |
| Narrator: | Porker turned left and skipped down the path. (pause) | Lift left hand; skip. |
| | Soon, he met a man selling bundles of straw. | |
| Porker: | I'm building my house today. Will you sell me a bundle of straw? (pause) | "Please; please!" |
| Seller of straw: | Yes, of course, if you can pay me one whole dollar. (pause) | Hold up one finger. |
| Porker: | Here's my dollar, sir. Thank you very much. (pause) | Pretend to be paying money. |
| | I'll build my house here under this big oak tree. (pause) | Pretend to build a house. |
| Narrator: | Straw houses are easy to build. Porker was done in just one hour. (pause) | Hold up one finger. |
| Porker: | I think I'll take a nap now in my pretty, new house. (pause) | Curl up and close eyes. |

# THE THREE LITTLE PIGS (continued)

Narrator: Hammy turned right, singing all the way. (pause) — Lift right hand; sing.

Soon he met a man selling bundles of sticks.

Hammy: I'm building my house today. Will you sell me a bundle of sticks? (pause) — "Please; please!"

Seller of sticks: Yes, or course, if you can pay me two whole dollars. (pause) — Hold up two fingers.

Hammy: Here's my two dollars, sir. Thank you very much. (pause) — Pretend to be paying money.

I'll build my house right here next to this strawberry patch. (pause) — Pretend to build a house.

Narrator: Stick houses are easy to build. Hammy was done in just two hours! (pause) — Hold up two fingers.

Hammy: I think I'll eat strawberries for lunch today in my nice, new house. (pause) — "Chomp! Chomp!"

Narrator: Baco didn't turn at all. Instead, she walked straight ahead. (pause) — Point straight ahead.

Her bags were heavy, and she walked slowly. (pause) — Bend over and walk slowly.

She stopped when she met a man selling bricks.

Baco: I'm building my house today. I hope you'll sell me some bricks. (pause) — Cross fingers as if wishing.

Seller of bricks: If you pay me three whole dollars, you can have them all! (pause) — Hold up three fingers.

You can even have this wood for your door.

Baco: Oh, thank you very much, sir! Here's my three dollars. (pause) — Pretend to be paying money.

I'll build my house right here by this little stream.

Narrator: Now building a brick house is hard work, and Baco worked all day. (pause) — Pretend to be laying bricks.

When finished, she went to the stream and filled a pot with water. (pause) — Pretend to carry a heavy pot.

Then she added vegetables and put the pot in the fireplace to cook. (pause) — Add things to pot and stir.

Then she read a book and waited for her soup to boil. (pause) — Pretend to be reading.

# THE THREE LITTLE PIGS (continued)

| Wolf: | Ha! Ha! Your Mama can't help you now! And I'm sooo hungry!!! (pause) | Rub stomach; lick lips. |
| Narrator: | First, he went to Porker's house and knocked on the straw door. (pause) | "Knock! Knock!" |
| Wolf: | Little pig, little pig, let me in! (pause) | Rub hands together. |
| Porker: | Not by the hair on my chinny-chin-chin! (pause) | Pull on chin and cry. |
| Wolf: | Okay, little pig. Then I'll just huff and puff, and blow your house down! (pause) | Blow hard. |
| Narrator: | Porker's house fell with a crash! (pause) | Bang hands on floor. |
| | He ran for his life, all the way to Hammy's house. (pause) | Run across room. |

| Wolf: | Silly pig, I'm right behind you. Now I can catch both of you! (pause) | Laugh loudly! |
| Narrator: | The wolf knocked loudly on Hammy's stick door. (pause) | "Knock! Knock!" |
| Wolf: | Little pigs, little pigs, let me in! (pause) | "Please! Oh, please!" |
| Porker & Hammer: | Not by the hairs on our chinny-chin-chins! (pause) | Pull on chin and cry. |
| Wolf: | Okay, little pigs. Then I'll just huff and puff, and blow your house down. (pause) | Blow hard. |
| Narrator: | Hammy's house fell with a crash! (pause) | Bang hands on floor. |
| | The two piggies ran for their lives, all the way to Baco's house. (pause) | Run across room. |

# THE THREE LITTLE PIGS (continued)

| | | |
|---|---|---|
| Wolf: | Silly pigs, I'm right behind you. Now I'll catch all of you! (pause) | Laugh loudly! |
| Narrator: | The wolf knocked loudly on Baco's wooden door. (pause) | "Knock! Knock!" |
| Wolf: | Little pigs, let me in! (pause) | Rub hands together. |
| The three pigs: | Not by the hairs on our chinny-chin-chins! (pause) | Pull on chins and giggle. |
| Wolf: | Okay, little pigs. Then I'll just huff and puff, and blow your house down. (pause) | |
| The three pigs: | Go ahead and blow! (pause) | Blow hard! |
| | | Dance in a circle and giggle. |
| Narrator: | The wolf blew and blew, but nothing happened! (pause) | Blow and blow! |

| | | |
|---|---|---|
| Narrator: | Suddenly, the wolf had a wonderful idea! (pause) | Snap fingers! |
| Wolf: | I'll show those pigs who's boss around here! (pause) | Put hands on hips. |
| Narrator: | Quickly, the wolf climbed up to the roof. (pause) | Climbing motion with hands. |
| | Then he slid down the chimney. (pause) | "Swoosh! Swoosh!" |
| Wolf: | OUCH! OUCH! I'm burning!!! (pause) | "Ouch!! Ouch!!" |
| Narrator: | When the wolf's big toe touched the hot soup, he cried in pain. (pause) | Howl and cry! |
| | He climbed back up the chimney as fast as he could and ran home. (pause) | Climbing motion with hands. |
| | So, now who's afraid of the big, bad wolf? | |
| Porker: | Not me!!! | |
| Hammy: | Not me!!! | |
| Baco: | Not me!!! | |

**Name** _____     **Date** _____

# WHO DID THAT?

**DIRECTIONS:** Complete each statement below with the name of one of the characters from the story "The Three Little Pigs."

**Characters:**  Mama Pig     Porker     Baco     Hammy     Wolf

1. _____ said goodbye to her three little pigs.

2. _____ built a house made of straw.

3. _____ built his house under an oak tree.

4. _____ ate strawberries.

5. _____ built a house made of bricks.

6. _____ saved Porker and Hammer from the wolf.

7. _____ huffed and puffed.

8. _____ made soup for dinner.

9. _____ took a nap after building his house.

10. _____ burned his big toe in a pot of hot soup.

11. _____ spent $1.00 to build his house.

12. _____ built a house the wolf couldn't blow down.

13. _____ slipped down a chimney.

14. _____ read a book.

15. _____ spent $2.00 to build his house.

16. _____ said, "Eat well, work hard, and build good, strong houses."

**Answers:** 1. Mama Pig; 2. Porker; 3. Porker; 4. Hammy; 5. Baco; 6. Baco; 7. Wolf; 8. Baco; 9. Porker; 10. Wolf; 11. Porker; 12. Baco; 13. Wolf; 14 Baco; 15. Hammy; 16. Mama Pig

© 1994 by The Center for Applied Research in Education

# MAKING A BOOK COVER

**ABOUT THIS STORY**

_____

_____

_____

_____

_____

## WHAT YOU NEED:

construction paper     paste

scissors               crayons

## WHAT TO DO:

1. Put these events in order:

____ a. The wolf runs away.

____ b. Porker buys straw and builds his house.

____ c. Mamma Pig says goodbye to her three little pigs.

____ d. The wolf fails to blow down Baco's brick house.

____ e. Baco buys bricks and builds her house.

____ f. The wolf blows down Porker's straw house.

____ g. Hammer buys sticks and builds his house.

____ h. The wolf slides down the chimney.

____ i. Baco makes a pot of soup.

____ j. The wolf blows down Hammer's stick house.

2. Fold a sheet of construction paper in half.

3. Then fold each edge, making a 3" wide flap.

4. Cut out and paste the lined portions of this page onto the flaps.

5. Tell the story of the three little pigs in your own words, writing on your book-cover flaps.

6. Write the title and draw a picture on the cover.

THE THREE PIGS

Cutting Line ↑

← Cutting Line

**Name** _____  **Date** _____

# THE BACO AWARD

WHAT DO YOU THINK?

1. Of the three little pigs, who worked the hardest? _____

2. What did that little pig do? _____

3. Why did Porker and Hammer come running to Baco's house? _____

_____

4. Write four words to describe Baco:

_____     _____

_____     _____

Do you work hard, too? Of course, you do!
Make a list of some of the work you do.
Then fill in the award below, and color it, too!
Cut it out and wear it the whole day through!

**THE BACO AWARD**
**FOR**
**HARD WORK**

**Your Name:** _____

**Today's Date:** _____

# FEBRUARY

Teacher Notes and Additional Activities
Monthly Activities
Emotions
The Five Senses
Story and Related Activities

# FEBRUARY
# Teacher Notes and Additional Activities

## It's February, February's Calendar

Encourage your students to decorate their calendars, noting important dates and birthdays. Make a large classroom calendar, as well, and celebrate any February birthdays.

Winter has settled in now. Take the children out for a walk and have them note what they see and hear. Be sure to ask what they don't see and hear, too, such as leaves and birds. Make chalk drawings.

## Groundhog Day: Hand Shadows

First, go outside on a sunny day so everyone can find his/her shadow—run with it, try to step on it, etc.

While outside, explain that we can measure the heights of tall trees and buildings, even each other, by measuring shadows. First, have them measure the shadow of a yardstick. It will be 9 feet long, or three times as long as the stick itself. It will be the same for everything they measure: the shadow will be three times as long as the object. For instance, if a flagpole's shadow is 60 feet long, then the flagpole itself is 20 feet long. They'll enjoy doing this with each other, as well.

Teach the song, "Me and My Shadow" (lyrics: Billy Rose; music: Al Jolson and Dave Dreyer), and Robert Louis Stevenson's poem, "My Shadow."

Have the children put on a shadow play: tape cut-out shapes of people and animals onto barbecue sticks and have the children hold their sticks in front of a flashlight. (The closer the light, the larger the shadow.)

Play **Shadow Buff**: Tape a sheet tightly between two walls. Place a strong lamp a few feet behind it, leaving enough room for a child to pass between the sheet and the light. Choose someone to be "Buffy" and seat that child in front of the sheet. The other children pass one at a time between the sheet and the light, disguising themselves as they do so. Buffy tries to identify each child. When successful, they switch places.

## Lincoln's Birthday: Honest Abe

First, find out what the children know about Lincoln, recording their responses. Talk about slavery, freedom, and the Civil War, and remind them about Martin Luther King, Jr., comparing and contrasting these two heroes.

## Valentine's Day: Be My Valentine

To set the stage, play **Broken Hearts**: Cut out one large red heart for every two students. Then cut each heart in half with a few bold, jagged cuts and hand out. The object is for the children to find the holder of their other half. The first pair to do so wins.

Find out what the children know about Valentine's Day; is it celebrated in their native countries? Talk, too, about the different kinds of love that exist between friends, family, etc.

Make a Valentine's Day bulletin board by cutting out large red hearts and have the children write "I love you" in their native languages and display on a bulletin board around a picture of the earth.

Have the children make and color their **Be My Valentine** cards, to be given to friends, etc. Or, you might have them send or take their cards to a retirement community or hospital.

Ask the children to bring in various "craft" items, such as stickers, candy wrappers, buttons, fabric scraps, and dried flowers. Along with some paper, such items can be turned into cards as a recycling project.

Give the children several strips of pink paper and let them write "I love you" messages on them. These can then be taken home and placed so that their loved ones can find them.

Make a Valentine's Day lunch: heart-shaped sandwiches, strawberry-flavored milk, and strawberry sundaes.

## Washington's Birthday: George Washington

Start by talking about "firsts:" first steps, first day in school, etc. Then find out what the children know about our first President and record responses. Talk about freedom and how we fought for it, led by men like Washington. Ask about honored heroes in their native countries. After doing this activity, add facts to your list.

## Lincoln or Washington?

This follow-up activity asks children to differentiate between the two men and test what they've learned.

Take the children to the library and have them select a book about one of these Presidents to read, or select these yourself and read them to the class. Next, give cut-outs of the two Presidents' heads on which can be written his name, his wife's name, home state, years in office, and two or three additional facts they've learned.

## Feelings

Brainstorm the word "feelings" and write their responses on the board.

After completing this activity, go over it together using an overhead. Next, let the children color their squares, applying a different color to each feeling. Then share. Any consensus? Explain sayings like "feeling blue," and "seeing red."

Play charades by giving each child a "feeling" to act out.

As a follow-up, have children portray these emotions using only their hands. Then only their faces.

## Another Kind of Feeling

Have the children make hand prints in clay to set the stage for the sense of touch.

Before doing this activity, be sure everyone understands words such as *cool, dry, soft,* etc. This is even more fun when each child is first blindfolded with another child recording their responses.

Have each child put a few textured items in a brown lunch bag. Then pair them up and let them exchange bags and see if they can guess, by touch alone, what each item in the bag is.

Have the children make "texture" books.

## Hot or Cold?

This activity demonstrates how we sense water temperature, showing how heat moves from our hand into water or from water into our hand, thus dictating what we "feel."

## Feeling and Hearing Sound!

To move from the sense of touch to hearing, record a collection of sounds, such as thunder, hands clapping, a barking dog, a cat's meow, an ambulance siren, and the like, and let the children try to identify them.

Through this activity your students will experience firsthand the relation between vibrations and sound.

## A String Telephone

Bring in a phone and pretend to talk to a friend. Then make an actual "call" using a string phone to demonstrate how, instead of being carried over a wire, their voices will vibrate and be carried over a piece of string. When they make their "phones," just make sure they remember to keep the string straight!

## Your Two Eyes

We now move from hearing to seeing, and this activity will show your students how our two eyes work in concert. They'll find they need both of their eyes to really see!

## You Won't Believe Your Eyes

Here your students will make a toy called a thaumatrope, tricking their eyes into seeing "moving" pictures.

Have each child roll up a 9"-square piece of newspaper into a 1"-diameter tube and tape down. Now, they should hold the tube up to their right eye using their right hand. At the same time, they'll put their left palm about 4" away from their left eye. A hole appears in their hand, because the brain puts the two images together!

Have the children put the tips of their index fingers together and hold their hands about 5" from their eyes. When they focus on something across the room, "sausages" will appear between their two fingers.

Pair the children up and have them put their foreheads and noses together. Then tell them to look straight ahead as if looking at something on the other side of the room. What they'll see is a Cyclops—a one-eyed monster!

## The Way Things Taste

We now move to the sense of taste and our taste buds, which sense sweet, sour, salty, and bitter. These will be easy for the children to identify. As a follow-up and to show children how our taste buds can send the wrong message, give each child a bit of toothpaste, followed by a sip of orange juice. They won't like it! That's because the detergent in toothpaste prevents the "sweet" taste buds from working, making the juice taste bitter and sour.

## Tasting Is Smelling, Too!

This activity sets out to prove that our sense of taste depends on our noses. As a follow-up, show the children a sliced apple and onion. Then blindfold them and tell them to hold their noses, too. Since they can't see or smell, it will be very hard for them to tell whether they are biting into the apple or the onion!

More Follow-up Activities:

Have the children make a list of sense and feeling verbs and their synonyms, such as *cry,* and act them out.

Brainstorm sense and feelings adjectives. Then turn the children loose with newspapers, circling all the related adjectives they can find and add these to the list and display—leads to much discussion, too!

Let the children make "sense" and/or "feelings" mobiles.

Write these headings on the board: Tastes, Smells, Sounds, Feelings, Textures, Sights. Then have the children brainstorm and correctly categorize their words.

Play **Pottsie**: With chalk, mark off a diagram with eight boxes, each about $2' \times 1'$. Put a different category in each box and number, such as animals, feelings, senses, colors, fruits, vegetables, holidays, and body parts. The first player rolls a ball into the first box, stopping it with hands and/or feet before it rolls out of the box, or else losing the turn. To progress further, the player names something fitting that first category, such as "pig" for the animal category. Then she/he bounces the ball into each of the next boxes, giving an answer while catching the ball. The first player to get through all the boxes without making a mistake or dropping the ball wins.

## "The Golden Touch"

Talk about "wishes" and then ask each child to make a wish, sharing it if they like. Would their lives change in any way? (Many children wish for wealth.) Explain that this is a story about a wish that comes true.

Brainstorm "gold," recording everything they can think of that is gold—even sunsets!

Ask if they think someone can be too rich, have too much gold.

Read the story several times to the class, acting out all the motions, etc., and pausing at the appropriate spots to let the children answer the questions that are posed, either orally or in writing. Once the children know the story well, assign parts. Pairing parts helps include even your shyest of students. (Please note that the ending is not given. The children will write their own endings in a follow-up activity.)

## One More Time

This cloze story frame gives the children an opportunity to summarize the story and use context clues by filling in the blanks. Then put this activity on an overhead and let the children read it out loud in its entirety. Note that each event is numbered to help the children follow the sequence of events.

## Story Strip

This activity reflects how each event is caused by the one before it. First, though, make sure your students understand the concept of cause and effect by giving them plenty of examples, such as: "The alarm goes off. You get up." Let them make up (and act out, too) some of their own.

Once assured that this concept is well understood, read the summary again to the class. Then give each child a copy of this activity. Following directions, your students should first correctly order the events that are listed and record these on the appropriate arrows. The strips can then be cut out and pasted together where indicated. This activity culminates on the next page with the children writing their own endings.

## The End!!!

Now, the children write their own endings, recording them in the box provided. After these are shared, have the children cut them out and attach to the end of their story strips for display.

Follow-up Activities:

Give each child a copy of the following graph to complete:

### Somebody    Wanted    But    So

After filling it in for "The Golden Touch," let the children make up story lines of their own that fit this outline and do some writing, either individually or in groups.

Using a Language Experience Approach, have the children write and illustrate a big book for this story.

Read Patrick S. Catling's *The Chocolate Touch,* handing out plenty of chocolate kisses, too!

Do a compare/contrast activity between these two stories using a Venn Diagram.

# IT'S FEBRUARY

Look at February's calendar on the next page and do the following:

1. Number the days on your calendar. February has 28 days, unless it's leap year. Then it has 29 days. This happens every four years, as in 1996, 2000, 2004, etc.

2. Cut and paste  on February 2nd. This is Groundhog Day.

3. Cut and paste 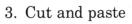 on February 12th. This is Lincoln's birthday.

4. Cut and paste  on February 14th. This is Valentine's Day.

5. Cut and paste  on February 22nd. This is Washington's birthday.

**Name** ———

**Date** ———

# FEBRUARY

| SUNDAY | MONDAY | TUESDAY | WEDNESDAY | THURSDAY | FRIDAY | SATURDAY |
|--------|--------|---------|-----------|----------|--------|----------|
|  |  |  |  |  |  |  |
|  |  |  |  |  |  |  |
|  |  |  |  |  |  |  |
|  |  |  |  |  |  |  |
|  |  |  |  |  |  |  |

# HAND SHADOWS

People say that on February 2nd the groundhog comes out of his hole and looks around. If he sees his shadow, he goes back to sleep, and winter will last another six weeks.

Now you can have some fun with shadows, too!

1. Turn on a bright lamp. Turn off all the other lights in the room.

2. Fix your hands as shown below. Then put them in the beam of light and watch the show! Can you make any other animals?

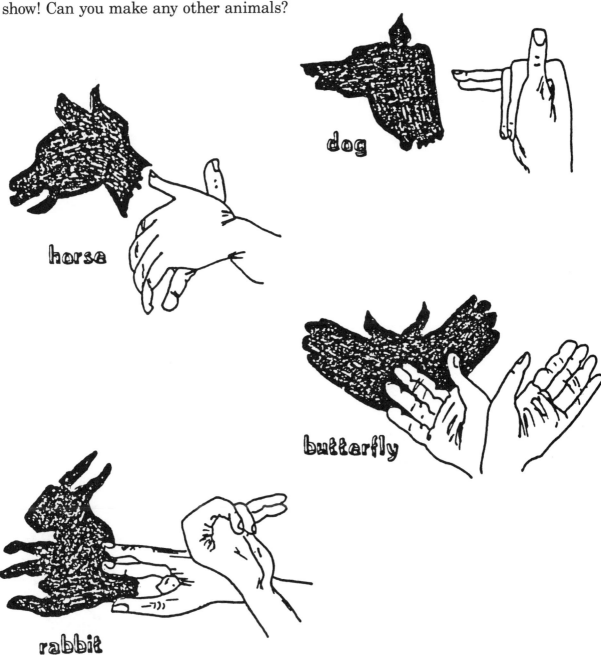

dog

horse

butterfly

rabbit

# "HONEST ABE"

Abraham Lincoln was born in a log cabin in Kentucky on February 12, 1809.

He always loved books, and when he grew up, he became a lawyer.

The one thing he hated was slavery and often spoke against it. He believed that all men and women should be free. Slavery was important in the south, though. These states would not give up their slaves.

When Lincoln became President in 1861, several southern states decided to break away and start their own country. It was called the Confederate States of America. Lincoln wanted the country to stay together. At the same time, he wanted to end slavery in America.

The result was the Civil War. It began in 1861 and did not end until April 1, 1865. The North won the war, and the South rejoined the United States.

On April 14, 1865, Lincoln and his wife, Mary, went to Ford's Theater to see a play. He needed to relax and was enjoying the play when shots rang out. John Wilkes Booth had shot the President. Lincoln died the next morning. Slavery finally ended in the United States on December 18, 1865.

What other facts or stories do you know about Abraham Lincoln?

_____

_____

_____

# BE MY VALENTINE!

1. Cut along —— solid lines.
2. Fold **back** along – – – broken line.
3. Fold **back** along · · · · dotted line.
4. Write your Valentine message inside your card.
5. To make the envelope, turn the page.

*Happy Valentine's Day*

# TO MAKE AN ENVELOPE

## CUT OUT THE ENVELOPE AND THEN . . .

1. Fold flap "A" along broken line (1).
2. Fold flap "B" along broken line (2).
3. Paste along edge of flap "C" (3).
4. Fold and paste down flap "C" (4).
5. Insert card.
6. Paste along edge of flap "D" (6).
7. Fold flap "D" along broken line (7).

*"Knock, Knock."*
*"Who's there?"*
*"Olive."*
*"Olive who?"*
*"Olive You!!!"*

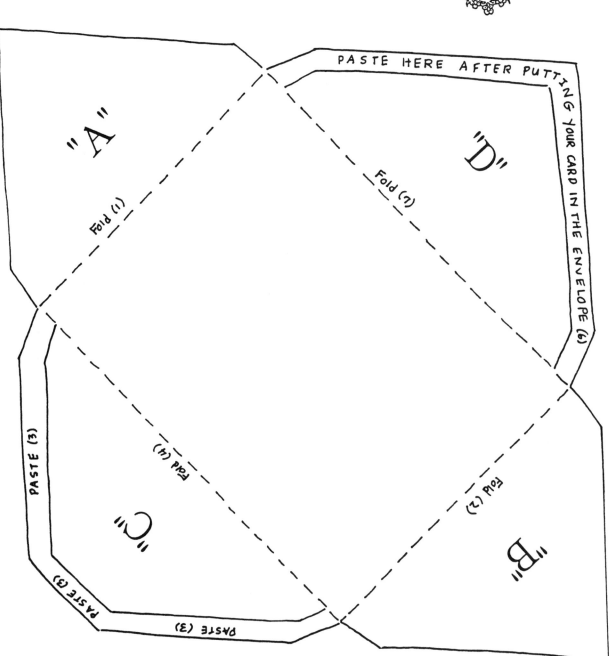

# GEORGE WASHINGTON

George Washington was born on February 22, 1732, in Virginia. To this day, he is known as "the father of our country." This is why:

Washington fought with the English to move the French out of the Ohio Valley. Known as the French and Indian War, fighting lasted from 1753 to 1758. When it was over, the English had won.

After the war, he married Martha Curtis. Together they went back to his home, Mt. Vernon, in Virginia, to raise their family.

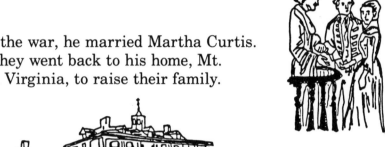

But in 1775, the American colonies went to war against England. They were fighting to be free. This war was called the American Revolution. Washington led the fight. The war ended in 1783. America was free, but it still needed Washington.

On April 30, 1789, he became our first president. He served for eight years, until 1797. Then he finally left public life and went back home to Mt. Vernon. Washington died two years later, on December 14, 1799.

Name _____ Date _____

# LINCOLN OR WASHINGTON?

**DIRECTIONS:** Fill in the blanks with either an "L" for Lincoln or a "W" for Washington.

_____ 1. I was born in a log cabin.

_____ 2. My birthday is February 22nd.

_____ 3. My birthday is February 12th.

_____ 4. I am known as the father of my country.

_____ 5. Virginia is my home state.

_____ 6. I helped to end slavery in America.

_____ 7. I helped America free itself of English rule.

_____ 8. I was a lawyer.

_____ 9. I was the first President of the United States.

_____ 10. I was born in Kentucky.

_____ 11. I fought in two great wars.

_____ 12. The Civil War was fought while I was President.

_____ 13. Mt. Vernon was my home.

_____ 14. My wife's name was Mary.

_____ 15. I married Martha Curtis.

_____ 16. I was shot and killed by John Wilkes Booth.

© 1994 by The Center for Applied Research in Education

**Answers: 1. L; 2. W; 3. L; 4. W; 5. W; 6. L; 7. W; 8. L; 9. W; 10. L; 11. W; 12. L; 13. W; 14. L; 15. W; 16. L.**

Name _____  Date _____

# FEELINGS

**DIRECTIONS:** Label each picture with the feeling it shows. Here are your choices:

happy    lonely    confused    worried    angry    sad    loving    tired

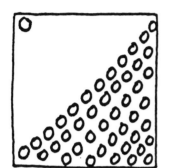

1. _____    2. _____    3. _____

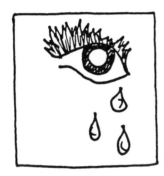

4. _____    5. _____

6. _____    7. _____    8. _____

**Answers: 1. lonely; 2. angry; 3. loving; 4. sad; 5. confused; 6. tired; 7. worried; 8. happy**

Name _____

Date _____

# ANOTHER KIND OF FEELING

1. Look around your classroom and the cafeteria. Look outside, too!

2. Collect some small objects, such as:

| ice cube | shell | rock | sponge |
| nail file | leaf | bread | hot water |
| pine cone | jello | brush | pencil |

. . . AND ANYTHING ELSE YOU LIKE!

3. Now, rub each object with your hand. How does it feel? Write your answers below. Some items will go in more than one category.

| Cool | Warm | Dry | Wet | Soft | Hard | Rough | Smooth |
|------|------|-----|-----|------|------|-------|--------|
|      |      |     |     |      |      |       |        |
|      |      |     |     |      |      |       |        |
|      |      |     |     |      |      |       |        |
|      |      |     |     |      |      |       |        |
|      |      |     |     |      |      |       |        |

**Name** _____     **Date** _____

# FEELING HOT OR COLD???

**WHAT TO DO:**

1. Fill 3 bowls with hot, warm, and cold water. Put them next to each other, with the warm water in the middle.

2. Put your right hand in the hot water and your left hand in the cold water.

   **How does your right hand feel?**

   _____

   That's because your hand was cooler than the hot water. Heat moved from the water into your right hand, making it hot.

   **How does your left hand feel?**

   _____

   That's because you hand was warmer than the cold water. Heat moved from your hand into the water, making it cold.

3. Now, put both hands in the bowl of warm water in the middle.

   **How does the warm water feel to your right hand?**

   _____

   That's because your right hand was hotter than the warm water. Heat moved from your hand into the water. This made your right hand feel cool.

   **How does the warm water feel to your left hand?**

   _____

   That's because your left hand was colder than the warm water. Heat moved from the water into your hand. This made your left hand feel warm.

**Name** _____ **Date** _____

# FEELING AND HEARING SOUND!

When you hear a sound, any sound, something is moving . . .

**YOU'LL NEED:**  a spoon     string
a knife     a glass
a fork

**NOW . . .**

1. Put your hand on your throat and sing a few notes. Feel the sound moving? Your vocal cords are moving, vibrating, inside your throat!

2. Rap a glass with a spoon. It will make a sound.

   Next, rap the glass with the spoon again, but this time touch the rim with your hand. Can you feel it move, vibrate? When the movements (vibrations) stop, the sound stops.

3. Now rap a fork against a table or desk. Then quickly bite down on the handle with your teeth. Feel it move? The vibrations moved through your teeth and bones to your ears! Loud, wasn't it?

4. Finally, make a spoon sound like a bell! Tie the string to the spoon's handle. Then hold the string tightly to the center of your ear. Let the spoon hang down. The sound vibrations will travel from the spoon up the string to your ear, and you'll hear the sound of a bell!

# A STRING TELEPHONE

**YOU WILL NEED:**

2 clean, empty (12-½ ounce) juice cans
a nail
a hammer
a piece of string about 20 feet long
a partner

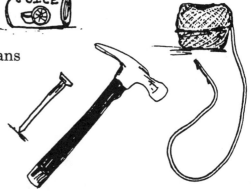

**NOW:**

1. Make a hole in the bottom of *each* can. (Hold the point of the nail against the bottom of the can and tap with hammer.)

2. Push one end of the string through the hole and tie a big knot.

3. Let the string slide back through the can. Tug on it to make sure your knot holds.

4. Push the other end of the string through the hole in the other can and tie a knot. Tug on it to make sure it holds.

5. Give one can to a friend. Walk away from each other until the string is pulled straight and tight. Don't let the string touch anything.

6. Take turns talking into the can and listening. Even if you whisper, your friend will hear you!

Name _____ Date _____

# YOUR TWO EYES

**WHAT YOU NEED:**

    a ball (a partner, too!)

**NOW . . .**

1. Close one eye.

2. At the same time, try to bring your two index fingers together, tip to tip.

    DID YOU MISS? _____

3. Do the same thing, but this time keep both eyes open.

    DID YOU MISS? _____

**NOW . . .**

1. Ask your partner to throw a ball up into the air.

2. At the same time, close one eye and try to catch the ball.

    DID YOU CATCH THE BALL? _____

3. Do the same thing, but this time keep both eyes open.

    DID YOU CATCH THE BALL? _____

**Two eyes really are better than one!!!**

# YOU WON'T BELIEVE YOUR EYES!!!

A thaumatrope is a toy that tricks your eyes into seeing two pictures at the same time. See for yourself . . .

**WHAT YOU WILL NEED:**

a 2-inch-square piece of construction paper
a pen
a pencil with an eraser
a push pin

**WHAT TO DO:**

1. Draw someone fishing on one side of the paper as shown. Don't forget the worm!!!

2. Turn the paper over and draw a fish near the lower left-hand side as shown.

3. Stick the paper to the pencil's eraser with the push pin.

4. Now hold the pencil between your palms.

5. Roll the pencil back and forth, faster and faster. As the paper flips from one side to the other, you will see the fish getting ready to eat that worm!

(You might also like to try putting a fish in a bowl or a bird in its cage.)

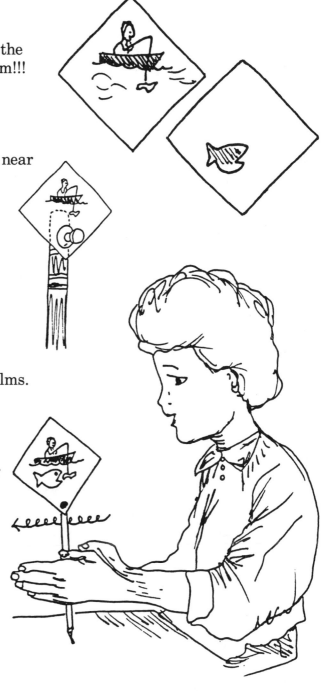

**Name** _____  **Date** _____

# THE WAY THINGS TASTE—SALTY, SWEET, SOUR, BITTER

Some tastes are easy to tell about . . .

**WHAT YOU NEED:**

glass of water
sugar
lemon slice
salty peanut
black coffee

1. Taste some sugar.

   How does it taste? _____

   RINSE YOUR MOUTH WITH WATER.

2. Taste a slice of lemon.

   How does it taste? _____

   RINSE YOUR MOUTH WITH WATER.

3. Taste a salty peanut.

   How does it taste? _____

   RINSE YOUR MOUTH WITH WATER.

4. Taste some black coffee.

   How does it taste? _____

   RINSE YOUR MOUTH WITH WATER.

**WHERE IT ALL HAPPENS:** The taste buds on your tongue bring these four tastes to you. This is where you find the different taste buds.

**Name** _____     **Date** _____

# TASTING IS SMELLING, TOO!

Only your nose knows what you are really eating. Find out for yourself!

### YOU WILL NEED:

4 different kinds of juice
a piece of cloth
a large glass of water
4 small glasses

### WITH YOUR PARTNER, DO THIS:

1. Pour each fruit juice into a small glass.

2. Cover your partner's eyes with the cloth.

3. Let your partner taste each juice, sipping some water after each taste.

4. What did your partner taste each time?

_____  _____  _____  _____

5. Now, have your partner hold his nose and taste the juices again. Remember to give him/her some water after each taste.

6. What did your partner taste each time?

_____  _____  _____  _____

(Now, you try it, too!)

Name _____  Date _____

# THE GOLDEN TOUCH

**Characters:**  Narrator      Marygold
King Midas    Stranger

| | |
|---|---|
| Narrator: | Once upon a time, there lived a king named Midas. He loved his ten-year-old daughter, Marygold, with all his heart. He also loved gold—bright, shiny gold! |
| Everybody: | (Touch hearts.) |
| Narrator: | Some people say he loved gold too much. Let's listen and find out. |
| Everybody: | (Cup hands over ears, as if listening.) |
| King Midas: | You're as good as gold, dear girl. |
| Everybody: | (Hugging motion.) |
| Marygold: | You always say that, Father! |
| Everybody: | Giggle. |
| King Midas: | Well, it's true. You're a good girl, a golden girl. I wish you were gold . . . |
| Everybody: | What did you say??? |
| Marygold: | What's that, Father? I didn't hear you. |
| King Midas: | Oh, nothing, dear. I was just talking to myself. Now pick a few roses and let's go inside. |
| Everybody: | Snip. Snip. |
| King Midas: | Your teacher will be here soon, and I have some work to do before breakfast. |
| Marygold: | Are you going to count your gold again before you even eat this morning? |
| Everybody: | 1 . . . 2 . . . 3 . . . 4 |
| King Midas: | Don't ask so many questions, child. We need gold. We need more gold. |
| Everybody: | (Shake index fingers.) |

**What do you think the king will do now?** _____

# THE GOLDEN TOUCH (continued)

| | |
|---|---|
| Narrator: | The king went straight to his treasure room and locked himself in. |
| Everybody: | (Pretend to put a key in a lock and turn it.) |
| King Midas: | Just look at you, my golden beauties! Let me touch you and hold you! |
| Everybody: | (Touching, hugging motions.) |
| Stranger: | Do you love gold more than anything in the world? |
| Everybody: | I really want to know. |
| King Midas: | Who are you, and how did you get in here? I know I locked that door! |
| Stranger: | Didn't you hear me? Tell me now, what would make you a happy man? |
| Everybody: | Tell me! Tell me! |
| King Midas: | Okay, I'll tell you. I want gold. I want everything I touch to turn to gold. |
| Stranger: | Really? Are you sure you want the Golden Touch? |
| Everybody: | Say, "NO!" Say, "NO!" |
| King Midas: | Of course, I'm sure. I'd be so happy if everything turned to gold. |
| Everybody: | What a wish! |
| Stranger: | Very well, then. I give you the Golden Touch. |
| King Midas: | Wait! Don't go! Who are you? |
| Everybody: | Come back! Come back! |
| King Midas: | My goodness, what a dream that was! But it seemed so real. |
| Everybody: | (Shake heads and rub eyes.) |
| King Midas: | Oh, well, I'd better meet Marygold for breakfast. I'll come back after I eat. |

**What do you think will happen next?** _____

_____

# THE GOLDEN TOUCH (continued)

Narrator: Midas was hungry and soon forgot about the Stranger in his treasure room.

King Midas: Marygold, pass me that plate of fish. The muffins look good, too!

Everybody: Um, um! The food looks so good!

Marygold: Here, Father. Have some orange juice, too.

Everybody: (Pretend to pour.)

King Midas: What's the matter here? This fish is so cold and hard I broke a tooth!

Everybody: Crack! Crack!

Marygold: Father, what's wrong with you? The fish is sweet and tasty!

King Midas: It's nothing, dear. Forget it. Let me just drink some juice. Oh, no!

Everybody: (Grab throats and cough.)

Marygold: Father, what is it? What's wrong?

King Midas: It's nothing, dearest. Just give me a hug, and everything will be fine.

**What is happening to King Midas?** _____

**What do you think will happen next?** _____

# THE GOLDEN TOUCH (continued)

Narrator:      As soon as he touched her, Marygold turned to gold—hard and cold!
Everybody:     (Stand like statues.)
King Midas:    Oh, no! Not my Marygold! What have I done?
Everybody:     Oh, no! Oh, no!

Narrator:      Suddenly, the Stranger appeared again.
Stranger:      You said you loved gold and wanted the Golden Touch. Now you have it.
Everybody:     (Point index fingers and shake them.)
King Midas:    How could you do this to me? Everything I touch turns to gold. I am hungry, but I cannot eat! And now even my Marygold is like a rock!
Everybody:     I hate you! I hate the Golden Touch!
Stranger:      It's what you wanted, is it not? All I did was give you your dream.
King Midas:    Take it away! Please, take it away. Make me a poor man if you want. Just give me back my daughter! Give me back my life! I beg you . . .

**What do you think the Stranger will do?** _____

_____

Name _____  Date _____

# ONE MORE TIME . . .

**DIRECTIONS:** Fill in the blanks to retell "The Golden Touch."

(1) King Midas was a good king who loved his daughter very much. Her name was

_____, and she was _____ years old. He also loved

_____. (2) In fact, he loved gold so much that he wished for the

_____  _____. He thought he would be happy if everything

he touched turned to gold. (3) The _____ made his wish come true.

(4) After the Stranger left him, King Midas went to eat _____ with

Marygold. But everything he tried to eat or drink turned to _____ in his

mouth. (5) Finally, he hugged _____. She also turned to

_____.

After that, King Midas cried and cried. What a fool to wish for the

_____  _____. Now, he hated it. Once again, the Stranger

came to him. (6) This time King Midas asked to be a poor man. He didn't want the

Golden Touch anymore. All he wanted was his life back. All he

wanted was Marygold back.

**Answers:** 1. Marygold, 10, gold; 2. Golden Touch, 3. Stranger; 4. breakfast, gold 5. Marygold, gold, Golden Touch

© 1994 by The Center for Applied Research in Education

# STORY STRIP

To make your story strip of "The Golden Touch," do the following:

1. Number the events in their right order.
2. Write these events in order on the arrows below.
3. Cut the strips out on the *solid* lines.
4. Paste the strips together as shown.
5. Then, go on to the next page.

___ King Midas wishes to be poor.
_1_ King Midas loves gold and wants more.
___ Marygold turns to gold.
___ The Stranger gives King Midas the Golden Touch.
___ King Midas asks the Stranger for the Golden Touch.
___ All the king's food turns to gold.

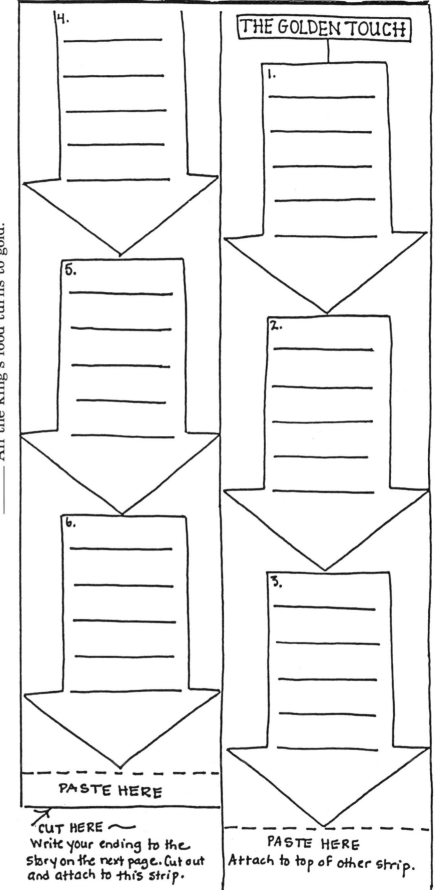

THE GOLDEN TOUCH

1.

2.

3.

PASTE HERE
Attach to top of other strip.

4.

5.

6.

PASTE HERE

CUT HERE
Write your ending to the story on the next page. Cut out and attach to this strip.

# THE END!!!

**DIRECTIONS:** Now you decide what happens to King Midas.

1. Write your ending below.
2. Cut box out along *solid* lines.
3. Paste your ending to your story strip.

The story ends when _____

THE GOLDEN TOUCH

1.

2.

3.

4.

5.

6.

The story ends when

# MARCH

Teacher Notes and Additional Activities
Monthly Activities
Spatial Prepositions
Houses and Floor Plans
Map Reading
Story and Related Activities

# MARCH
# Teacher Notes and Additional Activities

## Calendar

Encourage children to decorate their calendars, noting important dates and birthdays. Make a large classroom calendar, as well, and celebrate birthdays.

With the coming of spring, the landscape will begin to green again. Take a walk outside and note such things as the return of birds and budding trees.

Share some of the meanings of the word *march* and act the first two out.

> *to march* —to walk as soldiers do, in time, with steps of the same length
> *a march* —music meant for marching
> *March* —the third month of the year; comes from *Martius* meaning "the month of Mars"; Mars was the Roman god of war

## St. Patrick's Day Shamrock Mobile

Invite all the children to wear something green on March 17th. Then individually or in pairs, have the children answer such questions as:

(Turn into an illustrated book.)

1. What color do you think of when you think of spring?
2. What is the first thing you think of when you hear the word *green*?
3. What two colors combine to make green?
4. Name five words that contain the word green.
5. What are three things that are always green?
6. Write a definition for *green*.

Point out Ireland on a globe or world map and briefly tell the children the legend of St. Patrick—how he used a shamrock leaf when preaching and drove the snakes out of Ireland using a loud drum.

Talk about good and bad luck and making our own luck. Take a walk and look for four-leaf clovers.

## A Spring Pinwheel

Brainstorm *spring* and make a class list of "spring" words.

Create a "T" chart: Spring Looks Like/Feels Like and complete together.

To celebrate the new season, have the children make their pinwheels and then head outside.

Using a Venn Diagram (2 overlapping circles), have the children compare/contrast winter and spring.

## Peanut Butter

March is Peanut Butter Month, so let the children make peanut butter sandwiches with this simple recipe.

Purchase a packet of peanut seeds and plant together once the ground has thawed. Before long, children will be pulling peanuts out of the ground!

## Prepositions, It's Your Turn

First model these spatial prepositions, acting them out and then inviting the children to follow your lead. Turn into a game of Simple Simon.

Complete these two preposition activities, using an overhead.

Write these spatial prepositions on 3" × 5" index cards and hand one to each child to act out for the class. Plant a fallen tree branch in a bucket of sand. Have the children illustrate their cards and hang them on the branches.

Make an obstacle course in the room and write out directions, such as "Climb over the desk," and "Crawl under the table."

Have the children close their eyes while one child hides. The students then ask location questions using prepositions, such as "Is he near the flag?" You respond with "yes" or "no."

Have one student (or even yourself) leave the room and hide an object, such as a chalk eraser, somewhere in the room. When she/he returns, she/he asks individuals where the object is. For example, "Is the eraser under the teacher's desk?" and "No, it is not under the desk." (Everyone should use complete sentences.)

## All Around the House

These activities are designed to reinforce spatial prepositions while introducing household rooms and furnishings. Using an overhead is suggested.

Have students draw a picture of each room of their house/apartment on 4" × 6" cards. Then tape together to make an accordion book and hang on wall.

Divide class into groups to make a collage, assigning each group a different room.

Divide class into groups and give each group a shoe box and assign them a room. Have the groups then create and decorate their room and then put them all together to make a house. (Bring in fabric scraps.)

## "The Old Woman in a Shoe"

Put this well-known nursery rhyme on an overhead and read it several times, inviting the children to join in when ready. Act it out as you read it by doing such things as holding up a shoe, counting all the children in the room, slurping soup, shaking your head from side to side at the mention of bread, and finally shaking your finger at the group and hustling them all into a corner and making them lie down.

Once familiar with the story, complete this activity. Try turning the "Maybe" portion into a group or whole-class Language Experience Approach (LEA) activity with everyone contributing and embellishing their facts.

## Inside the Shoe: A Floor Plan

This activity introduces mapping by using a floor plan, while reinforcing "home" words and spatial prepositions. Can be done on an overhead.

On butcher-block/bulletin-board paper, have the children make a floor plan of the school and display.

## Where, Oh, Where?

This follow-up activity also uses the shoe's floor plan, asking the children to sort and categorize a list of household items. You can add to this list and/or invite the children to do so.

Have each child draw a classmate's name and decorate a shamrock for that child. Then everyone hides his/her decorated shamrocks somewhere in the school and draws a map with directions, such as "Turn left at the door and walk ten paces," etc. (First, demonstrate what is meant by a "pace.") Once found, put the shamrocks on a bulletin board. You might want to add a photograph of each child.

## Which Way?

This activity introduces map direction words using a simple picture.

For reinforcement, form groups of eight and have the children lie in circles, feet pointing in, with each child representing a map direction. Place a simple map on an overhead and make up a road-trip story, tracing your route on the map. Each time you change direction, the appropriate children sit up and call out their direction.

## Scales

This activity introduces the concept of *scales* as measuring devices to prepare the children for map scales. You might want to bring in some of these scales, such as a weight scale, and weigh each child, etc.

## Map Scales

Using a simple map and line drawings, this activity prepares children to use map scales. As a follow-up, bring in various maps with differing scales and demonstrate their use.

## My Town, Map Reading

Continuing with map-reading skills, these activities introduce map legends and provide additional practice applying map directions and scales.

Have the children make a map of their town/city/neighborhood, drawn to scale on bulletin board or butcher-block paper. Take photos of some well-known locations and attach to the map.

Distribute a state or national road map to each child and ask the children to find such items as an airport, state park, good vacation spot, etc. Use an overhead. A similar activity can be done with a town/city map.

Give each child a state map and various props, such as a gas-station credit card, etc. Then concoct a traveling story such as, "We stopped on Route 73 in Norristown for gas." The children follow along on their maps and hold up the appropriate props.

## "Thumbelina"

Bring in pictures of a mouse, toad, swallow, and mole.

Teach the "Thumbelina" song, holding up your thumb as you sing.

Have the children decorate their thumbs to look like a girl.

Read this simplified version several times, adding lots of action and sound effects in your telling, until the children are fully acquainted with the story. Have the children volunteer for parts. Some children may feel more comfortable reading in pairs. Shy/less fluent students will, of course, contribute to the "Everyone" parts.

Make a Story Map, displaying the setting and characters, first problem and solution, second problem and solution, and resolution. Have the children illustrate these.

Make a PMI chart with these headings: *P*luses, *M*inuses, *I*nteresting. The children then think about being the size of a thumb and come up with the advantages, disadvantages, reasons why it might be interesting to be that size.

## Make a Book

First, have the children sequence the events, thus briefly summarizing the story before making their little books.

## Acting Out

A variation of this activity is to group the class, assigning each group a different part of the story. This way, everyone will have a part in the "play."

## Following Thumbelina

This activity provides a follow-up to both mapping skills and "Thumbelina."

Have the children make up their own maps and scales for Thumbelina's travels. Then ask them to add questions and swap. These can later be colored in and displayed.

It's
March!!

Look at March's calendar on the next page and do the following:

1. Number the days on your calendar. March has 31 days.

2. Cut and paste  on March 17th. This is St. Patrick's Day.

3. Cut and paste  on the first day of spring, March 21st.

4. Cut and paste    on special March birthdays.

(March is National Peanut Month)

**Name** _____

**Date** _____

## MARCH

| SUNDAY | MONDAY | TUESDAY | WEDNESDAY | THURSDAY | FRIDAY | SATURDAY |
|--------|--------|---------|-----------|----------|--------|----------|
|        |        |         |           |          |        |          |
|        |        |         |           |          |        |          |
|        |        |         |           |          |        |          |
|        |        |         |           |          |        |          |
|        |        |         |           |          |        |          |

**Name** _____  **Date** _____

# SHAMROCK WISH MOBILE

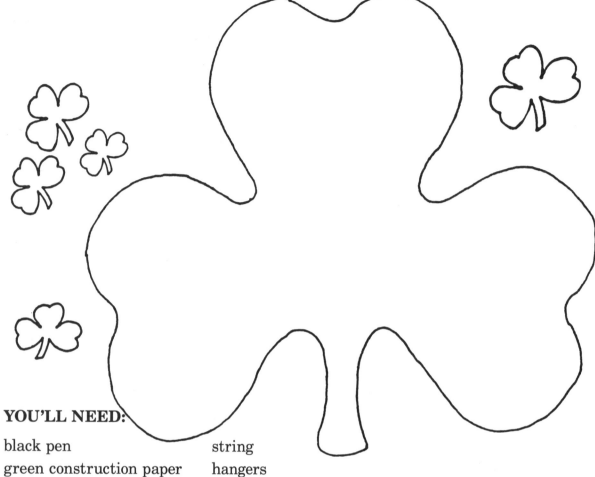

**YOU'LL NEED:**

black pen                           string
green construction paper            hangers
magazine pictures                   photos

**NOW . . .**

1. Make 6 wishes:

   a. _____

   b. _____

   c. _____

   d. _____

   e. _____

   f. _____

2. Cut out 6 shamrocks.

3. Write a wish on each shamrock.

4. Using string, hang your shamrocks from a hanger—pictures, too!

**Name** _____   **Date** _____

# A SPRING PINWHEEL

**YOU'LL NEED:**    crayons        straight pin            tape
                    scissors       pencil with an eraser

**WHAT TO DO:**

1. Color the pinwheel different colors.
2. Cut out the square along the ——— solid lines.
3. Cut into the square along the ——— solid lines—*but not inside the circle.*
4. Bend (don't fold down) each of the corners marked with an "X" along the – – – dotted lines. Tape in place.
5. Put a straight pin through the 4 corners and the center of the circle.
6. Put the pin into the eraser of a pencil.
7. Take your pinwheel outside. It will spin when you run with it, or blow on it!

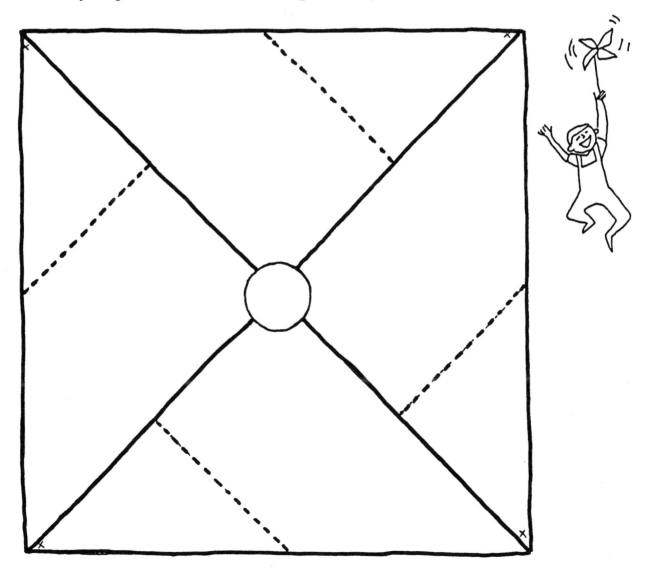

## YOU WILL NEED:

electric blender
rubber spatula
measuring cup
measuring spoons
mixing bowl

1 cup peanuts
2 tablespoons oil
¼ teaspoon salt

## NOW, TO MAKE YOUR PEANUT BUTTER, ALL YOU DO IS:

1. Grind the peanuts in the blender until powdery.
2. Scrape peanuts into the bowl.
3. Add oil and salt.
4. Stir until well blended—AND ENJOY!!!

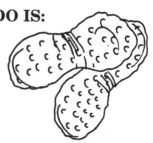

# PREPOSITIONS

**LOOK AT THESE PICTURES AND LEARN SOME PREPOSITIONS:**

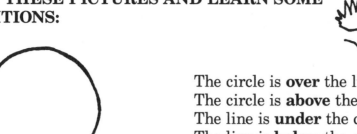

The circle is **over** the line.
The circle is **above** the line.
The line is **under** the circle.
The line is **below** the circle.
The line is **beneath** the circle.
The line is **underneath** the circle.

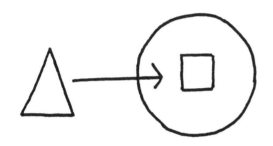

The circle is **around** the square.
The square is **in** the circle.
The square is **within** the circle.
The square is **inside** the circle.
The arrow is going **into** the circle.
The square is **in front of** the arrow.
The triangle is **behind** the arrow.
The arrow is **between** the triangle and the circle.

The square is **near** the circle.
The square is **beside** the circle.
The square is **next to** the circle.
The square is **by** the circle.

The circle is **on** the square.
The straight arrow (→) is going **up** the square.
The wavy arrow (↝) is going **down** the square.
A straight line is leaning **against** the square.
A dotted (– – –) line runs **across** the bottom.

# IT'S YOUR TURN!

1. Draw two squares **next to** each other **on** this circle.
2. Draw a small circle **between** the two squares.
3. Draw a wavy (⤳) line **under** the two squares.
4. Draw a straight (→) line **above** the two squares.
5. Draw a small triangle **inside** each square.
6. Draw a small rectangle **over** this circle.
7. Draw a small square **beneath** this circle.
8. Draw a circle **around** this circle, your square and your rectangle.
9. Draw an arrow going **into** both circles.
10. Draw a triangle **behind** the arrow and two circles.

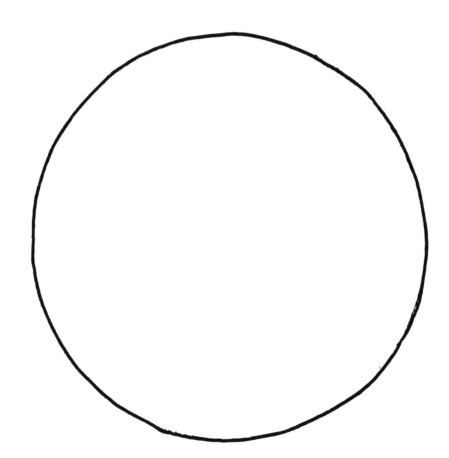

**Color your shapes, too!**

Name —————————

Date —————————

# ALL AROUND THE HOUSE

## CIRCLE THE RIGHT ANSWERS:

1. The roof is **over/below** the house.

2. The walkway is **inside/outside** the house.

3. The shutters are **beside/in** the windows.

4. The door is **between/within** two windows.

5. The garage is **next to/under** the house.

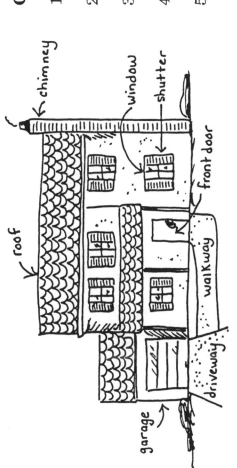

## CIRCLE THE RIGHT ANSWERS:

1. The refrigerator is **near/beneath** the stove.

2. The microwave oven is **below/above** the stove.

3. The sink is **in/over** the counter.

4. The drain is **outside/inside** the sink.

5. The drawers are **beside/under** the stove.

Name _____

Date _____

# ALL AROUND THE HOUSE

THE DINING ROOM

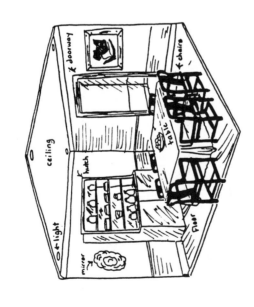

## CIRCLE THE RIGHT ANSWERS:

1. The wood is **across/within** the fireplace.

2. The fireplace is **over/under** the pictures.

3. Books are **on/below** the bookcases.

4. The sofa is **into/between** the bookcases.

5. The coffee table is **behind/in front of** the sofa.

---

## CIRCLE THE RIGHT ANSWERS:

1. The hutch is **behind/beneath** the table.

2. The chairs are **inside/around** the table.

3. The table is **within/on** the floor.

4. The lights are **on/above** the ceiling.

5. The mirror is **between/beside** the hutch.

THE LIVING ROOM

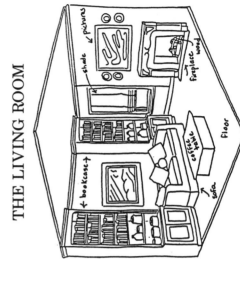

# ALL AROUND THE HOUSE

## CIRCLE THE RIGHT ANSWERS:

1. The floor is **underneath/over** the rug.

2. The bureau is **above/below** the windows.

3. The mirror is **across/between** the windows.

4. A box is **under/near** the bureau and the bed.

5. A lamp is hanging **over/near** the floor.

THE BEDROOM

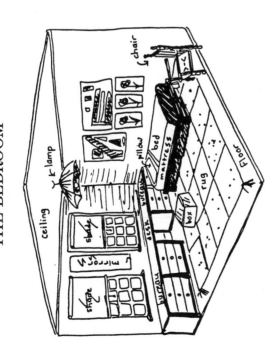

## CIRCLE THE RIGHT ANSWERS:

1. The bathtub is **underneath/next to** the vanity.

2. The windows are **behind/in front of** the shades.

3. The toilet is **beside/around** the towel rack.

4. The mirror is **above/under** the sink.

5. The plants are **in front of/behind** the windows.

THE BATHROOM

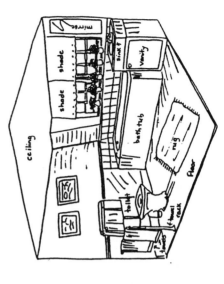

Answers: 1. underneath; 2. below; 3. between; 4. near; 5. over.
1. next to; 2. behind; 3. beside; 4. above; 5. in front of.

Name _____  Date _____

# THE OLD WOMAN IN THE SHOE

There was an old woman who lived in a shoe.
She had so many children she didn't know what to do.
She gave them some soup, without any bread,
Then scolded each one and sent them to bed.

**YOU KNOW THAT . . .**

1. This story is about _____

2. She had **few/many** children. (Circle one.)

3. They live in a _____

4. For supper, the children ate _____

5. Did the children also eat some bread? **YES/NO** (Circle the right answer.)

6. Did the children have ice cream for dessert? **YES/NO** (Circle the right answer.)

7. The old woman **kissed/scolded** her children. (Circle one.)

8. After that, the children **played outside/went to bed.** (Circle one.)

**MAYBE . . .**

1. The old woman is _____ years old and her name is _____

2. She has _____ (#) children living with her.

3. The children ate this kind of soup: _____

4. Their mother scolded them because they _____

_____

_____

**Answers: 1.** an old woman; **2.** many; **3.** shoe;
**4.** soup; **5.** no; **6.** no; **7.** scolded; **8.** went to bed

Name _____   Date _____

# INSIDE THE SHOE: A FLOOR PLAN

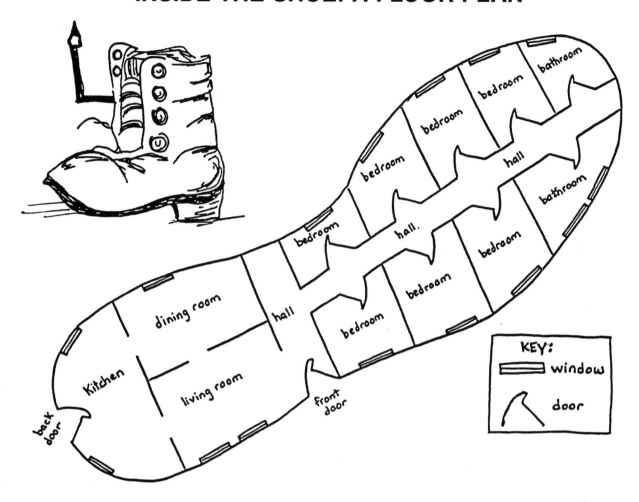

A floor plan is a map of a house—or a shoe. Take a look and answer these questions.

1. How many windows do you see? _____ How many doors do you see? _____

2. There are _____ bathrooms. Are the bathrooms the same size? YES/NO

3. How many bedrooms do you see? _____

4. There are two beds in each bedroom. How many beds are in the shoe? _____

5. If you enter the back door, what room are you in? _____

6. If you enter the front door, what room is to your left? _____

7. Can you get to the kitchen from the hall? YES/NO

8. What two rooms are next to the kitchen? _____   _____

Name _____

## WHERE, OH, WHERE?

Try putting these words in the right rooms. Write on the floor plan.

| | | |
|---|---|---|
| hutch | pillow | table and chairs |
| vanity | refrigerator | microwave oven |
| bureau | towels | fireplace |
| sofa | coffee table | desk |
| | stove | bed | counter | bathtub |

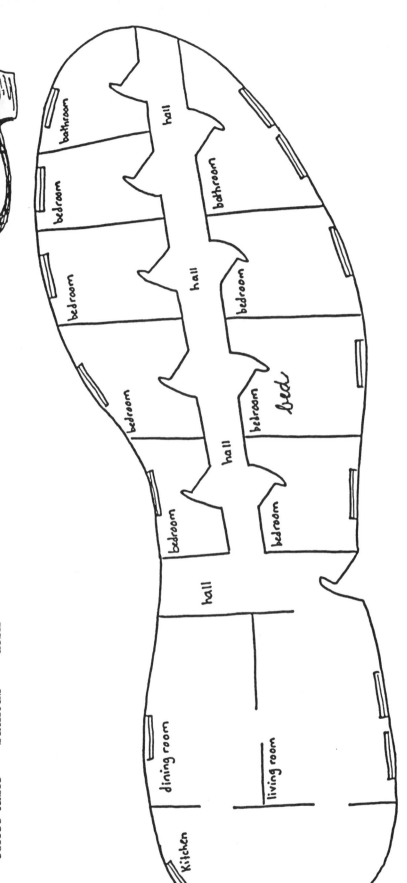

# WHICH WAY???

Study these directions:

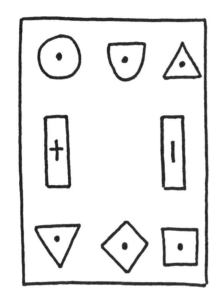

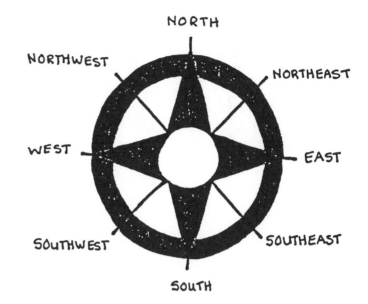

Now, look at this picture. Then answer the questions below. Circle your answer.

1. Is ⬆ in the NORTHEAST or NORTHWEST corner?

2. Is ⬥ in the NORTH or the SOUTH?

3. Is ⬜ in the SOUTHWEST or SOUTHEAST corner?

4. Is ⌣ in the NORTH or SOUTH?

5. Is ⬥ in the NORTH, the SOUTH, the EAST, or the WEST?

6. Is ● in the NORTHEAST or NORTHWEST?

7. Is ▽ NORTH, SOUTH, EAST, or WEST of ⬥ ?

8. Is ▯ NORTH, SOUTH, EAST, or WEST of ⊞ ?

**Answers:** 1. northeast; 2. south; 3. southeast; 4. north;
5. south; 6. northwest; 7. west; 8. east

Name _____     Date _____

# SCALES

A calendar is a *scale*. It measures time in days, months, and years.

What year is marked on this calendar? _____

What month? _____

What day of the week? _____

A clock is a *scale*. It measures time in seconds, minutes, and hours.

What time is it on this clock? _____

(And how many seconds? _____)

A thermometer is a *scale*. It measures body temperature in degrees.

The arrow points at "normal," or _____ degrees.

A ruler is a *scale*. It measures length in inches.

Do you know how many inches there are in a foot? _____

Weight *scales* measure how much you weigh in pounds.

How much do I weigh on this scale? _____

How much do you weigh? _____

© 1994 by The Center for Applied Research in Education

Name _____    Date _____

# MAP SCALES

Maps have scales, too. Map scales help you measure the distance between two places on a map. This scale tells you that one inch equals two miles.

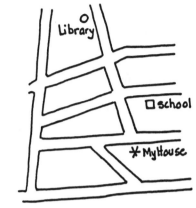

On this map, ☐ is _____ inch from ✳ .

That means, school is _____ miles from my house.

On this map, ✳ is _____ inches from ◯ .

That means, my house is _____ miles from the library.

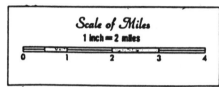

## WHAT IS THE DISTANCE BETWEEN THE DOTS?

Scale of Miles
1 inch = 1 mile
├─────────────┤

Distance between dots: _____ miles

Scale of Miles
1 inch = 25 miles
├─────────────┤

Distance between dots: _____ miles

Scale of Miles
1 inch = 100 miles
├─────────────┤

Distance between dots: _____ miles

Scale of Miles
1 inch = 300 miles
├─────────────┤

Distance between dots: _____ miles

Scale of Miles
1 inch = 500 miles

Cut out the ruler.

Distance between dots: _____ miles

**Answers:** ½ inch; one mile; 1-½ inches; 3 miles; one mile; 50 miles; 75 miles; 300 miles; 1000 miles

Name _____     Date _____

# MY TOWN

1 Sal's Pizza
2 Pat's Dress Shop
3 Toys for All
4 Movie Theater
5 Clem's Groceries
6 Doctor's Office
7 The Shoe Stop
8 One-Stop Bakery
9 Burger Heaven

 My house

 Park

 School

 Library

 Hospital

 Stores

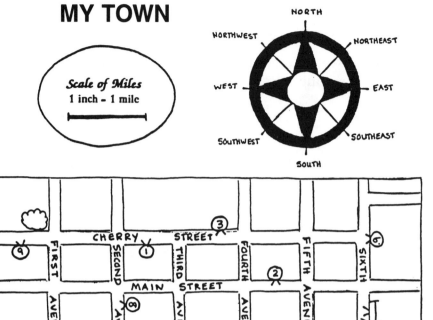

Scale of Miles
1 inch – 1 mile

## FILL IN THE BLANKS AND CIRCLE THE ANSWERS:

1. I live on _____ Street. Clem's Groceries is about _____ mile(s) EAST/WEST of my house. The park is NORTH/SOUTH of my house.

2. The grocery store is SOUTHEAST/SOUTHWEST of Burger Heaven. They are about _____ mile(s) apart.

3. The library and my school are on _____ Street. I live about _____ mile(s) from there.

4. After seeing the doctor, I traveled EAST/WEST to Toys for All on _____ Street. About how many miles did I walk? _____ Then I stopped at Sal's for pizza. How far is the toy store from Sal's? _____ miles

5. Mom is going to drive me to the movies tonight. The theater is _____ miles EAST/WEST of my home. After the movies, we'll stop at Burger Heaven for dinner. That's _____ miles from the theater. It is in the NORTHEAST/NORTHWEST.

Cut out the ruler.

**Answers: 1. Sunny, 1 mile, east, north; 2. southeast, 1-3/4 miles; 3. Broad, 2-1/2 miles; 4. west, Cherry, 2 miles, one mile; 5. 3 miles, east, 3-1/4 miles, northwest.**

Name _____  Date _____

# MAP READING

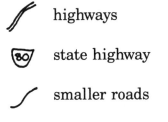

- ● cities
- ✸ capital
- ⟋ highways
- 🛡80 state highway
- ⟋ smaller roads
- ↗ airport
- ✕✕✕ railroad

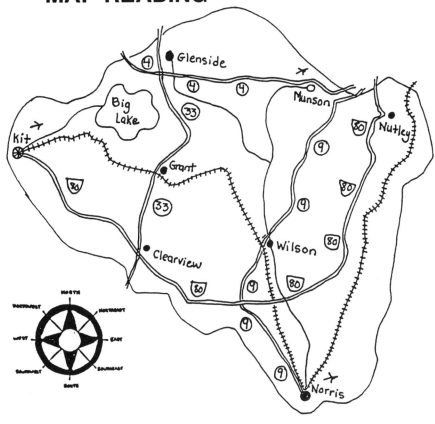

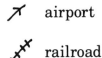

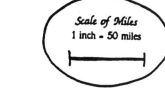

*Scale of Miles*
1 inch = 50 miles

1. You can fly to three cities: _____  _____  _____

2. You live in the capital. To go to Norris, you will travel SOUTHEAST/SOUTHWEST for
   _____ miles. What two highways will you drive on? _____  _____.

3. From Nutley, the train passes through _____  _____
   and _____ before going to Kit. Nutley is in the NORTHEAST/NORTHWEST.

4. From Glenside, Route 4 takes you _____ miles EAST/WEST to Munson.

5. From Glenside, Route 33 takes you _____ miles NORTH/SOUTH to Grant.

6. From Clearview, Route 33 takes you _____ miles NORTH/SOUTH to Grant.

Cut out the ruler.

# THUMBELINA
## by Hans Christian Andersen
## (A Class Activity)

**CHARACTERS:**  Thumbelina   Mrs. Mole   Mr. Swallow
              Toad       Mrs. Mouse   Flower King

**Everybody:** (Follow the directions.)

| | |
|---|---|
| **Narrator:** | Once upon a time, in the forest beside Winding River, there lived a girl no bigger than your thumb. Her name was Thumbelina. (pause) | Hold up your thumb. |
| **Toad:** | I've decided. I want you to marry my son today. He needs a wife. (pause) Someone small and pretty—just like you! So, come along! (pause) | Put hands on hips. Point finger, reach out to grab. |
| **Thumbelina:** | Never, Mrs. Toad! Never! I don't love him, and I won't marry him! (pause) | "Never! Never!" |
| **Toad:** | Yes you will, my dear, so stop fussing. You're giving me a headache! (pause) | Rub forehead; grabbing motion |
| **Thumbelina:** | Let go of me, Toad! (pause) | Twist and turn and cry out. |
| **Narrator:** | Thumbelina twisted and turned. When Mrs. Toad finally let go, she ran away. (pause) | Pound hands quickly on floor. |
| **Thumbelina:** | Oh, dear! Oh, dear! Where am I? I ran so far, I've lost my way. And now it's starting to snow. Oh, dear! Oh, dear! (pause) | Cover face with hands; crying sounds |
| **Narrator:** | Now remember that Thumbelina is the size of your thumb. Each snowflake knocked her to the ground. Her tears turned to ice. (pause) | Make teeth chatter. Hug yourself to keep warm. |

# THUMBELINA (continued)

Mrs. Mouse: Who are you, child? And what are you doing out here in the snow? Don't you know you'll freeze out here? (pause) — Bend down and reach out.

Thumbelina: My name is Thumbelina. Mrs. Toad said I had to marry her awful son. So I ran away. Now I don't know where I am. (pause) — Rub eyes and wipe away tears.

Mrs. Mouse: Oh, you poor dear! It's a good thing I found you. Come inside and let me take care of you. (pause) — Put out a helping hand.

Narrator: Thumbelina loved living with Mrs. Mouse, and they became good friends. (pause) — Hug a friend. "Uh, oh!"

Mr. Mole: Marry me, Thumbelina. I have big house, and I'll feed you only the best bugs. You'll be happy, Thumbelina. You must say yes. (pause) — "Please, oh, please!"

Thumbelina: I hate bugs, Mr. Mole, and I don't love you. And your house is under the ground. I cannot live without the sun. (pause) — "No! No!"

Mr. Mole: Of course, you can, my dear. Now, please, come with me. (pause) — "Come! Come!"

Mrs. Mouse: Go with him, my dear. He'll make you a fine husband. (pause) — "Go on! Go on!"

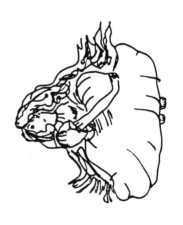

# THUMBELINA (continued)

| | | |
|---|---|---|
| Narrator: | Thumbelina finally said yes and followed Mr. Mole to his house under the ground. (pause) By the door, she found a swallow tied to the root of a tree. (pause) | "Sob! Sob!" "Oh, my!" |
| Thumbelina: | You poor thing. You're so cold and hungry. (pause) When Mr. Mole goes out, I'll bring you some food and blankets. (pause) | "Poor thing!" "I will! I will!" |
| Narrator: | Every day Thumbelina fed the swallow. Soon they became good friends. (pause) | Shake hands with a friend. |
| Mr. Swallow: | You made me strong again, Thumbelina, and now I want to leave this awful place. Come with me to a place where it is always spring. (pause) | "Come fly with me!" |
| Narrator: | Thumbelina quickly climbed on the swallow's back. Up, they flew, (pause) high into the sky. When they finally landed, Mr. Swallow put Thumbelina on a rose petal. Next to her stood a little man as small as Thumbelina. (pause) | Flying motion. |
| Flower King: | Pretty lady, I have been waiting for you all my life. Will you marry me? (pause) | "Oh, so good-looking!" "I love you. I love you." |
| Thumbelina: | Yes! Yes! Of course, I'll marry you! (pause) | Big smiles. Hugging motion. |
| Narrator: | On every leaf and flower stood a little man or woman. They clapped and clapped for Thumbelina and her king. (pause) And in a treetop above them, Mr. Swallow sang for his friend, Thumbelina. (pause) | Clap your hands! "Chirp! Chirp!" |

Name _____     Date _____

# MAKE A BOOK

**YOU'LL NEED:**
    paste
    scissors
    stapler

**NOW:**
1. Cut out the box below and on page 216.
2. Paste the two boxes together, back to back.
3. Cut along dotted line.
4. Fit the pages together to make a book.
5. Fill in the pages.

---

THUMBELINA
by Hans Christian Andersen

    This book was made
          by

_____

8

1

---

    We flew and flew, coming down in

the Land of the Flowers. My story

ends there _____

_____

_____

_____

_____

_____

    I lived near the _____

River. I was very happy. Then Toad

wanted me to marry her son. This is

what happened next: _____

_____

_____

_____

_____

_____

6

3

**Name** _____  **Date** _____

My name is Thumbelina.

This is my picture.

2

7

I ran so fast that soon I was lost. It started to snow and then _____

_____

_____

_____

_____

_____

_____

4

I liked living with Mrs. Mouse. Then Mr. Mole took me to his home under the ground. There I met _____.

This is what we did: _____

_____

_____

_____

_____

_____

5

**Name** _____  **Date** _____

# ACTING OUT

## WHAT YOU WILL NEED:

tongue depressors or popsicle sticks
construction paper
felt-tip pens/crayons
scissors
paste

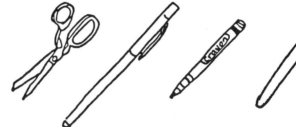

## WHAT TO DO:

1. With a partner, reread "Thumbelina."
2. Choose your favorite part.
3. Draw and color the heads of the characters in that part of the story.
4. Cut out the heads and paste them on tongue depressors or popsicle sticks.
5. Act out your story for your classmates.

**Name** _____    **Date** _____

## FOLLOWING THUMBELINA

Follow Thumbelina. Put the houses, palace, and rose petal in the right places.

1. Toad lives ¼ mile east of Thumbelina's house on the Winding River.
2. Thumbelina ran one mile southwest from her house to Mrs. Mouse's house.
3. Mr. Mole lives ½ mile southeast of Mrs. Mouse's house.
4. Mr. Swallow took Thumbelina from Mr. Mole's house to the Flower Kingdom:
   a. First he flew three miles east.
   b. Next he flew two miles north.
   c. Then he flew two and one-half miles northwest to the rose petal.
   d. The King's palace is ½ mile west of the rose petal.

○ Thumbelina's house
◠ Toad's House
◇ Mrs. Mouse's House
▽ Mr. Mole's House
◇ Rose Petal
🏰 King's Palace

# APRIL

Teacher Notes and Additional Activities
Monthly Activities
World Languages
Getting to Know You
Story and Related Activities

# APRIL
# Teacher Notes and Additional Activities

### It's April, April's Calendar

Encourage your students to decorate their calendars, noting important dates and birthdays—and then celebrate them. Make a large classroom calendar, as well.

Spring is really in the air now and subtle changes can be seen everywhere, from the budding of trees to the returning of robins, etc. Take a walk and have students list the sights and sounds of spring.

Chart the temperature, taking a reading every day at the same time and recording it on a large chart. Then use the chart for math activities, such as finding the difference between the warmest and coolest days.

### April Fool's Day: April Fool's Day Trick

Some background: Many scholars believe April Fool's Day began in France, because New Year's Day used to be celebrated on April 1st. Then, in 1582, the king adopted our current calendar, moving the holiday to January 1st. However, many people forgot or chose to forget the new date, and they were called April fools. Start by wishing everyone a Happy New Year and then telling them this story.

Talk about the words "fool" and "trick," so that everyone understands them fully. Then do a few "tricks" of your own, such as calling on a student, saying that if she/he can tear a piece of paper into four equal parts, you'll give them a quarter—a quarter of the paper! Or, tell everyone to line up with their heads, left shoulder, left side, and left foot against a wall. Then have them lift their right foot off the floor. It's impossible!

Ask if anyone knows any tricks of their own.

Do this activity with the children.

### Passover: Making Matzo

(Passover, like Easter, sometimes falls in March.)

Matzo, much like a cracker, is the traditional bread of Passover, symbolizing the Jews' hasty departure from Egypt, with no time to let their bread rise. Bring in yeast and some bread to explain "rising" bread.

Invite children to talk about holidays celebrated by their own cultures.

### Easter: A Cone-Shaped Easter Basket

These simple paper baskets are easy to make and can be filled with nuts and raisins or candy.

Hard boil some eggs and let the children decorate and hide them for an egg hunt. Afterwards, make egg salad or deviled eggs and serve with matzo.

Make paper bunnies by stapling a small white paper plate to a large one, adding face, ears, and tail.

Fill a jar with jelly beans and let the students guess how many there are.

## Humpty Dumpty

Talk about things that break and how some can be repaired and some not. Make a class list of both.

This classic rhyme serves as a follow-up to all those Easter eggs. Read it several times to the children until they know it so well they can repeat it themselves, complete with actions. If using raw eggs to dramatize Humpty's plight, be sure to drop them into a bowl and save for scrambling later.

Let the children write some verses of their own—acting them out before pasting them on oval cutouts.

## Earth Day: Saving the Earth

Let a faucet drip slowly into a bucket to help children see how quickly it fills up. Then do this activity together to build awareness of how natural resources are misused by all of us. Talk about the environment, community recycling efforts, the garbage problem, etc. Teach the children to look for these two symbols:

Made of Recycled Materials

Made of Recyclable Materials

Make a bulletin board display using plastic bottles, Styrofoam cups, etc.

Encourage children to stop their junk mail by writing to:

> Mail Preference Service
> Direct Marketing Association
> 11 West 42nd Street, P.O. Box 3861
> New York, New York 10163-3861

Have the children decorate 3" × 5" index cards reminding everyone to turn off lights. Photocopy, laminate, and place by all light switches in the school.

Plant a class tree.

Make Earth Day banners and place in hallways.

Rent **Fern Gully**, an animated film about our endangered rainforests. Then sponsor a schoolwide fund raiser to adopt acres of rainforest—$35 per acre. For more information, write to:

> The Earth's Birthday Project
> 170 Joralemon Street
> Brooklyn, New York 11201

## Important Languages of the World

This activity launches a unit about "self" and our various cultures by having children study a graph to answer some questions. Be sure to remind children that these are just a *few* of the world's languages.

Make a list of the languages spoken in your classroom. Have the children write common expressions, such as "Hello" and "I love you," on index cards in their native languages and teach them to one another.

## Coming to America

Use a globe with this activity, letting everyone come up and locate his/her native country. Let volunteers share their recollections of their coming here, what they like most, dislike most, miss most, etc.

Extend this activity by making a long time line on butcher-block paper and having the children record all the important dates in their lives and then illustrate it for display.

Have the children make mobiles, with a map and flag of their native country, and some facts, such as major cities, climate, exports, etc.

Share newspaper articles about recent trends in immigration.

Have the children draw special places in their native countries on 4" × 6" blank index cards, taping them together to make a postcard book.

Have each child bring in a recipe from her/his native country and make a class recipe book. Photocopy so everyone can have a copy. Put one in the library, too! Invite them to bring these foods in and have a party.

Teach the children the song, "It's a Small World."

## My Family

Continuing the theme of "self" and in preparation for the next activity, ask the children to draw pictures of their family members, pasting them on balloon cutouts. The pictures can also be pasted onto real balloons and tied together.

Give children an opportunity to talk, too, about relatives and friends they may have left behind, and about the concept of "extended family."

## Your Family Tree

Ask the children to interview family members to learn as much as they can about their roots before completing this activity. Encourage them to bring in pictures of their families, as well.

This activity can be extended by letting children make their own family trees on poster board, giving them plenty of room to attach photos.

Encourage your students to tape record or, if possible, videotape their conversations with older family members, such as grandparents, to save for their own children. Some will probably want to share a few of the stories they are told. These can also be written up into a diary or book and shared.

If within reach, take the children to Ellis Island and the Statue of Liberty.

## My Mondala

This activity asks children to think about themselves in terms of pictures/symbols. Model the activity first on the board or overhead by doing your own Mondala and explaining why these particular pictures and symbols represent you. Then talk about the seasons and their preferences before generating a class list of the children's various talents and lifelong goals. When done, these can be cut out and pasted on colored paper for display.

## Grow Some Beans

This springtime activity brings us back to the idea of the earth and renewal, the need for clean air, water, and soil for growing and well-being. It also serves as a lead-in for "Jack and the Beanstalk" which follows. When the seedlings have grown several inches, and it is warm enough (usually around mid-May), either plant a class garden at school or encourage the children to take their seedlings and plant them in a home garden.

As a follow-up, bring in some raw green beans for the children to snack on. You might also want to make a big salad, adding raw beans and/or bean sprouts.

Let the children actually watch the beans germinate and grow by soaking some in a solution of water (one quart) and bleach (one tablespoon). Then fold a dampened paper towel so it covers the bottom quarter of a zipper-seal bag. Place a few beans near (not touching) each other and watch them grow. Moisten every 2–4 days.

## "Jack and the Beanstalk"

This story gives you a chance to talk about such things as wealth and poverty, disobeying our parents, buying and selling, and how advertisers get us to buy their products even if they're not in our best interest. Talk, too, about taking things that don't belong to us, as well as hurting others.

Then, read the story several times to the class, dramatically acting out the parts and motions. Once everyone is very familiar with the story, assign parts. Pairing children helps include even your shyest student.

As a follow-up, have the children write different endings for the story.

Do a "*P*ositive, *M*inus, *I*nteresting" (PMI) activity on the question, "What would it be like to have a hen that lays golden eggs?" Here, the children will make a list of the advantages and disadvantages of such a possession, as well as what would be interesting about owning such a thing.

Have the children develop ads for a handful of beans, trying their hands at selling.

## One Thing Leads to Another

This activity provides the children with an opportunity to think not only about the sequence of major events in the story, but cause and effect, as well. To begin, be sure to provide lots of examples of cause and effect, such as "I didn't hear my alarm clock go off this morning. Therefore, I was late for school."

Group the children and let each group choose its favorite part, adding details and then acting it out.

Have a "Jack and the Beanstalk" day with everyone dressing up as his/her favorite character, staying in character for at least part of the day. Make and serve a three-bean salad for a special treat.

## Flip Book

Flip books are fun and easy to make, but first be sure to model the steps to make sure everyone understands the directions. After the books are made, have the children illustrate the covers, complete with the title.

# IT'S APRIL

**April showers
Bring May flowers.**

Look at April's calendar on the next page and do the following:

1. Number the days on your April calendar on the next page.

2. Cut and paste  on April Fool's Day. This is April Fool's Day.

3. Cut and paste  on the first day of Passover. When does Passover begin this year? Is it in March or April?

4. Cut and paste  on Easter Sunday. Easter falls between March 22nd and April 25th.

5. Cut and paste  on April 22nd. This is when we celebrate Earth Day.

6. Cut and paste   on April birthdays.

Date —————————

## APRIL

| SUNDAY | MONDAY | TUESDAY | WEDNESDAY | THURSDAY | FRIDAY | SATURDAY |
|--------|--------|---------|-----------|----------|--------|----------|
|  |  |  |  |  |  |  |
|  |  |  |  |  |  |  |
|  |  |  |  |  |  |  |
|  |  |  |  |  |  |  |
|  |  |  |  |  |  |  |

# AN APRIL FOOL'S DAY TRICK

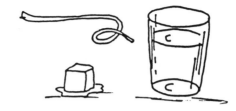

**WHAT YOU'LL NEED:**

6-inch piece of string
ice cube
glass of cold water
salt

**NOW . . .**

1. Put the ice cube in the glass of cold water.

2. Give the piece of string to a friend. Ask your friend to lift the ice out of the water using only the string and without tying any knots.

**IT CANNOT BE DONE, SO NOW DO A LITTLE MAGIC!**

3. Place the end of the string over the ice cube.

4. Sprinkle a line of salt over the top of the ice cube and the string.
   (The salt will melt the ice cube a little.
   Then it will refreeze around the string.)

5. Wait a few minutes.
   Then lift the string—and the ice cube—out of the water!!!

Why did the April fool get mad at his alarm clock?

Answer: It was always going off when he was asleep!

# MAKING MATZO

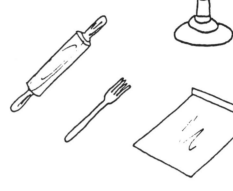

When the Jews were freed from slavery in Egypt a long time ago, they left quickly. They did not wait for their bread to "rise" before baking it. The flat bread they took with them is called **matzo**.

## TO MAKE MATZO, YOU'LL NEED:

flour       baking tray
cold water   rolling pin
large bowl   fork
measuring cup

## NOW:

1. Place 2 cups of flour into a bowl.
   Make a well in the center.

2. Pour ½ cup cold water into the well.

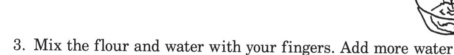

3. Mix the flour and water with your fingers. Add more water if needed. Keep mixing until the dough is soft and smooth.

4. Divide the dough into 4 pieces.
   On a floured table, **knead** each piece 10 times.
   If the dough is too sticky, add more flour.

   *2. With your palm, push it away. Give the dough a quarter turn.*

   *To Knead Dough:*

   *1. Place dough on lightly floured table. Fold it toward you.*

   *3. Continue until dough is smooth and not sticky.*

5. Roll each piece out with a floured rolling pin so that it is ⅛" thick or less.
   Prick with a fork.

6. Place the rolled dough on the baking tray.
   Bake at 500 degrees for 4 to 8 minutes on each side, depending on thickness. The matzo is done when it is dry and has golden-brown patches and edges.

7. Enjoy your matzo!

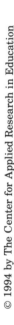

# A CONE-SHAPED EASTER BASKET

**TO MAKE A BASKET, YOU'LL NEED:**

construction paper
string
a plate
crayons
tape
scissors

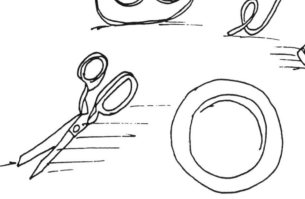

**NOW:**

1. Draw a circle on a piece of construction paper. (Use the plate to help you.)

2. Cut out the circle and fold in half.

3. Cut the circle in half along the fold line.

4. Decorate your half circle.

(bottom)

5. Twist the half circle into a cone and tape.

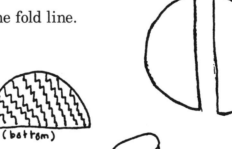

6. Use the string for the handle. Tape the ends of the string in place as shown.

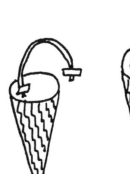

# HUMPTY DUMPTY
## (A Class Activity)

**Everybody:**
(Follow the directions.)

Sit on your desk.

Fall off your desk and lay on the floor.

Gallup around room.

"So sorry! So sorry!"

Humpty Dumpty sat on a wall (pause),

Humpty Dumpty had a great fall (pause).

All the King's horses and all the king's men (pause)

Couldn't put Humpty together again. (pause)

Make up a verse of your own, like "Humpty Dumpty sat in a car . . ."

# SAVING OUR EARTH!

## MATCH THESE "STEPS" WITH THEIR EFFECT:

1. If we all stop getting junk mail . . .

a. we'll save 250 million trees every year!

2. If we all lower our heat setting by 6 degrees . . .

b. you'll save up to 9 gallons of water each time!

3. If you use a low-flow shower head . . .

c. we'll save 500,000 barrels of oil every day!

4. If we all recycle our newspapers . . .

d. we'll save 1.5 million trees every year!

5. If you turn off the water when brushing your teeth . . .

e. you'll save up to 35 gallons of water each time you bathe!

## DID YOU KNOW THAT?

1. The average American spends 8 full months of his/her life opening junk mail?
2. More energy is used for heating than anything else in our homes?
3. A running faucet uses 3 to 5 gallons of water a minute?
4. Each of us throws away 580 pounds of paper a year, including newspapers?

**Answers: 1. d; 2. c; 3. e; 4. a; 5. b**

© 1994 by The Center for Applied Research in Education

Name _____    Date _____

# IMPORTANT LANGUAGES OF THE WORLD

**DANKE**

**Gracias**

**Grazie**

**TAK**

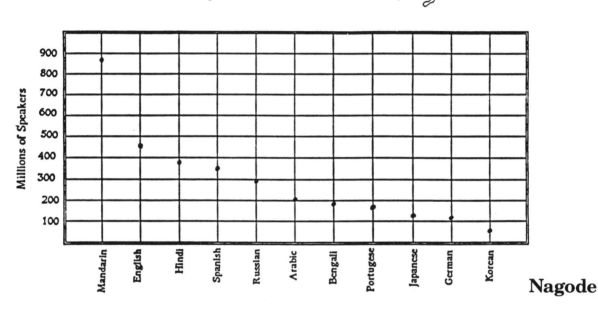

**Nagode**

**DIRECTIONS:** Look at the chart carefully. Then answer "yes" or "no" to these questions:

1. More people speak English than any other language. (YES) (NO)
2. Mandarin is spoken by more than 800 million people. (YES) (NO)
3. Fewer people speak Arabic than the other languages. (YES) (NO)
4. Spanish is spoken less than English. (YES) (NO)
5. About 100 million people speak German. (YES) (NO)
6. More than 200 million people speak Bengali. (YES) (NO)

謝 謝

**Merci**

**Thank You**

Name _____

Date _____

# COMING TO AMERICA

Fill in the blanks about you.

I was born on _____ in the town/city of _____, which is in the country of

_____. I came to America in _____ (month), _____ (year), when I was _____ years old. I came

here with the following people: _____

We traveled by _____ (ship/train/plane)

**MY TIME LINE:** (Mark the important dates in your life on this time line).

| 1975 | 1980 | 1985 | 1990 | 1995 | 2000 |
|------|------|------|------|------|------|

# MY FAMILY

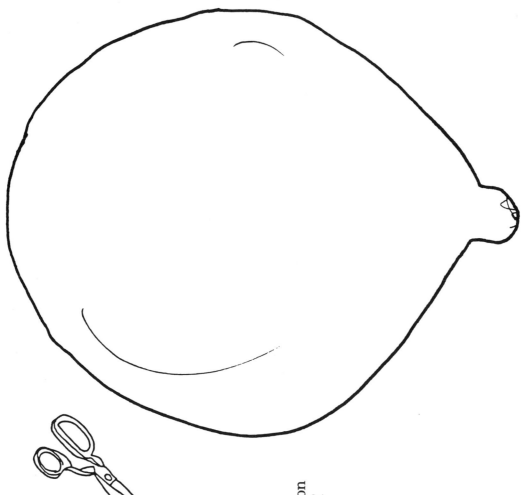

## YOU'LL NEED:

construction paper

pencil

crayons

tape

string

scissors

## NOW:

1. Cut out the large balloon.

2. Trace several balloons on construction paper—one balloon for each member of your family, and, of course, yourself!

3. Draw each family member on a balloon.

4. Tie a string around the end of each balloon.

5. Tape onto a large sheet of construction paper.

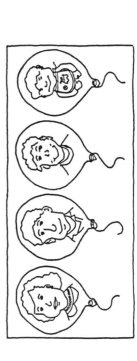

Name ______________________ Date ______________________

# YOUR FAMILY TREE

TO MAKE YOUR FAMILY TREE, FILL IN THE LINES WITH THE NAMES OF YOUR FAMILY MEMBERS.

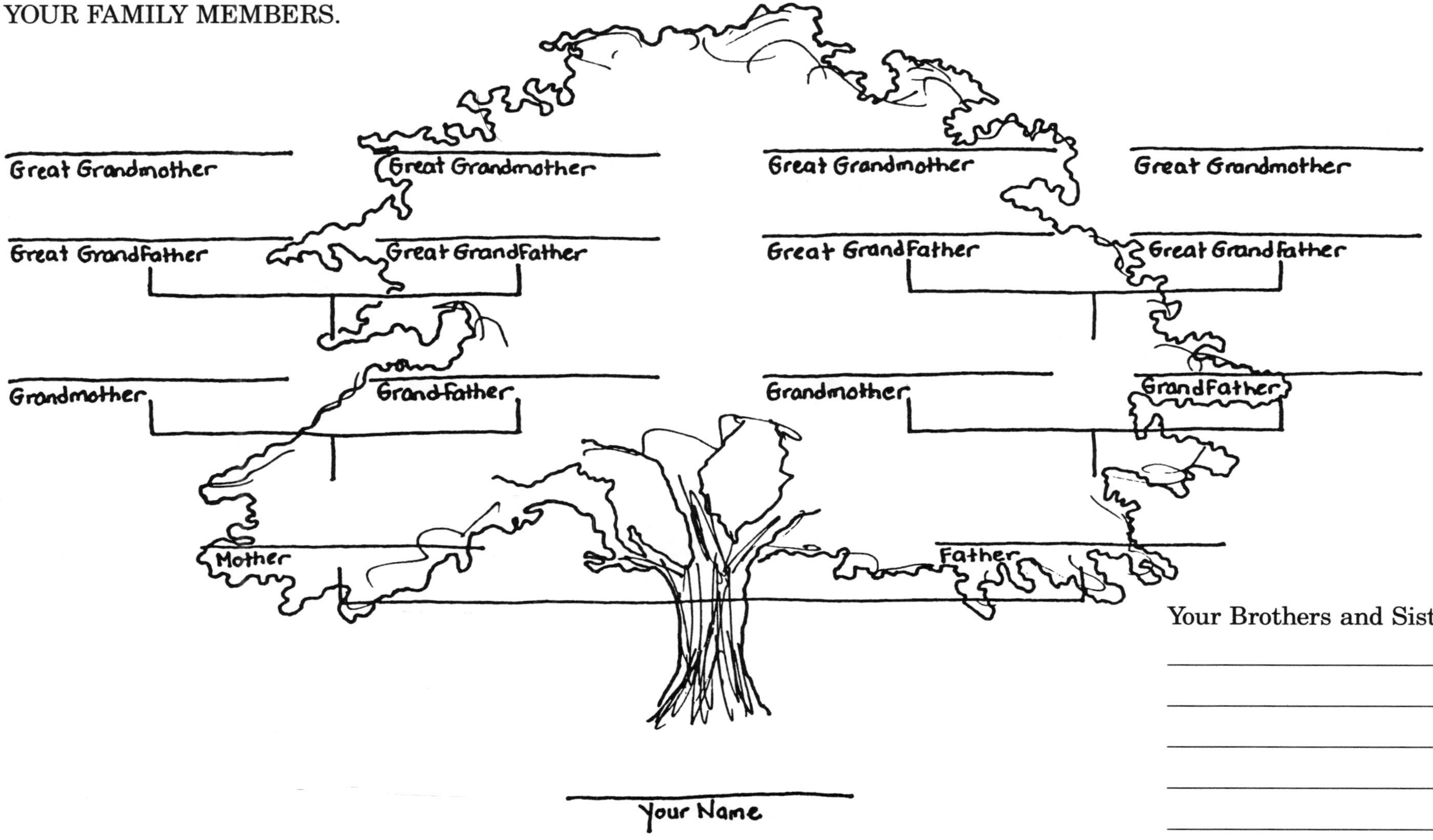

Great Grandmother
Great Grandmother
Great Grandmother
Great Grandmother
Great GrandFather
Great GrandFather
Great GrandFather
Great Grandfather
Grandmother
Grandfather
Grandmother
GrandFather
Mother
Father
Your Name


Your Brothers and Sisters:

______________________

______________________

______________________

______________________

______________________

**Name** _____   **Date** _____

# MY WORLD, MY MONDALA

**YOU'LL NEED:**   pencil   tape   crayons

A mondala is a circle that is divided into four quarters. Each quarter tells something about you in pictures. Look at the sample below. Then make your own mondala on the next page.

**NOW, ON THE NEXT PAGE . . .**

1. Find a picture of yourself and tape it on the first quarter.
2. In the second quarter, draw your favorite season: winter, spring, summer, or fall.
3. In the third quarter, draw a picture of something you do well, such as read or draw.
4. In the last quarter, draw a picture of what you want to be when you grow up, such as a teacher, carpenter, nurse, or doctor.

    This is my mondala. First, you see my picture. I am ___11___ years old, and I'm in the ___6th___ grade. In the next quarter, I drew a(n) _snowflake_. This is because _winter is my favorite season. I love to skate and play in the snow_. Next, I drew a(n) _treble clef and notes_, because I am good at _singing and playing the piano. I love music_. Finally, I drew a picture of _an apple, chalk, and a blackboard_. This is because I want to be a(n) _teacher_ when I grow up. So, as you can see, this mondala tells a lot about me.

CONTINUED . . .

**Name** _____   **Date** _____

## MY MONDALA

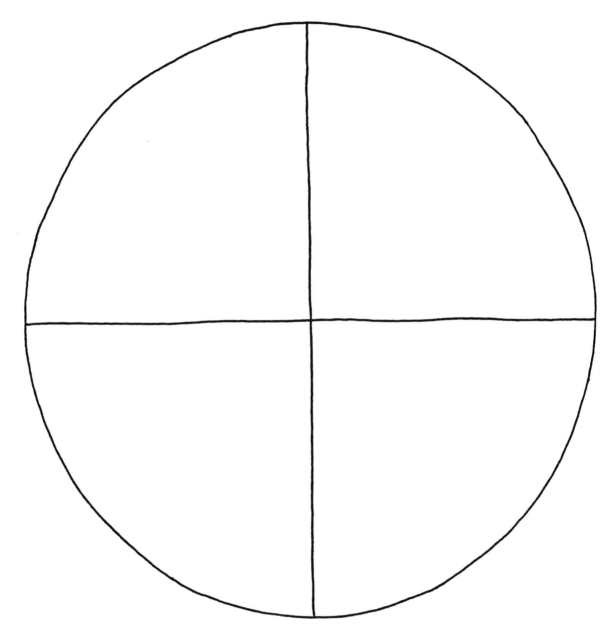

This is my mondala. First, you see my picture. I am _____ years old, and I'm in the

_____ grade. In the next quarter, I drew a(n) _____. This is because

_____.

Next, I drew a(n) _____, because I am good at _____.

Finally, I drew a picture of _____. This is because I want to be a(n)

_____ when I grow up. So, as you can see, this mondala tells a lot about me.

# GROW SOME BEANS!

## YOU WILL NEED:

an empty egg carton
potting soil
bean seeds
water

## NOW . . .

1. Remove the top half of the egg carton.

2. Fill each "cup" of the egg carton with soil.

3. *Gently* press one bean seed in each cup.

4. Cover each seed with a little soil.

5. Sprinkle each cup with a little water.

6. Place in a sunny window.
   Sprinkle with a little water every day.

7. Soon, the seedlings will begin to grow into little bean plants. When it is warm enough, plant them outside.

# JACK AND THE BEANSTALK
## (A Class Activity)

**Characters:** Jack   Mother   Stranger   Clara   Giant

**Parts:**

**Everybody:**
(Follow the directions.)

| | |
|---|---|
| Narrator: | Once upon a time, a poor woman lived with her son, Jack, in a small cottage north of town. The only thing they owned was Bessie, their cow. |
| Jack: | I'm so hungry, Mother. Bessie hasn't given us a drop of milk in days! |
| Mother: | We have to sell her, dear. We simply must! Take her to market and get a good price for her, you hear? |
| Narrator: | On the way, Jack met a strange old man. |
| Stranger: | Is that your cow, young man? Sure is skinny! Still, I guess maybe I could give you my magic beans and take her off your hands. Maybe. Maybe not. |
| Jack: | My Bessie is a good cow! Too good for a handful of silly beans, that's for sure! I'd never make such a trade! |
| Stranger: | Ah, but what if those silly beans could grow up to the clouds? |
| Jack: | Up to the clouds you say? Then, if you'll take Bessie, it's a deal! |

"It's story time!"

Rub belly.
"What can we do?"

"I hear! I hear!"
"Uh, oh!"

"Moo! Moo!"

"Never! Never!"
"Oooh! Ahhh!"

# JACK AND THE BEANSTALK (continued)

"He's back!"
Pat your own back.
Put hands on hips.
Grabbing action.
Throwing action.
Stretch all over.
Rub eyes.

| | |
|---|---|
| Mother: | Oh good, you're back. Give me the money, Jack. |
| Jack: | These beans are better than money, mother! |
| Mother: | You idiot! How can we live on a few ugly beans? |
| Narrator: | She grabbed the beans and threw them out the window! |
| | |
| Narrator: | The next morning, Jack got up early. |
| Jack: | I can't believe it. He was right! The beanstalk grew past the clouds. I've got to climb it! |

# JACK AND THE BEANSTALK (continued)

| | |
|---|---|
| Narrator: | Jack climbed high into the clouds. At the very top he saw a castle and walked up to the door. |
| Clara: | Who is that knocking on my door? |
| Jack: | I'm Jack, and I'm very hungry. Can you feed me? |
| Clara: | Go away, boy! If the Giant sees you, he'll eat you up! |
| Jack: | Just a bite to eat, and I'll be on my way. I promise. |
| Clara: | Very well, but be very quiet. And if you hear a thump, thump, thump, run for your life, child! |
| Narrator: | Jack stuffed his mouth with bread and cheese. It tasted so good. He closed his eyes and chewed. (pause) Then suddenly he heard a THUMP! THUMP! THUMP! |
| Giant: | Fee-fi-fo-fum! I smell the blood of an Englishman! |
| Clara: | Quick, Jack! Hide under the table! |
| Giant: | Where is he? I know he's here somewhere! |
| Clara: | All you smell is bacon frying, foolish giant. Here, eat! |

**Climbing action.**

**Knock on floor.**
**"It's Jack! It's Jack!"**
**Rub belly.**
**"Uh, oh!"**
**"Shhh! Shhh!"**

**Close eyes & chew.**

**Pounds hands on floor!**
**"Run, Jack!"**
**"Oh, no!"**
**Hide your head.**
**Look all around.**

# JACK AND THE BEANSTALK (continued)

| | |
|---|---|
| Chew loudly. | **Giant:** Ummmm! Bring me more food, wife. This is good—but a boy would be better! Maybe tomorrow I'll get lucky. While you're at it, bring me my golden hen, too. I feel like playing. |
| | **Clara:** Here, Giant. Here is more food and your golden hen, too! |
| Keep chewing loudly. | **Giant:** Hen, Hen, lay me a golden egg! Yes! Yes! Now, lay me another. Lay. Lay. Lay. |
| "Cluck! Cluck!" | **Narrator:** Soon the Giant grew tired and fell asleep. Jack peeked out of his hiding place. |
| "Such pretty eggs!" | **Jack:** I can't believe my eyes. A hen that lays golden eggs. I must have it! |
| Make snoring sounds. | **Narrator:** The Giant was snoring loudly, and Clara was washing dishes. Jack tiptoed across the |
| Tip-toe around room. | room and grabbed the hen. |
| Grabbing motion. | **Jack:** I've got you now, golden hen, but first, we've got to get out of here! |
| "Cluck! Cluck!" | **Narrator:** Unfortunately, the hen's clucking woke the Giant up. |
| "Uh, oh!" | **Giant:** Fee-fi-fo-fum! I smell the blood of an Englishman! And I hear him! And I see him! And I can't wait to taste him! |
| Point to your nose, | **Narrator:** Jack scrambled down the beanstalk. The Giant was right behind him. |
| ears, eyes. Lick lips. | As soon as Jack touched the ground, he grabbed an axe. |
| Chopping motion. | **Narrator:** Down came the beanstalk, Giant and all! The golden hen made Jack and his mother very rich, and they lived happily ever after. |

Name _____  Date _____

# ONE THING LEADS TO ANOTHER

**DIRECTIONS:** In "Jack and the Beanstalk," one event leads to another. Do you know what happened next? Use these choices to fill in the blanks.

1. Jack's mom throws the beans out the window.
2. Jack sells Bessie for a handful of beans.
3. Jack and his mom live happily ever after.
4. Jack eats bread and cheese in the castle.

5. Jack steals the golden hen.
6. Jack cuts down the beanstalk.
7. Jack climbs the beanstalk.
8. Jack hides under the table.

Bessie stops giving milk, so...  _____

Jack's mom is angry about the beans, so...  _____

Jack sees the tallest beanstalk ever, so...  _____

Jack tells Clara he's hungry, so...  _____

Jack hears a THUMP, THUMP, so...  _____

Jack sees the hen lay golden eggs, so...  _____

The Giant chases Jack, so...  _____

Jack gives his mom the golden hen, so...  _____

## A FLIP BOOK

To make a flip book, you will need scissors and crayons.

**NOW:**

1. Color in the pictures.

2. Cut box out along solid (——) lines.

3. Write what's happening below each picture.

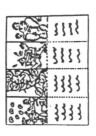

4. Cut between pictures as shown. Stop at center fold.

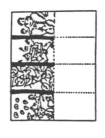

5. Fold cut pieces down at center fold.

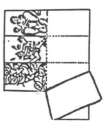

6. Make a cover for your flip book.

# MAY

Teacher Notes and Additional Activities
Monthly Activities
Indians
America
Story and Related Activities

# MAY
## Teacher Notes and Additional Activities

### It's May, May's Calendar

Encourage your students to decorate their calendars, noting important dates and birthdays—and then celebrate them. Make a large classroom calendar, as well.

Flowers are in full bloom now. Take a walk outside and collect wild flowers for pressing. Once dried and mounted, have the children look them up and label them. Turn into a big book.

Have the children write "May" or "Spring" poetry, perhaps in the form of a Haiku with only 3 lines and 17 syllables—5 in the first and third lines, and 7 in the second. These can then be illustrated.

Continue recording daily temperatures and designing related math activities.

### May Day Basket

First celebrated by the ancient Romans or perhaps the Druids, this holiday, though often ignored, welcomes the rebirth of flowering spring. Today, May Day is often celebrated by children who visit friends and leave little baskets of flowers on their doorsteps. These easy-to-make envelope baskets carry on that tradition.

You might also want to make a Maypole, using a broom stick and letting the children decorate ribbons with tissue-paper flowers to hang from it.

### Mother's Day: Roses for Mom

Make a list of synonyms for *mother* and ask if this is influenced at all by their mood, such as saying "Mother" when angry but "Mommy" when we want something or are ill.

Brainstorm and make a list of all the things mothers do for us, mean to us.

Even better than saying, "I love you" is showing that love. Here children will come up with ways they can help their moms, not just on Mother's Day but every day.

### Memorial Day

This is our saddest holiday, commemorating our fallen soldiers. This activity provides some background and asks a few follow-up questions. Do this together with an overhead.

Talk about why people—and countries—fight, and why peace seems so hard to live with.

Using a world map, point out some of the places where there is fighting and talk about the reasons why.

Make a list of the wars fought by America and those fought by the children's native countries.

## The First Americans

This activity builds on the work done in April that emphasized the individual, family, and heritage. Now, however, the focus is on America, beginning with the Indians. First discover what the children already know about Indians, how we treated them, and the reservations established for them. Then use an overhead and help the students see where the major tribes once lived.

Bring in lots of books about Indians, so that your students can see how different the tribes were in everything from housing and language to how they sustained themselves.

Let the children do a little reading about one tribe and tell or write a story based on their learning.

## An Indian Headband

Here the children will create their own headbands using some Indian symbols. To extend this activity, have them also make oak-tag totem poles.

## Corn Meal Crackles

Indians introduced white settlers to corn, and it has become one of our most important and versatile crops. Have the children brainstorm *corn* and all the things made from it, from oil to corn chips. Then make this snack together and have an Indian party with everyone wearing their headbands.

## "The Coming of the Indians"

This is presented as a Silent Directed Reading Thinking Activity that asks the children to predict outcomes as they read. You might want to read the story aloud as the children read along, pausing for them to make their predictions, which should then be shared.

Tie this story in with the environment, since the Sun demanded that the Indians be good to each other, the land, and all living things. Are we keeping that promise? How? Why? Why not?

## Getting to Earth

This follow-up game can be done with two or three players. Encourage the children to read their direction cards out loud as they play. Corn chips make a great award for winners and losers alike!

To extend these activities, have the children write Indian legends on their own. Begin by having them make a list of possible story lines, such as "Why birds fly" and "Why the moon only shines at night."

## My Passport

Now we leave the Indians and come to present-day America, starting with passports. First, though, make sure that everyone understands what a passport is, perhaps bringing in your own to show them and asking how many children have their own passports. This passport is, of course, very different, filled with personal questions for the children to answer before it is assembled and shared.

## Welcome to America

The Statue of Liberty symbolizes America in many ways, welcoming newcomers with the promise of freedom and opportunity. If a trip to the Statue is not possible, bring in lots of books and pictures. As a follow-up, let the children draw the Statue themselves and write about what America means to them.

Teach the children the song, "This Land Is Your Land."

## These United States

This activity presents the different regions of the United States and asks your students to study a map and then answer questions based on it. Use an overhead with this activity and let the children develop their own questions.

Extend this activity by having the children work in groups and choose a region and read about it, sharing what makes it unique. Then compare and contrast the regions—including dialects.

## Telling Time in America

Our country is so vast that, with Alaska and Hawaii, it encompasses six time zones! Use an overhead with this activity. Then let the children make up questions for each other, using the regional map, as well.

Have the children plan trips around the country, determining times of departure and arrival.

## Make a State Plate

Moving now to individual states, be sure to explain how each state is different, with its own symbols and license plates. Then let your students choose a state (not necessarily their home state), look it up in an encyclopedia to discover its symbols, and then create their own state plate. Let them also draw their state, locating major cities, mountains, and rivers on it.

Follow up by having the children write a song or rap about their chosen state.

## My Two Countries

The children will again need an encyclopedia to help them answer these simple questions contrasting America with their native countries.

Extend this activity by having children think of other ways America is similar and different from their native countries and record their responses on a Venn Diagram.

## Dear Ugly Duckling

This pre-reading activity is in the form of letters from the Ugly Duckling to your students. In America, it is not always easy to be different, to not quite fit in. Most immigrant children know this only too well, and this will give them an opportunity to get in touch with their feelings. Read the letters out loud and then let the children write their responses, preparing them for the story.

## "The Ugly Duckling"

This timeless Hans Christian Andersen tale has been simplified, with "Everybody" parts included. Read it several times to the children until everyone is very familiar with the story. Then let the children take over the "Everybody" parts. You might also ask for volunteers to read the different sections.

Then talk about the Ugly Duckling, why he met with such rejection. Ask questions such as was he right to run away and what would have happened to him if he had stuck it out on the farm. Ask, too, how your children would have treated the Ugly Duckling. Lots of talking will surely ensue.

## Endings

This follow-up activity asks the children to consider possible endings, using "If . . . Then . . ." questions. Once completed, have them share their responses and write their own conclusion to the story.

## My Recipe for Happiness

Brainstorm **happiness**. It means different things to different people, but most will agree that a sense of belonging, of being loved, and of having friends are all important ingredients. So it was for the Ugly Duckling, and so, based on his story and your students' insights and feelings, have them come up with a recipe for happiness. First, though, show some sample recipes, explaining ingredients, amounts, and the directions for putting it all together.

As a follow-up, have your students write letters to Hans Christian Andersen and/or the Ugly Duckling.

Make a big book out of the story for the children to write and illustrate.

Using a Venn Diagram, ask how the Ugly Duckling and the swan he became are still the same and how they differ. Has he really changed or has just his appearance? How would he now treat an "ugly duckling"? What if he had never been transformed into a beautiful swan?

Have a character day where everyone dresses up and acts like one of the characters in the story, including the barnyard animals.

Look at May's calendar on the next page and do the following:

1. Number the days on your May calendar on the next page.

2. Cut and paste  on the first day of May. This is May Day.

3. Cut and paste  on the second Sunday in May. This is Mother's Day.

4. Cut and paste  on the last Monday in May. This is Memorial Day.

5. Cut and paste    on special birthdays.

Name _____

Date _____

## MAY

| SUNDAY | MONDAY | TUESDAY | WEDNESDAY | THURSDAY | FRIDAY | SATURDAY |
|--------|--------|---------|-----------|----------|--------|----------|
|        |        |         |           |          |        |          |
|        |        |         |           |          |        |          |
|        |        |         |           |          |        |          |
|        |        |         |           |          |        |          |
|        |        |         |           |          |        |          |

# A MAY DAY BASKET

Celebrate May's flowers this May Day with an easy-to-make envelope basket. Then fill it with some paper flowers and give it to a friend.

**YOU'LL NEED:**

a large envelope        scissors
ruler                   crayons

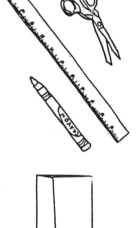

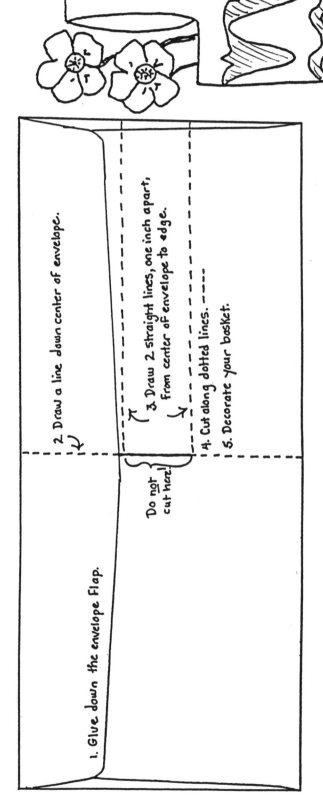

1. Glue down the envelope flap.

2. Draw a line down center of envelope.

Do not cut here!

3. Draw 2 straight lines, one inch apart, from center of envelope to edge.

4. Cut along dotted lines. ------

5. Decorate your basket.

Name _____

Date _____

## ROSES FOR MOM

Show Mom how much you love her with these roses that promise you'll help her—today and every day! Write some promises of your own. Then cut them out and give them to your mom for a happy Mother's Day.

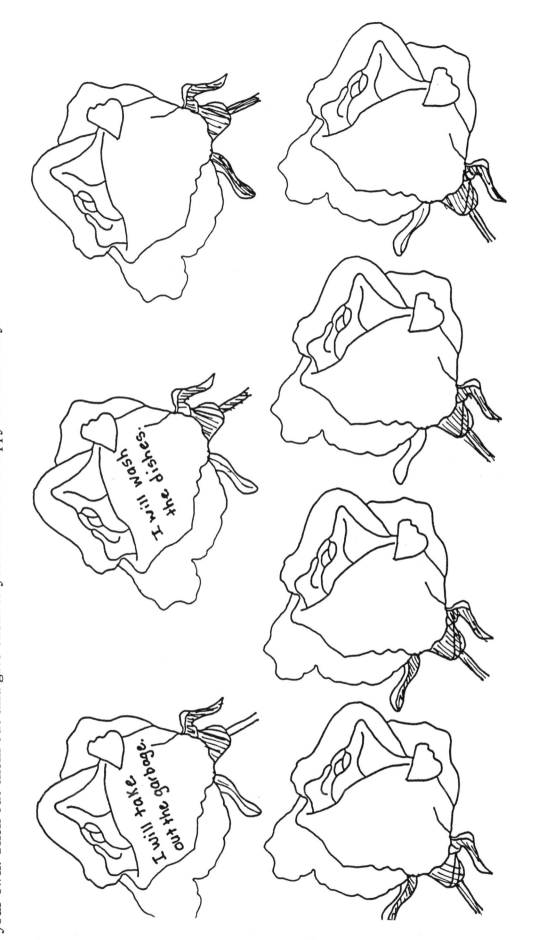

Name _____   Date _____

# MEMORIAL DAY

On this sad day, we remember the men and women who have died fighting for our country.

It started with a parade on May 5, 1866. Back then it was called Decoration Day, and it honored the soldiers of the Civil War. In that war, America was divided, and the North and South went to war.

In 1882, the name was changed from "Decoration" Day to "Memorial" Day. Then finally, in 1971, President Richard Nixon made it a national holiday to be celebrated on the fourth Monday in May.

On that day, soldiers fire rifles into the air, sailors throw flowers into the ocean, and Americans everywhere join in parades and place flowers and small flags on soldiers' graves.

## FILL IN THE BLANKS:

1. This holiday was first called _____

2. President _____ made Memorial Day a national holiday.

3. Whom do we honor on Memorial Day? _____

4. Memorial Day is celebrated on the _____ (#) Monday in May.

5. Soldiers fire their _____ and sailors throw _____ into the ocean on Memorial Day.

**Answers: 1. Decoration Day; 2. Nixon; 3. those who died in war; 4. 4th; 5. rifles, flowers**

Name _____    Date _____

# THE FIRST AMERICANS

When Christopher Columbus landed in the New World in 1492, he thought he was in India. That's why he named the people living there "Indians." At that time, 850,000 Indians lived in this country. Today there are about 650,000.

Where some of the Indians lived:

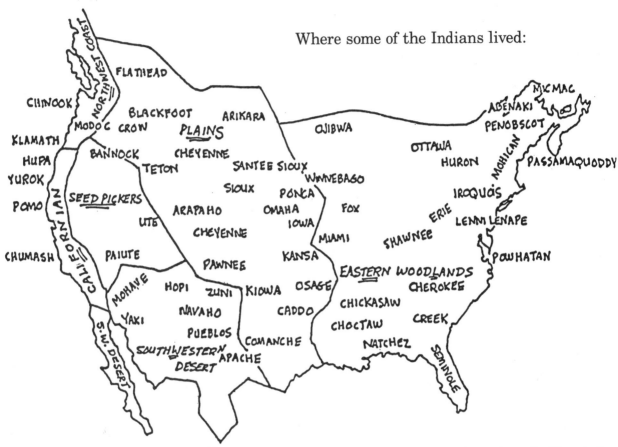

Look carefully at the map above showing some of the important American Indian tribes and where they lived. Then answer YES or NO to the following questions:

1. The Comanche, Iowa, and Sioux were Plains Indians.    YES/NO

2. The Ute were Seed Pickers.    YES/NO

3. The Navaho and Apache lived in the Eastern Woodlands.    YES/NO

4. The Pueblo Indians lived in the Northwest Coast area.    YES/NO

5. The Seminole Indians lived in what is now called Florida.    YES/NO

Answers: 1. yes; 2. yes; 3. no; 4. no; 5. yes

# AN INDIAN HEADBAND

**YOU'LL NEED:**

construction paper    tape
string                scissors
paste                 crayons

**NOW . . . .**

1. Use the string to measure your head.

2. Draw a rectangle that is the same length as your string and two inches wide.

3. Decorate your headband with a few of these Indian symbols.

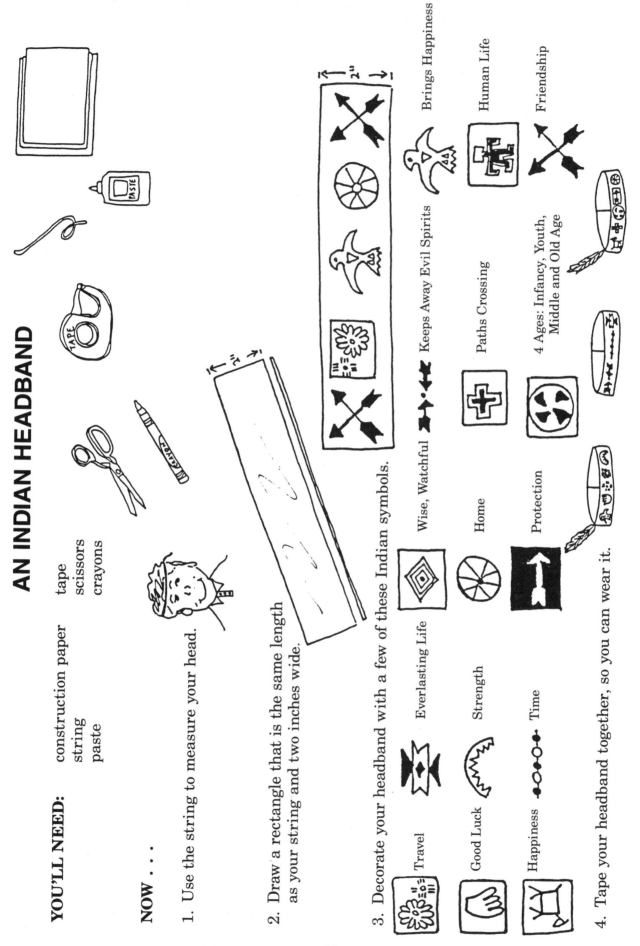

Travel

Everlasting Life

Wise, Watchful

Keeps Away Evil Spirits

Brings Happiness

Human Life

Good Luck

Strength

Home

Paths Crossing

Friendship

Happiness    Time

Protection

4 Ages: Infancy, Youth, Middle and Old Age

4. Tape your headband together, so you can wear it.

# CORN-MEAL CRACKLES

The Indians taught the white settlers how to grow corn.

## YOU'LL NEED:

1 cup yellow corn meal
½ cup sifted flour
¼ teaspoon salt
¼ teaspoon baking soda
⅛ teaspoon paprika
2 tablespoons oil
⅓ cup milk

1 tablespoon melted butter
salt

large bowl
measuring cup
measuring spoons
rolling pin
baking tray
pastry brush

© 1994 by The Center for Applied Research in Education

## NOW:

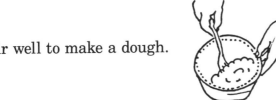

1. Preheat oven to 350 degrees.
2. Combine all the ingredients EXCEPT the butter.

3. Stir well to make a dough.

To Knead Dough:

Place dough on lightly floured table. Fold it towards you.

4. Knead dough for about 10 minutes.

With your palm, push it away. Give the dough a quarter turn.

5. Roll dough into 1-inch balls.

Continue until dough is smooth and not sticky.

6. Roll balls out until paper thin.

7. Bake for 15 minutes.
8. Remove from oven. Brush with butter and sprinkle with salt.

# THE COMING OF THE INDIANS

The Indians tell us that once upon a time people lived on the clouds. That's right! They lived on the clouds, rocking happily from morning until night, and from night until morning. But some people were not happy. They wanted more, as people always do. They asked, "What does the Sun do all day? Where does it go at night?"

Brave Shadoweg decided to find out. He told his people, "Let's follow the Sun to the place where it sleeps and catch it there with this strong rope."

Some people said, "Shadoweg is crazy. Don't follow him." But others said, "Yes! Let's go and catch the Sun!"

The brave hunters followed the Sun across the sky. At first, its rays felt warm and good. Closer and closer they went. Soon the rays grew hot and burned their skin. But no one ran away. Then Shadoweg cried, "Now!" and they threw their rope around the Sun.

What do you think will happen to Shadoweg and his hunters?

© 1994 by The Center for Applied Research in Education

## THE COMING OF THE INDIANS (continued)

The Sun roared like a lion. It tugged on the rope and got hotter and hotter. But the people did not let go. The Sun then roared again, setting the night on fire. More people came to help, even children, but the Sun was very strong.

Lightning flashed, and the sky rocked back and forth. Shadoweg and his people fell over, but still they did not let go. They hung down from the sky on their rope like ants. "We will surely die," they all cried.

What do you think will happen to Shadoweg and his people now?

# THE COMING OF THE INDIANS (continued)

The mighty Sun looked down at the people hanging on their rope and said, "I should let you all fall and die. But you are very brave. Even when I burned your skin and made it red, you did not run away. Brave redskins, from now on you shall be called *Indians,* and I will give you a country all your own. Take care of the land. Take care of each other and all living things."

As the Sun spoke, the Indians felt their rope drop slowly to the Earth. When everyone had landed safely, Shadoweg told his people, "The Sun has given us a new life and a beautiful new land. Go and pitch your tents and light your fires and be happy. But never forget what you have learned this day. Be good to each other. Be good to the land. Be good to all living things on this Earth."

The Indians never forgot those words. They told this story to their children, who told their children, and on and on. Now, I have told it to you.

© 1994 by The Center for Applied Research in Education

# GETTING TO EARTH!

**DIRECTIONS:**

1. Cut out the playing cards on the next page.
2. Choose a partner.
3. Get a small marker, such as a penny, and place it on START.
4. Choose a card and move that many spaces forward.
5. If you land on a circle with a dot, move back 2 spaces.
6. Continue playing until one of you reaches EARTH first.

PLACE CARDS HERE

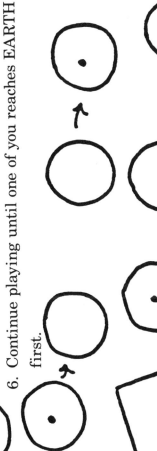

START

END

| | |
|---|---|
| You are a brave hunter. Move ahead 3 spaces. | You are not afraid of the sun. Move ahead 1 space. |
| Shadoweg needs your help. Move ahead 2 spaces. | The sun is hot, but you do not leave Shadoweg's side. Move ahead 2 spaces. |
| You want to help catch the sun. Move ahead 1 space. | The rope burns your hand, but you do not let go. Move ahead 2 spaces. |
| Friends are important to you. Move ahead 2 spaces. | The sky shakes and lightning flashes, but you hold on to the rope. Move ahead 1 space. |
| You love the earth and care for it. Move ahead 2 spaces. | You will keep your promise to the sun. Move ahead 3 spaces. |
| Animals are your friends. Move ahead 1 space. | The sun burned you and now your skin is red. Move ahead 1 space. |
| You are tired of living on a cloud. Move ahead 2 spaces. | You tell your friends that Shadoweg is not crazy. Move ahead 2 spaces. |
| All people are your brothers and sisters. Move ahead 2 spaces. | You are a good friend. Move ahead 3 spaces. |

Cut out these game cards.
Then play "Getting to Earth."

# MY PASSPORT

**TO CREATE YOUR OWN PASSPORT, YOU'LL NEED** scissors, a pencil, paste, and stapler.

## NOW:

1. Paste your picture on the cover.
2. Fill in the blanks.
3. Cut out each page along the solid (——) lines.
4. Put the pages together and staple.

PASSPORT

Your Photo Goes Here

UNITED STATES OF AMERICA

13 MAR MAR 87
PASSPORT AGENCY
PHILADELPHIA, U.S.A.

---

My birthday is _____, and I am _____ years old.

I was born in _____. When I was _____ years old,

I came to America with these people: _____

_____

I have been in America for _____ months/years.

---

I love _____ ice cream, and my favorite colors are _____

and _____. The best season for me is _____,

because I like _____ weather. As a _____ grader, my best

subject is _____. When I grow up, I want to be a

_____ or a _____.

**Name** _____ **Date** _____

# WELCOME TO AMERICA!

The Statue of Liberty stands on Liberty Island in New York Harbor and welcomes all newcomers to America. She was a gift from the French to celebrate our one-hundredth birthday. *Liberty* is another word for *freedom*. In fact, the word *liberty* comes from the Latin word *liber,* which means *free*.

What does freedom mean to you? _____

_____

I weigh 450,000 pounds.

I am about 305 feet tall.

My mouth is 3 feet wide.

My nose is 4 feet 6 inches long.

My right arm is 42 feet long.

Forty people can stand in my head.

Twelve people can stand in my torch.

The Statue of Liberty weighs _____ pounds and is _____ tall. _____ people can stand in her head and _____ people can stand in her torch. Her mouth is _____ wide and her nose is _____ long. She was given to America by the French for our _____ birthday. The word *liberty* means _____.

© 1994 by The Center for Applied Research in Education

Name _____ Date _____

# THESE UNITED STATES

In 1776, the 13 colonies broke away from England, and the United States was born. Today, we are made up of 50 states, covering 3,615,211 square miles, with a population of about 213,650,000 people.

Study the map below showing our different regions.

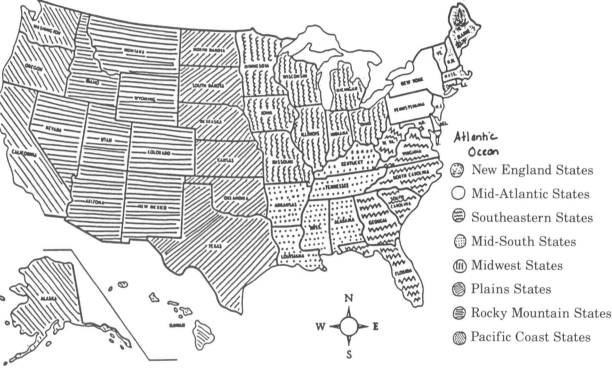

Atlantic Ocean

⦾ New England States
◯ Mid-Atlantic States
⊜ Southeastern States
⊕ Mid-South States
⧈ Midwest States
◎ Plains States
⊜ Rocky Mountain States
◉ Pacific Coast States

1. The United States was born in _____.

2. There are _____ different sections of the United States.

3. _____ is the largest New England state.

4. The Rocky Mountain states are east/west of the Plains states.

5. _____ is the largest of the Plains states.

6. New York is one of the _____ states.

7. Alaska and Hawaii are _____ states.

8. Iowa is one of the _____ states.

9. Florida is a _____ state.

**Answers: 1. 1776; 2. 8; 3. Maine; 4. west; 5. Texas; 6. Mid-Atlantic; 7. Pacific Coast; 8. Midwest; 9. Southeastern**

Name _____ Date _____

# TELLING TIME IN AMERICA

As we travel east, time is later in the day.
As we travel west, time is earlier in the day.

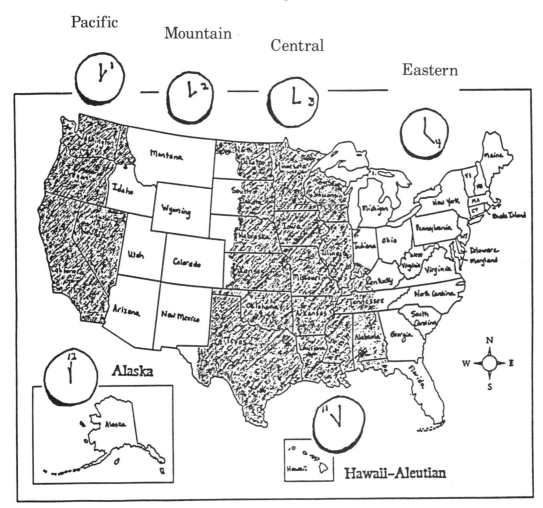

1. What are the 6 time zones? _____ _____

_____ _____ _____

2. It's 3 o'clock in New York. What time is it in Virginia? _____ in Utah? _____

3. It's one o'clock in Ohio. What time is it in Iowa? _____ in Hawaii? _____

4. It's 2 o'clock in Iowa. What time is it in California? _____

5. It's 4 o'clock in eastern Tennessee, what time is it in western Tennessee? _____

6. It's 4 o'clock in southern Idaho, what time is it in northern Idaho? _____

© 1994 by The Center for Applied Research in Education

## MAKE A STATE PLATE

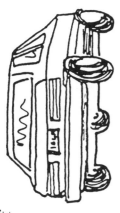

Each state in the United States has its own capital, flag, bird, tree, and flower. Choose one of the 50 states and look it up in an encyclopedia. It will tell you all about your chosen state. Use that information to draw your own state license plate.

PENNSYLVANIA

Harrisburg

THE KEYSTONE STATE

# MY TWO COUNTRIES

Name _____

Date _____

Go to the library to find the answers:

## AMERICA:

Population: _____

Area: _____

Major Cities: _____
_____
_____
_____

Capital: _____

Unit of Money: _____

Language(s): _____

National Anthem: _____

## MY NATIVE COUNTRY:

Population: _____

Area: _____

Major Cities: _____
_____
_____
_____

Capital: _____

Unit of Money: _____

Language(s): _____

National Anthem: _____

Answers: America—1. 247,100,000 (1990); 3,618,772 square miles;
3. New York, Los Angeles, Chicago, Houston, Philadelphia;
4. Washington, D.C.; 5. Dollar; 6. English;
7. Star-Spangled Banner

# DEAR UGLY DUCKLING

## BEFORE YOU READ ABOUT THE UGLY DUCKLING, PLEASE WRITE AND TELL HIM WHAT TO DO . . . .

Dear Student,

Nobody likes me here on the farm. The animals scratch and peck at me. My brothers and sisters don't want to swim with me, and my mother calls me the Ugly Duckling. What should I do?

Love,

*The Ugly Duckling*

Dear Ugly Duckling,

_____

_____

_____

_____

_____

Dear Student,

I finally ran away from the farm. Now I live alone on a pond. I'm okay, but winter is coming, and I am cold and afraid. What should I do?

Love,

*The Ugly Duckling*

Dear Ugly Duckling,

_____

_____

_____

_____

_____

Love,

_____
Your Name

# THE UGLY DUCKLING
## By Hans Christian Andersen
## (A Class Activity)

One by one, Mama Duck's eggs cracked and out popped her little ducklings.

Everybody: "Cheep! Cheep!"

All the eggs cracked, except one. "Why won't this egg hatch?" asked Mama Duck.
"That egg is too big!" squawked the chicken.
"That's a turkey egg if ever I saw one," cackled the goose.

Everybody: "Oh, dear! Oh, dear!"

Crack! Pop! Crack! Finally, the last egg opened up. "But what's this?" quacked Mama Duck. "You're so big! So ugly! I'll just have to call you my Ugly Duckling!"

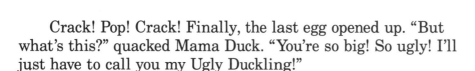

Everybody: "Cheep! Cheep!"

"You're an ugly duckling! You're an ugly duckling!" cheeped his brothers and sisters. "Stay behind us when we swim. We don't want you near us."

Everybody: "Ugly! Ugly! Ugly!"

The cat scratched the Ugly Duckling. The turkey clawed the Ugly Duckling. The chicken pecked at the Ugly Duckling.

Everybody: "Ugly! Ugly! Ugly!"
Scratch, claw, and peck.

"Everybody hates me. I can't stay here anymore," sobbed the Ugly Duckling, and he ran away. He ran as fast as his little webbed feet could take him—right into a lake next to some wild ducks.

Everybody: Pat thighs quickly. "Splash! Splash!"

# THE UGLY DUCKLING (continued)

"Get out of our lake, Ugly Duckling, and never come back!" snapped the ducks, and they chased him away.

Everybody: "Ugly! Ugly! Ugly!"

Once again, the Ugly Duckling ran as fast as his little webbed feet could take him. He didn't stop until he landed in an empty pond.

Everybody: Pat thighs quickly.
"Splash! Splash!"

"My new home sure is lonely," thought the Ugly Duckling looking all around. "Now, if I were a beautiful swan, I would have lots of friends. But I'm ugly, so nobody loves me at all."

And so the Ugly Duckling talked to himself every day as he swam around and around the empty pond. And every night he cried himself to sleep.

Everybody: Make crying sounds.

Then one night winter came. The wind blew snow everywhere and the pond turned to ice. "Oh, no! I'm stuck in the ice and can't move. I'll die out all by myself! HELP! HELP!"

Everybody: Wriggle and Squirm.

Luckily, a hunter heard him crying and ran to the pond. "You poor thing," he said, as he broke the ice and saved the Ugly Duckling. "From now on, little one, remember to stay out of the water at night. Next time I might not be nearby to help you and you will surely freeze!"

Everybody: "Stay out! Stay out!"

# THE UGLY DUCKLING (continued)

Every day the Ugly Duckling grew sadder and colder—but he never froze in the pond again. Then, finally, the sun peeked through the clouds, and it was spring again. The leaves turned green, birds sang, and the wild ducks came back to the pond. The Ugly Duckling watched them play and bob for food. And when they stretched their wings and flew away, he said, "I wish I could do that!"

Everybody: Flap your arms.

He flapped his wings and suddenly he was in the air. "I'm flying!" he squealed happily. "I'm really flying!"

Just then some swans flew by and he followed them down to the pond. "I know I'm ugly," he said to them, "but please don't fly away. I've been alone for so long."

"You're not ugly at all! Look in the water and see for yourself. You're beautiful!" they all said, and they kissed him with their bills.

Everybody: Make kissing sounds.

"Huh? Me beautiful?" he asked. And then he looked in the water. "Why can't I see myself? All I see is a beautiful swan."

"That's you! That's you!"

"It can't be. Everybody says I'm ugly. I'm the Ugly Duckling."

"Look again, friend," they all said. "You're a swan just like us!"

The Ugly Duckling looked in the water again and cried out, "It's really me! I'm a swan! I'm a swan!" And his heart filled with a happiness that is known by anyone who was once an ugly duckling!

Everybody: "Yes! Yes!"

Name _____

Date _____

# ENDINGS

"I have friends! I can fly! I am beautiful! But what do I do now?" asks the Ugly Duckling.

| THEN THIS WILL HAPPEN . . . |
| THEN THIS WILL HAPPEN . . . |
| THEN THIS WILL HAPPEN . . . |

IF I stay alone on my pond . . . .

IF I go back to the farm . . . .

IF I fly away with the swans . . . .

# MY RECIPE FOR HAPPINESS

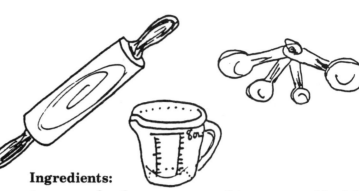

**Ingredients:**
1. one cup family
2. one cup friends
3. three tablespoons sunshine
4. ½ cup books
5. one cup good health
6. one teaspoon sugar
7. two teaspoons toys
8. ¾ cup laughter

**Directions:**
1. Preheat oven to 375 degrees.
2. In large bowl, combine family and friends with laughter.
3. Spoon in good health.
4. Add remaining ingredients and stir well.
5. Pour into cake pan and bake for one hour.

## (Ingredients) WHAT YOU NEED TO BE HAPPY:

1.

2.

3.

4.

5.

6.

7.

8.

## (Directions) NOW DO THIS:

1.

2.

3.

4.

5.

# JUNE

Teacher Notes and Additional Activities
Monthly Activities
Team Sports
Healthful Eating and Exercise
Dinosaurs
Wild Animals
Story and Related Activities

# JUNE
# Teacher Notes and Additional Activities

## It's June, June Calendar, July Calendar, August Calendar

Encourage students to decorate their calendars, noting important dates and birthdays—and then celebrate them. Make large classroom calendars, as well.

Write the four seasons on the board and have the children come up with related words. Then group according to their favorite season. Each group can then make seasonal murals on bulletin-board paper.

## The American Flag

Briefly explain our flag's history and how Flag Day was made an official holiday by President Truman.

Have the children draw the flag provided, perhaps attaching a short poem or story. Such writing can be done individually or in groups. Suggest that the same be done for the flags of their native countries.

## A Father's Day Card

Before making these thank-you cards, brainstorm "father" and all the things dads do. Using a Venn Diagram, compare and contrast "father" and "mother."

## It's Ice-Pop Time

Welcome summer with these easy-to-make ice pops and ask about your students' vacation plans. Do a Language Experience Approach (LEA) writing activity about summer vacation.

Teach summer songs, such as Jerry Keller's "Here Comes Summer," and have the children write their own verses and/or songs, or, perhaps, a summertime rap.

## The Liberty Bell

Find out what *freedom* and *dependence/independence* mean to your students, adding an analysis lesson at the same time: *in = not; de = from; pend = hang; ence = noun suffix ending.*

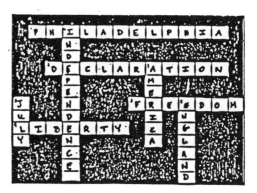

Briefly tell the story of the 13 colonies, British rule, the Declaration of Independence, and the Revolution. Review the word *symbol*, providing examples, such as McDonald's golden arches, and how and why the Liberty Bell symbolizes American freedom and independence.

If possible, travel to Philadelphia to see Independence Hall and the Liberty Bell.

## Name That Team Sport

The focus shifts to health, athletics, and belonging to a team. Since games are an important part of American culture and are offered by most schools, your students are probably familiar with most of these.

Tape sports news broadcasts and game segments to show your students.

To further prepare for this activity, which highlights major team sports and related terms, begin by bringing in sports equipment, such as a baseball and a hockey puck. Talk, too, about the multiple meanings of such words as diamond and court.

Bring in pictures from sports magazines, etc., and make sports collages.

Find out what team sports your students are involved in and encourage more participation. Find out about the sports played in the children's homelands, too.

## Another Look at Team Sports

This review activity asks the children to identify the sport and the one word that does NOT belong in each category. Works well with an overhead.

Give each child a sport to act out for their classmates, as in charades.

Have the children make a mobile, drawing pictures and attaching related words.

Other group games you can play:

**Call Ball**: Form a circle around IT, who tosses the ball in the air and calls out someone's name. That person tries to catch the ball before it bounces a second time. If successful, that player becomes IT.

**Word Lightning**: A player is assigned a letter and has one minute to call out as many words as possible beginning with that letter. The player who comes up with the most words wins.

**Coffeepot**: One player is IT. A second player chooses a verb and whispers it to everyone else. With a 2–3 minute time limit, IT questions each player in turn to discover the verb, substituting "coffeepot" for the unknown word, as in "Do you coffeepot outdoors?"

## Counting Calories

We now move to healthy eating and calorie counting. Ask the children to list their favorite foods and talk about healthier alternatives, such as popcorn instead of chips, skim milk instead of whole milk, etc.

Bring in calorie counters and have the children start keeping a record of their daily food intake for several weeks, recording calories as they go along.

## Eat Right and Exercise, Too!

Enlarge the Food Guide Pyramid for the overhead and explain it carefully. Then have the children analyze their own eating habits to see how their diets measure up and what changes, if any, need to be made.

Along with a healthful diet goes exercise, and this page also presents some forms of exercising. Poll the class to see if and how the children are exercising and make a bar graph. Encourage everyone to begin an exercise plan and add their times/distances to their food journals. Monitor progress periodically.

## How Long Does It Take?

This activity allows the children to get an idea of how long they have to do a certain exercise in order to burn off the calories they've consumed. Study the table together to discover the most and least efficient forms of exercise, etc. Then answer the questions together. Have children write questions of their own and trade these.

Have the children make mobiles or collages of their favorite exercise.

## From the Beginning

No discussion of the animal world would be complete without some mention of dinosaurs. Here a geological time line is provided, showing when different life forms appeared/disappeared and the very late appearance of man. Write 100, 1,000, and 1,000,000 on the board to impress upon everyone the Earth's age.

Write the 4 eras on the board and go over their meanings before completing this activity.

## Looking Back

This activity refers to the geologic time line on page 297. Work together and then have the students write out and share additional questions of their own.

The largest of all dinosaurs, Brachiosaurus, is also introduced here. Talk about the information provided and have the children draw pictures of Brachiosaurus next to a 4-story building and/or a person.

Have the children do a bit of dinosaur research, discovering when these various creatures appeared (Triassic, Jurassic, or Cretaceous periods). Explain *extinct* and ask the children for possible explanations for their extinction. Then let them draw their favorite dinosaur and attach an information card to it.

## Dinomarkers

This activity has the children turn their favorite dinosaur into a bookmark. Laminate if possible.

## The Animal Kingdom Today

This information page categorizes today's animal kingdom. (Explain that dinosaurs were reptiles.) Go over terms such as warm- and cold-blooded, to ensure understanding. Bring in lots of animal pictures and have the children sort them by category. These can then be turned into mobiles and/or collages.

## Looking Again at Animals

Besides cutting and pasting pictures of animals beside their descriptors, a semantic feature analysis chart is provided. Putting (+) in a box means the descriptor applies; (−) means it does not. Enlarge for the overhead.

For spelling practice, scramble the letters of the different categories for the children to unscramble.

Have everyone make his/her own crossword puzzle or word search to trade and complete.

## Mammals, Mammals, Mammals

First, review mammalian attributes, reminding everyone that we are mammals, too.

Have everyone draw her/his favorite animals. Tape a strip of cardboard on the back to make them stand.

Bring in grocery bags that the children can turn into animal masks.

Make "Concentration" game cards, matching the animal's name with its picture or description.

## Animal Chains

First, have the class make up lists of words associated with all their favorite animals.

Play "What Animal Am I?" with one child choosing an animal and everyone asking questions, such as "Can you fly?" as they try to guess the animal.

Hide animal crackers around the room and tell each child what animal she/he must find. A box of animal crackers can be the prize for those who are successful.

Let the children make various animals out of clay and label their zoo.

Tape an animal's name to each child's back, and they then ask each other questions to find out who they are.

Have each child move like a particular animal with classmates guessing the animal.

## "Goldilocks and the Three Bears"

Talk about antonyms, starting with big/little. See how many the children can come up with.

EVERYBODY parts have been included in this version of the story. First, read it several times, changing your voice as indicated. When everyone is familiar with the story line, let the children take over.

Have the children write different endings, such as having Goldilocks staying for dinner or coming back to pay for the damage she caused.

Talk about Goldilocks and what she did. Was she right in barging into the bears' house? Would she make a good friend? Is she an honest/honorable person? etc.

Make character strips by having the children draw each character on a strip of paper and writing descriptive words underneath.

Have a character day where everyone chooses one of the characters to imitate for an hour or two and then go on a bear picnic: Staple round bear ears to paper plates and let the children draw bear faces on their plates; make bear-shaped peanut butter sandwiches, even homemade lemonade (2 cups water or soda water, ½ cup lemon juice, and 2 or more tablespoons of honey).

Play some picnic games, such as:

**Going on a Picnic**: One player begins by saying, "I'm going on a picnic and I'm bringing _____," filling in the blank with an item that begins with the letter "a." The next player repeats all that and adds an item that starts with "b," and so on.

**I Packed My Bag**: The first player completes the phrase, "I packed my bag and in it I put a(n) _____," filling in the blank with some item. The next player repeats all that and adds another item, and so on.

## Make a Sequence Chain

Here the children are asked to go back to the story and order the events in their proper sequence. Check their work before they paste their "bears" and connect them with arrows. Ask what details were omitted.

Have the children write summaries of the story and illustrate them.

Write and illustrate a Three Bears big book.

## Bear Puppets

After the puppets have been made, group the children and have them put on the story for their classmates and/or present a sequel.

It's June!

Look at June's calendar on the next page and do the following:

1. Number the days on your June calendar (next page).

2. Cut and paste  on June 14th. This is Flag Day.

3. Cut and paste  on the 3rd Sunday in June. This is Father's Day.

4. Cut and paste  on June 21st. This is the first day of summer.

5. Cut and paste    on special birthdays.

**Name** _____

**Date** _____

# JUNE

| SUNDAY | MONDAY | TUESDAY | WEDNESDAY | THURSDAY | FRIDAY | SATURDAY |
|--------|--------|---------|-----------|----------|--------|----------|
|        |        |         |           |          |        |          |
|        |        |         |           |          |        |          |
|        |        |         |           |          |        |          |
|        |        |         |           |          |        |          |
|        |        |         |           |          |        |          |

# JULY

| SUNDAY | MONDAY | TUESDAY | WEDNESDAY | THURSDAY | FRIDAY | SATURDAY |
|--------|--------|---------|-----------|----------|--------|----------|
|  |  |  |  |  |  |  |
|  |  |  |  |  |  |  |
|  |  |  |  |  |  |  |
|  |  |  |  |  |  |  |
|  |  |  |  |  |  |  |

Follow these directions to complete your calendar for July.

1. Number the days on your July calendar above.

2. Cut and paste  on July 4th. This is Independence Day.

3. Cut and paste  on special July birthdays.

# AUGUST

| SUNDAY | MONDAY | TUESDAY | WEDNESDAY | THURSDAY | FRIDAY | SATURDAY |
|--------|--------|---------|-----------|----------|--------|----------|
|        |        |         |           |          |        |          |
|        |        |         |           |          |        |          |
|        |        |         |           |          |        |          |
|        |        |         |           |          |        |          |
|        |        |         |           |          |        |          |

Follow these directions to complete your calendar for August.

1. Number the days on your August calendar above.

2. Cut and paste   on special August birthdays.

# THE AMERICAN FLAG

**You'll need:**
red, white, and
blue crayons

one stripe for
each of the
original 13
colonies

one star for
each of the 50
states

Then cut out
your flag.

**Name** _____  **Date** _____

# A FATHER'S DAY CARD

Dad does so much:

1. Goes to work.
2. 
3. 
4. 
5. 

**NOW:**

1. Cut along solid (——) lines.
2. Fold along dotted (– – –) lines.
3. Color the cover.
4. Write a note and thank your dad.
5. Make the envelope on next page.

# MAKING AN ENVELOPE

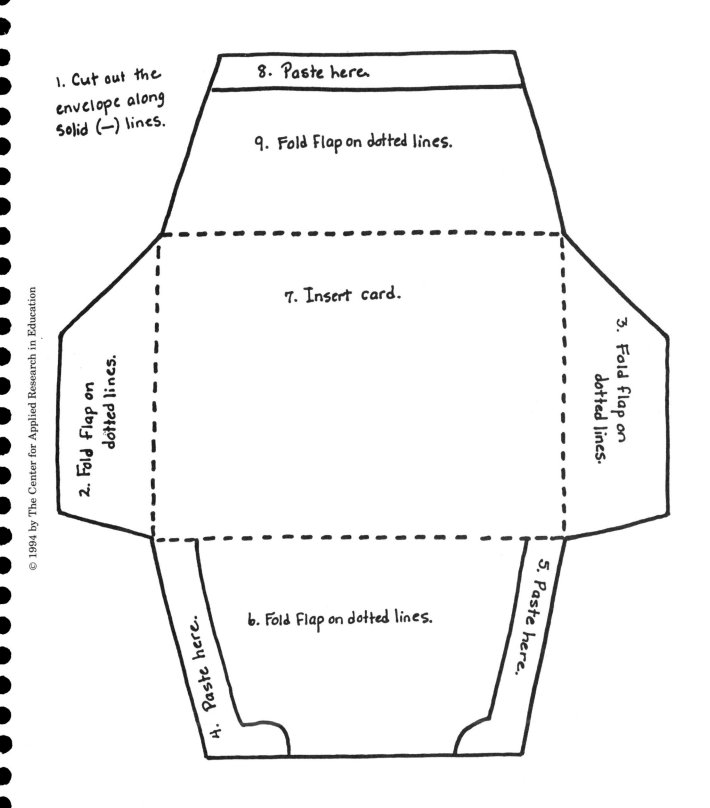

1. Cut out the envelope along Solid (—) lines.

8. Paste here.

9. Fold Flap on dotted lines.

7. Insert card.

2. Fold Flap on dotted lines.

3. Fold flap on dotted lines.

4. Paste here.

6. Fold Flap on dotted lines.

5. Paste here.

# IT'S ICE-POP TIME!

**YOU'LL NEED:**

    small paper cup(s)
    popsicle stick(s)
    fruit juice (any kind)

**WHAT TO DO:**

1. Pour juice into paper cup(s) and place in freezer.

2. Let the juice harden a little. Then, put the popsicle stick
in the center of the cup.

3. Put ice pops back in freezer till frozen hard.

4. Peel away the paper cup and ENJOY!!!

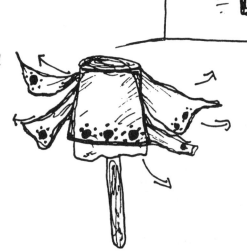

© 1994 by The Center for Applied Research in Education

# THE LIBERTY BELL

READ THIS AND THEN DO THE CROSSWORD PUZZLE BELOW.

*Liberty* means *freedom,* and *independence* means *being free from another (country's) rule.* In July 1776, the Declaration of Independence was signed in Philadelphia, Pennsylvania. The Declaration was a public statement that told the world that the 13 colonies now belonged to Americans, not England. The Liberty Bell rang out the news.

Years later, in 1835, it cracked when ringing at the funeral of John Marshall, Chief Justice of the Supreme Court. It cracked again when it rang on George Washington's birthday in 1846. The Liberty Bell's home is still in Philadelphia.

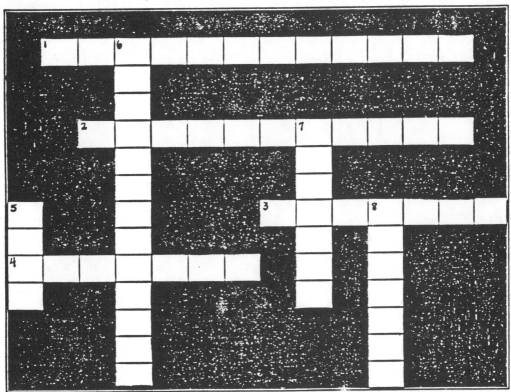

## ACROSS

1. The Liberty Bell lives here.
2. This is a public statement.
3. Another word for *liberty.*
4. Another word for *freedom.*

## DOWN

6. I mean "freedom from another's rule."
7. The United States; begins with "A"
8. This country once ruled America.

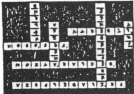
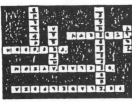

# NAME THAT TEAM SPORT!

Look at these pictures and related words. Then name the sport being played.

**CHOICES:**   tennis        field hockey    basketball    soccer
               football      ice hockey      baseball

I am playing _____.

$\left\{\begin{array}{ll}\text{base} & \text{hit} \\ \text{bat} & \text{strike out} \\ \text{ball} & \text{pitch} \\ \text{diamond} & \text{catch} \\ \text{outfield} & \text{run} \\ \text{home run} & \text{throw}\end{array}\right.$

I am playing _____.

$\left\{\begin{array}{ll}\text{court} & \text{throw} \\ \text{jump shot} & \text{bounce} \\ \text{ball} & \text{block} \\ \text{hoop} & \text{dribble} \\ \text{points} & \text{jump} \\ \text{basket} & \text{shoot}\end{array}\right.$

I am playing _____.

$\left\{\begin{array}{ll}\text{field} & \text{block} \\ \text{gridiron} & \text{catch} \\ \text{ball} & \text{throw} \\ \text{goal posts} & \text{tackle} \\ \text{touchdown} & \text{kick} \\ \text{field goal} & \text{run}\end{array}\right.$

(Continued)

**Name** _____  **Date** _____

# NAME THAT TEAM SPORT!

**CHOICES:**  tennis    field hockey    basketball    soccer
football    ice hockey    baseball

I am playing _____.
{ field    hit
ball    shoot
stick    scoop
goal    dribble
net    run
swing }

I am playing _____.
{ ice rink    skate
puck    shoot
stick    stride
skates    balance
net    swing
goal    push off }

I am playing _____.
{ ball    kick
goal    dribble
net    shoot
field    tackle
head    volley }

I am playing _____.
{ court    hit
racket    serve
ball    swing
net    volley
points    bounce }

(Continued)

Name _____ Date _____

# ANOTHER LOOK AT TEAM SPORTS

**CHOICES:**  tennis       field hockey   basketball   soccer
              football     ice hockey     baseball

**DIRECTIONS:**

1. Look carefully at each group of words. Then, on the line, name the sport.
2. Look again at the words. Circle the ONE word that doesn't belong!

   The first one has been done for you.

1. Sport: ___baseball___

| | |
|---|---|
| base | (net) |
| ball | pitch |
| home run | catch |

2. Sport: _____

| | |
|---|---|
| goal posts | touchdown |
| ball | stick |
| block | throw |

3. Sport: _____

| | |
|---|---|
| stick | field |
| racket | goal |
| run | hit |

4. Sport: _____

| | |
|---|---|
| ball | head |
| goal | water |
| field | kick |

5. Sport: _____

| | |
|---|---|
| court | basket |
| hoop | ball |
| bounce | touchdown |

6. Sport: _____

| | |
|---|---|
| court | ball |
| racket | kick |
| net | serve |

7. Sport: _____

| | |
|---|---|
| ice | rink |
| goal | base |
| puck | skate |

Answers: 1. baseball; net 2. football; stick 3. field hockey; racket 4. soccer; water 5. basketball; touchdown 6. tennis; kick 7. ice hockey; base

# COUNTING CALORIES

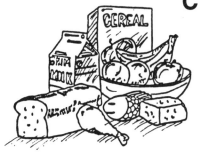

*Oh, dear! Oh, dear! I ate too much again and now I've gained 5 more pounds!!!*

How many calories* are in some of your favorite foods?
Use this CALORIE CHART to find out!

| Johnny Food: | Calories: | Jimmy Food | Calories: |
|---|---|---|---|
| ¼ cup dry cereal | 70 | 1 cup whole milk | 150 |
| 3 pancakes | 180 | 1 cup skim milk | 120 |
| 1 fried egg | 115 | 1 cup cola (soda) | 145 |
| 10 french fries | 135 | 1 cup orange juice | 120 |
| 1 cheeseburger | 518 | 1 cup ice cream | 270 |
| 1 hot dog | 291 | 4 cookies | 200 |
| 1 slice of pizza | 145 | 1 cup popcorn (unbuttered) | 25 |
| 1 cup spaghetti and sauce | 260 | 15 potato chips | 150 |
| ⅔ cup tuna fish salad | 210 | 1 medium apple | 70 |
| 4 ounces baked chicken | 205 | 1 medium banana | 100 |
| 2 slices white bread | 140 | 1 medium orange | 65 |

## ADD UP JOHNNY'S CALORIES:

Breakfast: 3 pancakes _____

1 cup orange juice _____

Lunch: 20 french fries _____

1 cheeseburger _____

1 cup whole milk _____

4 cookies _____

Dinner: 3 slices of pizza _____

2 cups cola (soda) _____

1 cup ice cream _____

Snacks: 30 potato chips _____

**TOTAL CALORIES:** _____

## ADD UP JIMMY'S CALORIES:

Breakfast: ¼ cup dry cereal _____

1 cup skim milk _____

1 cup orange juice _____

Lunch: ⅔ cup tuna salad _____

2 slices white bread _____

1 cup skim milk _____

1 medium apple _____

Dinner: 1 cup spaghetti _____

1 cup skim milk _____

1 medium orange _____

Snacks: 1 cup popcorn _____

**TOTAL CALORIES:** _____

Who is eating better, more healthfully? _____

*A calorie is a unit of energy we get from food.

Answers: Johnny's Total, 2,733; Jimmy's Total, 1,320; Jimmy is eating better.

**Name** _____   **Date** _____

# EAT RIGHT . . .

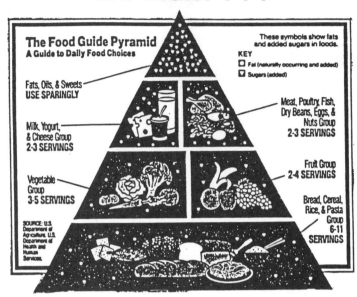

Look at this Food Guide Pyramid and answer YES or NO to these questions.

1. Eat more bread, rice and pasta than chicken and eggs.   YES   NO
2. Eat more fruits than vegetables.   YES   NO
3. Eat less milk, yogurt, and cheese than vegetables.   YES   NO
4. Use "sparingly" means eat only small amounts of these foods.   YES   NO
5. Eat one or two servings of vegetables every day.   YES   NO

. . . AND EXERCISE, TOO!!!

**Answers: 1. YES 2. NO 3. YES 4. YES 5. NO**

**Name** _____  **Date** _____

# HOW LONG DOES IT TAKE?

## Number of Minutes Needed to Burn These Calories

| Food | Calories | Running | Swimming | Biking | Walking | Aerobics |
|------|----------|---------|----------|--------|---------|----------|
| cereal | 70 | 5 | 9 | 11 | 18 | 11 |
| orange juice | 120 | 9 | 15 | 19 | 32 | 18 |
| french fries | 135 | 10 | 17 | 21 | 36 | 20 |
| cheeseburger | 518 | 39 | 64 | 82 | 136 | 78 |
| pizza | 145 | 11 | 18 | 23 | 38 | 22 |
| cola | 145 | 11 | 18 | 23 | 38 | 22 |
| ice cream | 270 | 20 | 33 | 43 | 71 | 41 |
| apple | 70 | 5 | 9 | 11 | 18 | 11 |
| potato chips | 150 | 11 | 19 | 24 | 39 | 23 |
| popcorn | 25 | 2 | 3 | 4 | 7 | 4 |

## HOW MANY MINUTES?

1. To burn off both a cheeseburger and french fries, you must RUN for _____ minutes.

2. To burn off the ice cream, you'll have to do AEROBICS for _____ minutes or BIKE for _____ minutes.

3. You must SWIM for _____ minutes to burn off a glass of orange juice.

4. One slice of pizza takes _____ minutes to WALK off.

5. It would take _____ minutes to SWIM off those potato chips.

6. You must RUN _____ minutes if you ate popcorn and an apple for snacks today.

7. How many minutes of AEROBICS must you do if you drink a cup of cola? _____

Answers: 1. 49; 2. 41, 43; 3. 15; 4. 38; 5. 19; 6. 7; 7. 22

# FROM THE BEGINNING

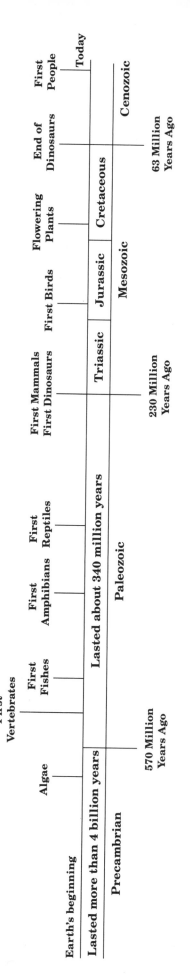

| | Earth's beginning | First Vertebrates | First Fishes | First Amphibians | First Reptiles | First Mammals First Dinosaurs | First Birds | Flowering Plants | End of Dinosaurs | First People | Today |
|---|---|---|---|---|---|---|---|---|---|---|---|
| | Algae | | | | | | | | | | |

| Precambrian | Paleozoic | Triassic | Jurassic | Cretaceous | Cenozoic |
|---|---|---|---|---|---|
| Lasted more than 4 billion years | Lasted about 340 million years | Mesozoic | | | |

570 Million Years Ago

230 Million Years Ago

63 Million Years Ago

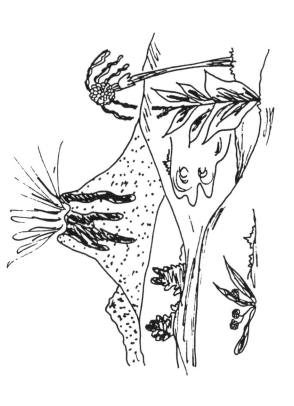

## WHAT THIS CHART TELLS YOU:

1. The Earth is very old. In fact, it is over 4 billion years old.

2. There are four major eras (periods of time):

   a. *Precambrian* means "before life."

   b. *Paleozoic* means "old life."

   c. *Mesozoic* means "middle life."

   d. *Cenozoic* means "recent life."

3. Algae (water plants) came first. Then, in the Paleozoic era, came the first vertebrates (animals with backbones) and fish.

4. Dinosaurs lived during the Mesozoic era, starting about 230 million years ago. They died off about 63 million years ago.

5. The Mesozoic era is divided into three periods: Triassic, Jurassic, and Cretaceous.

6. People are newcomers on Earth. We came on the scene during the Cenozoic era.

# LOOKING BACK

| Earth's beginning | | First Vertebrates | First Fishes | First Amphibians | First Reptiles | First Mammals First Dinosaurs | Triassic | Jurassic | Flowering Plants First Birds | Cretaceous | End of Dinosaurs | First People | |
|---|---|---|---|---|---|---|---|---|---|---|---|---|---|

Algae

| Lasted more than 4 billion years | Lasted about 340 million years | | | |
|---|---|---|---|---|
| Precambrian | Paleozoic | Mesozoic | Cenozoic | |

570 Million Years Ago   230 Million Years Ago   63 Million Years Ago   Today

## NOW, MEET THE BIGGEST DINOSAUR OF ALL . . . .

I am called Brachiosaurus (brack-ee-o-SAW-rus).
I lived during the Jurassic Period, about 140 million years ago.
I was a plant-eater. My long neck helped me reach the tops of trees.
I also ate the soft plants that grew in swamps.
My nose was in a bump on the top of my head. (Nobody knows why!)
I was taller than a 4-story building.
I weighed about 77 tons. (1 ton = 2,000 pounds)

Look at the time line again and then answer these questions with a YES or NO:

1. Algae was the first plant, and grows in water. YES NO

2. Dinosaurs lived during the Mesozoic era. YES NO

3. The Jurassic Period was in the Paleozoic era. YES NO

4. The first fish appeared after the first birds. YES NO

5. The Earth is about 3 billion years old. YES NO

6. The first people appeared during the Cenozoic era. YES NO

**Answers: 1. Yes 2. Yes 3. No 4. No 5. No 6. Yes**

# DINOMARKERS

**YOU'LL NEED:**

construction paper
hole puncher
pencil
crayons
scissors
yarn

**NOW . . .**

1. Look through some books about dinosaurs and find your favorite, such as . . .

Stegosaurus (Steg-owe-saw-rus)
Walnut-sized brain
Plant-eater
Length: 23 feet
Weight: 1-½ tons

BRACHIOSAURUS
Nose on top of head
Plant-eater
Weight: 77 tons

Jurassic

Triceratops (Try-serra-tops)
3-horned beast
Length: 30 feet
Plant-eater
Weight: 5 tons

Tyrannosaurus (Tie-ran-owe-saw-rus)
"King of Dinosaurs"
Biggest flesh-eater
Length: 46 feet
Weight: 7 tons

2. Make and cut out your dinomarker!

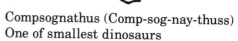

Compsognathus (Comp-sog-nay-thuss)
One of smallest dinosaurs
Flesh-eater
Length: over 2 feet
Weight: 6-½ pounds

# THE ANIMAL KINGDOM TODAY

## SPECIAL TERMS:

cold-blooded:    The animal's blood changes with changes in the air or water.
warm-blooded:    The animal's blood stays about the same all the time.
mammals:    Animals with mammary glands that give milk to their young.
marsupials:    Mammals that carry their young in a pouch (pocket).

**BIRDS:**

warm-blooded
backbone
wings
feathers
lays eggs
land animal

**REPTILES:**

cold-blooded
backbone
most covered with scales/plates
land animal

**AMPHIBIANS:**

cold-blooded
backbone
moist skin (slightly wet)
can live on land or in water

**FISH:**

cold-blooded
backbone
most covered with scales
fins for swimming
water animal

**INSECTS:**

cold-blooded
no backbone
antennae for touch, taste, smell
3 pairs of legs
wings
land animals

**MAMMALS:**

warm-blooded
backbone
mammary glands
most are land animals
water animals: whales, dolphins

**MARSUPIALS:**

mammals
carry young in pouch
land animals

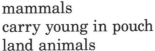

**Name** _____ **Date** _____

# LOOKING AGAIN AT ANIMALS

**DIRECTIONS:** Put a (+) or (−) in the boxes to show if the word applies or not. *Insects* has been done for you.

| ANIMALS | warm blooded | cold blooded | lives on land | lives in water | backbone | wings | scales | feathers | fins | pouch | mammary glands |
|---|---|---|---|---|---|---|---|---|---|---|---|
| BIRDS | | | | | | | | | | | |
| REPTILES | | | | | | | | | | | |
| AMPHIBIANS | | | | | | | | | | | |
| FISH | | | | | | | | | | | |
| INSECTS | − | + | + | − | − | + | − | − | − | − | − |
| MAMMALS | | | | | | | | | | | |
| MARSUPIALS | | | | | | | | | | | |

**DIRECTIONS:** Cut out the pictures below and paste them in the correct boxes.

1. I'm a cold-blooded animal, all covered with scales.
   The water is my home and swimming is what I do.

2. Like you, I'm a warm-blooded animal, with a strong backbone, too.
   I have mammary glands that give milk to my babies.

3. I fly all around and have lots of legs, too.
   Thanks to my antennae, I can smell, taste, and touch.

4. Like other mammals, I'm warm-blooded, with mammary glands, too.
   But unlike you, I carry my baby in a pouch.

5. I'm a cold-blooded animal, with skin that is soft and moist.
   I'm at home on land and in water, too.

6. I'm a cold-blooded animal and am usually scaly, too.
   But unlike fish, I make my home on land.

7. I'm a warm-blooded animal, all covered with feathers.
   When I flap my wings, I fly high in the sky.

# MAMMALS, MAMMALS, MAMMALS!

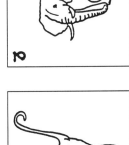

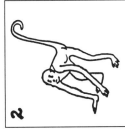

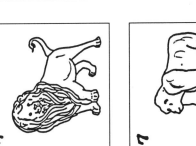

**DIRECTIONS:** Match the picture with the animal.

___ GIRAFFE: I'm the tallest animal on earth—17 feet tall as a matter of fact.

___ RHINOCEROS: My name means "nose-horned," because I have a horn on top of my nose. See it?

___ BEAR: I'm big and furry and look very cute, but I'm not very nice, so stay away from me!

___ ELEPHANT: I'm the biggest animal on earth, with a long trunk and white tusks, too!

___ HIPPOPOTAMUS: My name means "river horse," but I look more like a big pig with short legs.

___ ZEBRA: I look like a plump horse, but I'm covered with black and white stripes.

___ TIGER: I'm the largest member of the cat family. My yellow fur is covered with black stripes.

___ LION: I'm a fast and powerful yellow cat, and around my head I wear a big mane of hair.

___ LEOPARD: I'm smaller than lions and tigers, but just as mean. My yellow fur is covered with black spots.

___ APE: My body is a lot like a human being's. I don't have a tail and I walk on 2 legs like you!

___ MONKEY: I use my long tail like an extra hand. My favorite foods are insects, leaves, and fruit, too.

**Answers: 5, 6, 11, 3, 1, 10, 9, 4, 8, 7, 2**

# ANIMAL CHAINS

**YOU'LL NEED:**

construction paper    pen
ruler               scissors
                   paste

**NOW . . .**

1. Choose your favorite animals.
2. Make a list of words that describe each animal.
   For example:

**SNAKE:**
reptile
cold-blooded
scales
long
thin
no legs
crawl

**BEAR:**
mammal
warm-blooded
furry
meat-eater
honey
4 legs
winter nap

3. Now make a paper chain for each animal:
   a. Cut out 1" × 6" strips of paper.
   b. Write the animal's name on the first strip.
   c. Write one descriptive word on the other strips.
   d. Paste your chain together.

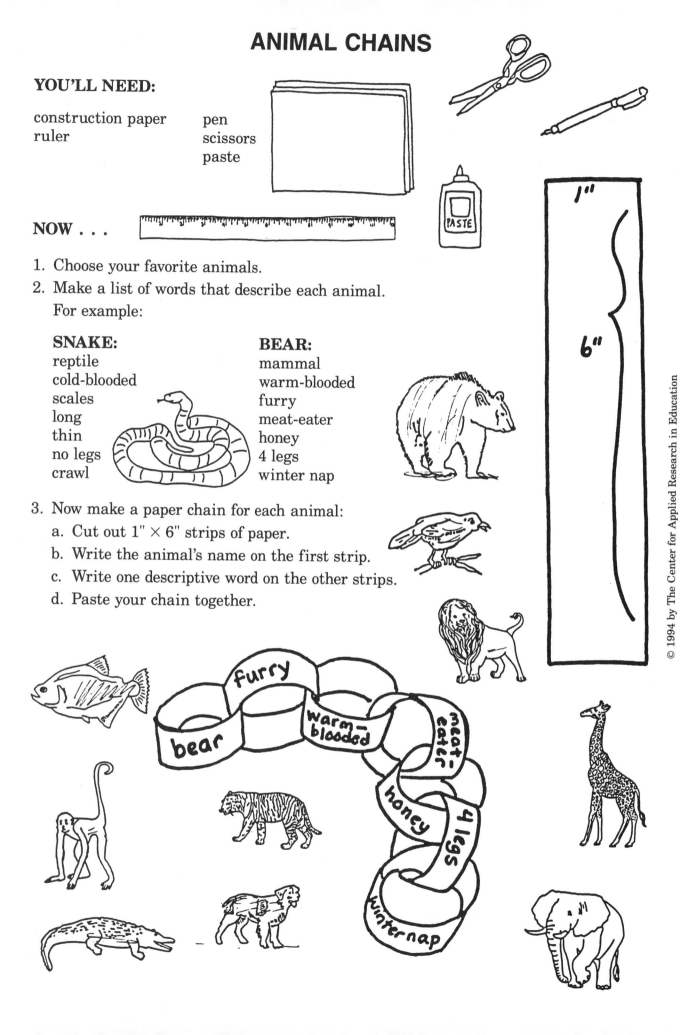

# GOLDILOCKS AND THE THREE BEARS
## (A Class Activity)

**EVERYBODY:** (Follow the directions.)

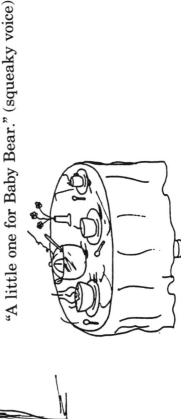

"Hello!" (deep voice)
"Hello!" (normal voice)
"Hello!" (squeaky voice)

"A great big one for Papa." (deep voice)
"A medium-sized one for Mama." (normal voice)
"A little one for Baby Bear." (squeaky voice)

"A great big one for Papa." (deep voice)
"A medium-sized one for Mama." (normal voice)
"A little one for Baby Bear." (squeaky voice)

Once upon a time, there were three bears:

Papa Bear (pause)
Mama Bear (pause)
Baby Bear (pause)

The three bears lived in a house in the forest.

They had three chairs. (pause)

Upstairs, they had three beds. (pause)

One morning, Mama Bear made some hot oatmeal.

# GOLDILOCKS AND THE THREE BEARS (continued)

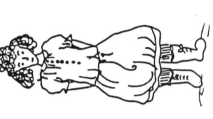

But it was too hot to eat! (pause)
So they went for a walk in the forest.

So did a little girl named Goldilocks.

And she walked right up to their door and knocked. (pause)
Of course, nobody was home, so she walked right in.

The first thing she did was sit in Papa's great big chair. (pause)
Next, she sat in Mama's medium-sized chair. (pause)
Finally, she sat in Baby Bear's little chair. (pause)

Then she saw the oatmeal and said . . . (pause)
First, she tasted Papa's oatmeal. (pause)
Next, she tasted Mama's oatmeal. (pause)
Finally, she tasted Baby Bear's oatmeal. (pause)

After eating all that oatmeal, Goldilocks yawned.
Sleepily, she went upstairs to the bedroom. (pause)
First, she tried out Papa's great big bed. (pause)
Next, she tried out Mama's medium-sized bed. (pause)
Finally, she tried out Baby Bear's little bed. (pause)

When the three bears came home, they took one look, and
Papa Bear said . . . (pause)
Mama Bear said . . . (pause)
Baby Bear said . . . (pause)

**EVERYBODY:**

"Too hot! Too hot!"

Knock on floor.

"But it was too hard!" (deep voice)
"But it was too soft!" (normal voice)
"And she broke it in half!" (squeaky voice)

"Boy, am I hungry!" (high voice)
"But it was too hot!" (deep voice)
"But it was too cold!" (normal voice)
"And she ate it all up!" (squeaky voice) "Slurp!"

"Clomp! Clomp! Clomp!"
"But it was too hard!" (deep voice)
"But it was too soft!" (normal voice)
"And she fell fast asleep!" (squeaky voice) Snore!

"Somebody's been sitting in my chair!" (deep voice)
"Somebody's been sitting in my chair!" (normal voice)
"Somebody's been sitting in my chair and broke it
in half!" (squeaky voice) "Sob! Sob!"

# GOLDILOCKS AND THE THREE BEARS (continued)

## EVERYBODY:

"Somebody's been eating my oatmeal!" (deep voice)
"Somebody's been eating my oatmeal!" (normal voice)
"Somebody's been eating my oatmeal and ate it all
up!" (squeaky voice) "Sob! Sob!"

"Somebody's been sleeping in my bed!" (deep voice)
"Somebody's been sleeping in my bed!" (normal voice)
"Somebody's been sleeping in my bed and there she
is!" (squeaky voice)

"Help! Help!" (high voice)
Jumping motion.
"Thump! Thump! Thump!"
Slap hands on thighs.

"1—2—3—4!"

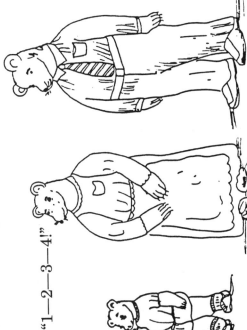

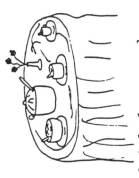

Then they looked at the table, and
Papa Bear said . . . . (pause)
Mama Bear said . . . (pause)
Baby Bear said . . . (pause)

Finally, the three bears went upstairs to their bedroom, and
Papa Bear said . . . (pause)
Mama Bear said . . . (pause)
Baby Bear said . . . (pause)

Goldilocks opened her eyes and sat straight up in bed.
She saw the three bears and screamed . . . . (pause)
And jumped off that bed! (pause)
Then she bounded down the stairs . . . (pause)
And ran right out the door! (pause)

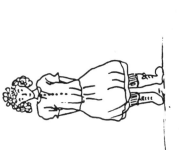

And that, my friends, is the story of Goldilocks and the three bears!

# MAKE A SEQUENCE CHAIN

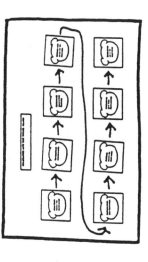

**YOU'LL NEED:**   scissors
paste
construction paper

**NOW:**   1. Read each "bear" carefully.
2. Cut out the title and all the squares.
3. Paste the squares IN THE RIGHT ORDER on construction paper.
4. Connect the squares with arrows as shown.

---

## GOLDILOCKS AND THE THREE BEARS

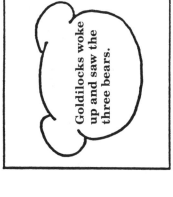

Goldilocks entered the bears' house.

The three bears went for a walk.

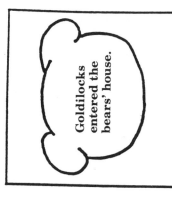

Mama Bear's oatmeal was too hot to eat!

Goldilocks woke up and saw the three bears.

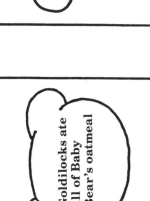

Goldilocks fell asleep in Baby Bear's bed.

Goldilocks ate all of Baby Bear's oatmeal

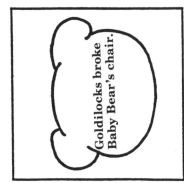

Goldilocks broke Baby Bear's chair.

Goldilocks ran out of the bears' house.

# BEAR PUPPETS

## YOU'LL NEED:

small brown paper bags
paste
string
crayons
old newspapers
scissors

## NOW . . .

1. Lay the bag down flat with the bottom facing away from you.

2. Draw and color in your bear face on the upper half of the bag.

3. Fill HALF the bag with newspaper.

4. Put your hand in the bag:
   a. push your first finger into the fabric
   b. make a mark where your thumb and second finger touch the sides and cut out holes. These will be the bear's arms.

5. Tie a string around the face, just below the face and above the armholes.

# BIBLIOGRAPHY

Adler, Irving. *Time in Your Life.* New York: The John Day Company, 1972.

Adler, Ruth, and Irving Adler. *Shadows.* New York: The John Day Company, 1961.

Ardley, Neil. *The Science Book of Light.* New York: Harcourt Brace Jovanovich, Publishers, 1991.

———. *The Science Book of Senses.* New York: Harcourt Brace Jovanovich, Publishers, 1992.

Arbuthnot, May Hill, compiler. *Time for Fairy Tales, Old and New.* Chicago: Scott, Foresman and Company, 1961.

Baker, James W. *April Fool's Day Magic.* Minneapolis: Lerner Publications Company, 1989.

Baynham, Mike. "Bilingual Folk Stories in the ESL Classroom." *ELT Journal,* XL (April, 1986), pp. 113–120.

Blossom, Grace. "Sing and Learn English." A 310 Special Demonstration Project, 1985.

Brady, Martha, and Patsy Gleason. *Are You Sure Shirley Temple Started This Way?* Flagstaff, Arizona: Heartstrings, 1990.

Brandenberg, Aliki. *My Visit to the Dinosaurs.* New York: Harper and Row, Publishers, 1985.

Burnett, Bernice. *Holidays: A Reference First Book.* New York: Franklin Watts, 1983.

Churchill, Richard E. *Holiday Hullabaloo.* New York: Franklin Watts, 1977.

Coulson, Zoe. *The Good Housekeeping Illustrated Cook Book.* New York: Hearst Books, 1980.

Dalgliesh, Alice. *The Thanksgiving Story.* New York: Charles Scribner's Sons, 1954.

Dolly, Martha R. "Integrating ESL Reading and Writing through Authentic Discourse." *Journal of Reading,* XXX (February, 1990), pp. 360–365.

Dupuy, Trevor Nevitt, editor. *Holidays: Days of Significance for All Americans.* New York: Franklin Watts, 1965.

Enright, D. Scott, and Mary Lou McCloskey. "Yes, Talking!: Organizing the Classroom to Promote Second Language Acquisition." *TESOL Quarterly,* XIX (September, 1965), pp. 431–453.

Epseland, Pamela. *The Story of King Midas.* Minneapolis: Carolrhoda Books, 1951.

Epstein, Sam, and Beryl Epstein. *The First Book of Maps and Globes.* New York: Franklin Watts, Inc., 1959.

———. *The First Book of Measurement.* New York: Franklin Watts, 1960.

Galeano, Karen. "Mother Goose in the ESL Classroom." Salt Lake City, Utah: Presented at Rocky Mountain Regional TESOL Conference. (October 1983.) (ERIC Document Reproduction Report #238262.)

Gilliatt, Mary. *The Decorating Book.* New York: Pantheon Books, 1981.

Graff, Henry F. *The Free and the Brave.* Chicago: Rand McNally & Company, 1980.

Guglielmino, Lucy Madsen. "The Affective Edge: Using Songs and Music in ESL Instruction." *Adult Literacy and Basic Education,* X (1986), pp. 19–25.

Harbin, E. D. *Games of Many Nations.* New York: Abingdon Press, 1954.

Haugaard, Eric Christian, translator. *The Complete Fairy Tales and Stories of Hans Christian Andersen.* New York: Doubleday & Company, 1974.

Haulman, April. "Fairy Tales in the ESL Classroom." Oklahoma City: Presented at International Conference on Second Language Acquisition by Children. (March 1985.) (ERIC Document Reproduction Report #279166.)

Heald-Taylor, Gail. *Whole Language Strategies for ESL Students.* Toronto, Ontario: Ontario Institute for Studies in Education, 1986.

Helfman, Harry. *Making Pictures Move.* New York: William Morrow & Company, 1969.

Henry, Edith H. "The Non-English Speaking Student in the Elementary Classroom: A Beginning." (August 1985.) (ERIC Document Reproduction Report #273087.)

Hoffman, Mark S. *The World Almanac and Book of Facts: 1992.* New York: Pharos Books, 1992.

Hornblow, Leonara, and Arthur Hornblow. *Prehistoric Monsters Did the Strangest Things.* New York: Random House, 1990.

Hulpach, Vladmir. *American Indian Tales and Legends.* London: Paul Hamlyn Drury House, 1965.

James, Lee J., and Ray Burns. *Draw 50 Holiday Decorations.* New York: Doubleday & Company, 1987.

Johnson, Patricia. "Effects on Reading Comprehension of Building Background Knowledge." *TESOL Quarterly,* XVI (December, 1982), pp. 503–517.

Jones, Linda, and Jim Rhinesmith. *Make-A-Book Workshop.* Thomas Jefferson School, 1992.

Kamen, Ruth. *The Complete Guide to Decorating Your Home.* Whitehall, Virginia: Betterway Publications, Inc., 1989.

Kaplan, Robert B. "Cultural Thought Patterns in Inter-Cultural Education." *Language Learning,* XVI (1966), pp. 1–21.

Keen, Dennis. "The Use of Traditional Reading Approaches with ESL Students." *Journal of Reading,* XXVI (November, 1983), pp. 139–144.

Kinnealy, Janice. *How to Draw Flowers.* Mahwah, NJ: Watermill Press, 1987.

Knight, David. *Let's Find Out About Sound.* New York: Franklin Watts, Inc., 1975.

Krashen, Stephen D. "The Input Hypothesis." In J. E. Alatis, ed., *Georgetown University Round Table on Languages and Linguistics.* Washington, DC: Georgetown University Press, 1980.

Krashen, Stephen D., and Tracy D. Terrell. "The Natural Approach: Language Acquisition in the Classroom." Hayward, CA: The Alemany Press, 1983.

Liberty, Gene. *The First Book of the Human Senses.* New York: Franklin Watts.

*Little Golden Book Library: Fairy Tales and Rhymes.* New York, Golden Press, 1969.

Livesey, Antony, and Stephanie Thompson. *Know Your Wild Animals.* New York: Rand McNally & Company, 1977.

Mackay, Ronald, Bruce Barkman, and R. R. Jordon, eds. *Reading in a Second Language.* MA: Newbury House Publishers, Inc., 1979.

Martin, Ann Aronson. "Effective Teaching of ESL Reading." Master's Thesis, Roosevelt University, 1984.

Matheidesz, Maria. "Communication Games—Are They Really Effective?" Edinburgh, Scotland: Presented at Annual Meeting of the International Association of Teachers of English as a Foreign Language. (April 1988.) (ERIC Document Reproduction Report #299820.)

McCauley, Joyce K., and Daniel S. McCauley. "Using Choral Reading to Promote Language Learning for ESL Students." *The Reading Teacher,* XLV (March 1992), pp. 526–533.

Miller, Leah D., and Kyle Perkins. "ESL Reading Comprehension Instruction." (1989.) (ERIC Document Reproduction Report #303779.)

Minicz, Elizabeth Watson. "A Bag Full of Newspaper Clippings and Other Tricks of the ESL Trade." *Lifelong Learning,* IX (September, 1985), pp. 2–3.

Norbeck, Oscar E. *Book of Indian Life Crafts.* New York: Association Press, 1966.

Petrimoulx, John. "Building an Airport and Other Fun ESL Learning Activities." Tampa, Florida: Presented at University of South Florida Linguistics Club Conference on Second Language Acquisition. (June 1986.) (ERIC Document Reproduction Report #283406.)

Piper, Terry. "Stories and the Teaching of Language in Grade Two ESL Classes." San Antonio: Presented at Annual Meeting of National Council of Teachers of English. (November 1986.) (ERIC Document Reproduction Report #278268.)

Pugh, Sharon L. "Literature, Culture, and ESL: A Natural Convergence." *Journal of Reading,* XXXII (January 1989), pp. 320–329.

Putnam, Mark Richard. "Using Proverbs and Sayings in the ESL/EFL Classroom." Master's Thesis, School for International Training, 1988.

Reidman, Sarah R. *The World Through Your Senses.* New York: Abelard-Schuman, 1962.

Rhodes, Dorothy. *How to Read a City Map.* Chicago: Children's Press, 1967.

Richek, Margaret Ann, Lynne K. List, and Janet W. Lerner. *Reading Problems: Assessment and Strategies.* Englewood Cliffs, NJ: Prentice Hall, Inc., 1989.

Ringel, Harry, and Jeanne H. Smith. "English as a Second Language: Language Experience Approach." Philadelphia: Nationalities Service Center. (1989.) (ERIC Document Reproduction Report #318275.)

Rinkoff, Barbara. *A Map Is a Picture.* New York: Thomas Y. Crowell Company, 1965.

Roop, Peter, and Connie Roop. *Great Mysteries: Dinosaurs—Opposing Viewpoints.* St. Paul, MN: Greenhave Press, Inc., 1988.

Royston, Robert. *Let's Look Up: Touch and Feeling.* Morristown, NJ: Silver Burdett Company, 1985.

Rupp, James H. "Whole Language in the Elementary ESL Classroom." Anaheim, CA: Annual Meeting of Teachers of English to Speakers of Other Languages. (March 1986.) (ERIC Document Reproduction Report #273121.)

Selsam, Millicent C. *How Animals Tell Time.* New York: William Morrow and Company, 1967.

Simpson, Anne. *How to Draw Wild Animals.* Mahwah, NJ: Watermill Press, 1992.

Smith, Frank, ed. *Psycholinguistics and Reading.* New York: Holt, Rinehart & Winston, Inc., 1973.

———. *Understanding Reading: A Psycholinguistic Analysis of Reading and Learning to Read.* New York: Holt Rinehart & Winston, Inc., 1971.

Snow, Marguerite Ann. "Common Terms in Second Language Education." Los Angeles: University of California. (1986.) (ERIC Document Reproduction Report #278259.)

Stahl-Gemake, and Francine Guastello. "Using Story Grammar with Students of English as a Foreign Language to Compose Original Fairy and Folk Tales." *The Reading Teacher,* XXXVII (November 1984), pp. 213–217.

Stocking, Elizabeth. "Art Activities for the ESL Classroom." Vermont: School for International Training. (September 1983.) (ERIC Documentation Report #244517.)

*Strategic Learning in Content Areas.* Madison, WI: Wisconsin Department of Public Instruction, 1989.

Taylor, Barry P. "Teaching ESL: Incorporating a Communicative, Student-Centered Component." *TESOL Quarterly,* March, 1983.

Thonis, Eleanor Wall. *Teaching Reading to Non-English Speakers.* New York: Collier Macmillan International, Inc., 1978.

Travers, John. "Tunes for Bears to Dance To." Chicago: Presented at Annual Meeting of Teachers of English to Speakers of Other Languages. (March 1988.) (ERIC Document Reproduction Report #299799.)

Wilkes, Angela, ed. *Dinosaurs and How They Lived.* New York: Dorling Kindersley, Inc., 1991.

*Young Students Encyclopedia.* Middletown, CT: Xerox Education, 1980.

Zaidenberg, Arthur. *How to Draw Wild Animals.* New York: Abelard-Schuman, 1958.